From
Educ

Mixed Sources
Product group from well-managed
forests and other controlled sources
www.fsc.org Cert no. TT-COC-2082
© 1996 Forest Stewardship Council
FSC

D1425525

LANGUAGES FOR INTERCULTURAL COMMUNICATION AND EDUCATION
Editors: Michael Byram, *University of Durham, UK* and Alison Phipps, *University of Glasgow, UK*

The overall aim of this series is to publish books which will ultimately inform learning and teaching, but whose primary focus is on the analysis of intercultural relationships, whether in textual form or in people's experience. There will also be books which deal directly with pedagogy, with the relationships between language learning and cultural learning, between processes inside the classroom and beyond. They will all have in common a concern with the relationship between language and culture, and the development of intercultural communicative competence.

Other Books in the Series

Developing Intercultural Competence in Practice
    Michael Byram, Adam Nichols and David Stevens (eds)
Intercultural Experience and Education
    Geof Alred, Michael Byram and Mike Fleming (eds)
Critical Citizens for an Intercultural World
    Manuela Guilherme
How Different Are We? Spoken Discourse in Intercultural Communication
    Helen Fitzgerald
Audible Difference: ESL and Social Identity in Schools
    Jennifer Miller
Context and Culture in Language Teaching and Learning
    Michael Byram and Peter Grundy (eds)
An Intercultural Approach to English Language Teaching
    John Corbett
Critical Pedagogy: Political Approaches to Language and Intercultural Communication
    Alison Phipps and Manuela Guilherme (eds)
Vernacular Palaver: Imaginations of the Local and Non-native Languages in West Africa
    Moradewun Adejunmobi
Foreign Language Teachers and Intercultural Competence
    Lies Sercu with Ewa Bandura, Paloma Castro, Leah Davcheva, Chryssa Laskaridou, Ulla Lundgren, María del Carmen Méndez García and Phyllis Ryan
Language and Culture: Global Flows and Local Complexity
    Karen Risager
Living and Studying Abroad: Research and Practice
    Michael Byram and Anwei Feng (eds)
Education for Intercultural Citizenship: Concepts and Comparisons
    Geof Alred, Mike Byram and Mike Fleming (eds)
Language and Culture Pedagogy: From a National to a Transnational Paradigm
    Karen Risager
Online Intercultural Exchange: An Introduction for Foreign Language Teachers
    Robert O'Dowd (ed.)
Deep Culture: The Hidden Challenges of Global Living
    Joseph Shaules

For more details of these or any other of our publications, please contact:
Multilingual Matters, Frankfurt Lodge, Clevedon Hall,
Victoria Road, Clevedon, BS21 7HH, England
http://www.multilingual-matters.com

LANGUAGES FOR INTERCULTURAL
COMMUNICATION AND EDUCATION 17
Series Editors: Michael Byram and Alison Phipps

From Foreign Language Education to Education for Intercultural Citizenship
Essays and Reflections

Michael Byram

MULTILINGUAL MATTERS
Clevedon • Buffalo • Toronto

Library of Congress Cataloging in Publication Data
Byram, Michael.
From Foreign Language Education to Education for Intercultural Citizenship:
Essays and Reflections / Michael Byram.
Languages for Intercultural Communication and Education: 17
Includes bibliographical references.
1. Languages, Modern–Study and teaching. 2. Multicultural education. 3. Intercultural
communication–Study and teaching. I. Title.
LB1578.B97 2008
418.0071–dc22   2008000289

British Library Cataloguing in Publication Data
A catalogue entry for this book is available from the British Library.

ISBN-13: 978-1-84769-079-1 (hbk)
ISBN-13: 978-1-84769-078-4 (pbk)

Multilingual Matters
UK: Frankfurt Lodge, Clevedon Hall, Victoria Road, Clevedon BS21 7HH.
USA: UTP, 2250 Military Road, Tonawanda, NY 14150, USA.
Canada: UTP, 5201 Dufferin Street, North York, Ontario M3H 5T8, Canada.

The policy of Multilingual Matters/Channel View Publications is to use papers that
are natural, renewable and recyclable products, made from wood grown in
sustainable forests. In the manufacturing process of our books, and to further support
our policy, preference is given to printers that have FSC and PEFC Chain of Custody
certification. The FSC and/or PEFC logos will appear on those books where full
certification has been granted to the printer concerned.

Typeset by Wordworks Ltd.
Printed and bound in Great Britain by the Cromwell Press Ltd.

Contents

Acknowledgements ix

Introduction 1

Part 1: Foreign Language Education 5

Purposes

1 Foreign Language Education in Context 5
   Defining Foreign Language Education. 6
   Foreign Language Education Policies 9
   Evaluation and Planning of Foreign Language Education 15
   Policies for Plurilingual Learners in Multilingual Environments . 16

2 Purposes for Foreign Language Education 21
   The Benefits of Foreign Language Education 23
   Purposes and Policies: Three Cases 32

Possibilities

3 Is Language Learning Possible at School? 43
   The Ambitions of Policy-makers 44
   Defining and Comparing 'Success' 46
   Expectations at the End of Compulsory Education 48
   Matching Policies with Possibilities. 53

4 The Intercultural Speaker: Acting Interculturally or Being
   Bicultural. 57
   Being Bicultural 60
   Acting Interculturally. 68
   A Comparison of Being Bicultural and Acting Interculturally. . 71

5 Intercultural Competence and Foreign Language Learning
   in the Primary School. 77
      Context and Content 78
      Learning Foreign Languages and Cultures in Primary Education 79
      Teachers of Language and Culture in Primary Education 83
      Curriculum Planning and Teaching Materials. 85
      Conclusion 87

6 Analysis and Advocacy: Researching the Cultural Dimensions of
   Foreign Language Education 91
      Analysis and Advocacy 91
      Analysis of Culture Learning and Language Learning 93
      Advocating Directions for Culture Learning. 96

Perspectives

7 Nationalism and Internationalism in Language Education 103
      'Language Educators'. 103
      Foreign Language Educators. 105
      Education In and Beyond the Nation State 106
      Socialisation and Social Identity 110
      National and International Identities 114
      Languages and Identities in the Curriculum 121

8 Language Learning in Europe 125
      A Political Aspiration 125
      European Identity as a Social Identity? 130
      Language and Identity 131
      Socialisation 133
      European Identity and Language Learning. 138

9 Foreign Language Teaching as Political Action 145
      Education for Teachers of Languages 150
      Education for Teacher Educators? 152

Part 2: Intercultural Citizenship Education 155

10 Language Education, Political Education and Intercultural
   Citizenship 157
      Politische Bildung 158

√ Critical Cultural Awareness 162
Conceptual and Linguistic Relativism. 166
Communication in Transnational Communities 169
Ethical Dimensions of Education for Intercultural Citizenship. 173

11 Education for Intercultural Citizenship 177
A Framework for Political and Language Education 177
√ Education for Intercultural Citizenship 186

12 Policies for Intercultural Citizenship Education 191
Citizens and Their Communities. 191
Education for Citizenship beyond the Nation State: Europe . . 197

13 Curricula for Intercultural Citizenship Education 205
Transnational Political Activity in Education 206
Levels of 'Acting Interculturally'. 212

14 Assessment and/or Evaluation of Intercultural Competence and
Intercultural Citizenship 219
'Assessment' and 'Evaluation' 219
Attributing Value 220
Portfolios and Profiles. 224

Conclusion 227

Appendix 1: Intercultural Competence 230

Appendix 2: Sources for Teacher Training for Intercultural
Competence 234

Appendix 3: Framework for Intercultural Citizenship 238

Appendix 4: Autobiography of Intercultural Encounters 240

Notes 246

References 258

Acknowledgements

The chapters of this book have multiple origins and intellectual sources. Many are acknowledged in the usual way in references, but there are always other influences that cannot be tied to a particular chapter or paragraph and it is those that I will attempt to include here – 'attempt' because I cannot always be sure why and how I have written what I have, especially over the many years this book has been in the making.

I could start at the very beginning with those who taught me at school and, for someone whose parents had minimal schooling, the privilege of a grammar school education was indeed a beginning. Like many people, I was particularly marked by my university years, and two people in Cambridge, who had little to do with language teaching, are nonetheless present in these pages. In my undergraduate days, Robert Bolgar was my supervisor and 'Director of Studies' whose erudition is still an inspiration. Elias Bredsdorff, my PhD supervisor, was a kind and modest man who gave me access to Scandinavian literature and the intellectual freedom of postgraduate studies. They both taught me literary criticism in their different ways and, through that, the value of scholarship and research that remained with me when I became a language teacher and teacher trainer.

My next opportunity to do research arose when I was appointed to the University of Durham after being a school teacher and adult educator for several years. Having first of all worked alone on the education of linguistic minorities, a happy coincidence led me to work on a first major project on language teaching with Pat Allatt, Veronica Esarte-Sarries and Susan Taylor, and thereafter I have been fortunate to research in teams in Durham and elsewhere, notably with Dieter Buttjes at the University of Dortmund.

Some years later, I had the opportunity to participate in workshops of the Council of Europe. This opportunity I initially owed to John Trim – who had also been influential in teaching me Linguistics in Cambridge. Then Jean-Claude Beacco and I were invited by Joe Sheils to become Advisers to the Language Policy Division. This has been for the last decade a wonderful stimulus intellectually, and a warm experience of collegiality. Over that period I have met many people but Geneviève Zarate, with whom I wrote our first text for the Council of Europe, was one of the most important.

In the early 1990s, Peter Doyé contacted me after he had read one of my articles, and we met at a café in Hamburg. There began a long friendship and professional partnership which has been a highlight of the years ever since.

On three occasions in the 1990s I was a Mellon Fellow at the National Foreign Language Center (NFLC) in Washington DC. The first time was the opportunity to write the book *Teaching and Assessing Intercultural Communicative Competence* and Miriam Met and Ross Steele, who were Fellows at the same time, were generous with their time and comments. On another occasion the NFLC was the haven where I could complete the *Routledge Encyclopedia of Language Teaching and Learning*, a task which brought me into contact with many colleagues throughout the world. I am grateful to the Centre and the colleagues I met there for the peace and quiet I so much enjoyed.

In the mid-1990s I met a number of people at conferences who were doing their PhDs on the cultural dimension of language teaching and were keen to talk, but rather than just talk to me, I thought they would benefit from knowing each other's work. I invited them to come to Durham for a weekend to give papers about their work in progress and the 'Cultnet' (Cultural Studies Network) was born and became an annual event. The group has grown, become self-organising, created its own website and produced a research project and publication. This is a wonderful example of the university as an international intellectual meeting place, where I have enjoyed listening to and learning from others.

One of the Cultnet members, Lynne Parmenter, completed her Durham PhD about education in Japan, and now lives in Japan. It was she who was instrumental in my becoming a Visiting Professor at Gakugei University in Tokyo for six months in 2004–05, and my wife and I remember with gratitude Lynne's and Yuichi's hospitality and constant help. That period of relative calm was the opportunity to start this book, and I am grateful to Gakugei University and to my friends at the Curriculum Centre for Teachers, especially Mitsuishi-sensei, for their hospitality and the chance to learn about education in Japan.

Back in Durham, we began to organise annual symposia in the late 1990s and my colleagues Geof Alred, Anwei Feng and Mike Fleming have been and continue to be a great team to work and publish with. The symposia have been particularly influential in the formulation of what I call 'intercultural citizenship', as will be evident in later chapters.

I have been a consultant on a number of projects and always learnt yet more about the interaction of theory and practice. I owe thanks to: the ICOPROMO team lead by Manuela Guilherme from the University of Coimbra in Portugal; the INCA project led by Anne Davidson-Lund at

CILT in London; the teams of the ILTE and *Imagens das Línguas na Comunicação Intercultural* projects led by Helena Sá at the University of Aveiro in Portugal; the Interculture Project led by Robert Crawshaw at the University of Lancaster in England; the LABICUM project at the University of Primorska in Slovenia, and remember in particular Neva Čebron and the evening we spent at a café in Piran working out the grids of objectives that became an appendix of this book.

I have had the pleasure of supervising many research students and, as every supervisor knows, the constant need to read and discuss new research with such enthusiastic and hardworking people is yet another fundamental source of ideas and new energy. I cannot mention them all and shall therefore mention none. They are all nonetheless present in these pages.

I am also very grateful to an anonymous Glaswegian reviewer who provided some excellent suggestions, disentangled some of my tortuous syntax, and noted the blemishes resulting from my inability to type. I remain of course responsible for whatever escaped this thorough reading.

And finally, I can trace my views on language teaching to their most important source: the pupils I taught in secondary schools in Kent and Durham in England and, even before that, in Mascara in Algeria. They are the ones who challenge the orthodoxy of beliefs about language teaching when they ask, 'Why are we doing this, sir?' I hope this book is an answer to that question.

Introduction

> *The social sciences are essentially 'applied sciences' designed, to use*
> *Marx's phrase, to change the world not merely to interpret it [...] That*
> *sciences in the past, and especially the social sciences, have been*
> *inseparable from partisanship does not prove that partisanship is*
> *advantageous to them, but only that it is inevitable. The case for the*
> *benefits of partisanship must be that it advances science.*
> Eric Hobsbawm, *On History* (1998)

At a conference of the Italian association of language teachers in Rome in November 2005, I gave a lecture on 'Foreign language education for intercultural citizenship' and afterwards a teacher came to say thank you because 'teachers need a vision' in the midst of their daily life. A few months later I spoke to a conference of teachers of language courses for the International Baccalaureate about the relationship of their work to the mission statement of the International Baccalaureate Organisation and again I was thanked by someone for 'making us think'. This gave me renewed energy to complete this book.

There are different kinds of language teachers: those who teach what is usually called 'mother tongue', the dominant language of a society (such as French in France, Japanese in Japan); those who teach a dominant language in a society to newcomers to the society for whom it is a 'second language'; those who teach a language spoken in another country and learnt only in schools, colleges and universities – a 'foreign' language. All these teachers are handling one of the most important elements of humankind, for it is language that is one of the distinctive features of being human, one of the most important facilitating factors in the formation of human social groups, and at the same time one of the factors that separates groups from one another. Language teachers have important responsibilities in ensuring that learners of any age – from kindergarten into schools and on into adult, lifelong education – acquire the practical skills of the languages they need. This includes reading and writing the language(s) they otherwise acquire naturally in their environment – their 'mother tongue(s)' or 'first lang-uage(s)' – because, although they will inevitably learn to speak, reading and writing do not come naturally and often do not come at all without great effort and application. Language teaching also includes teaching the practical skills in a language that are needed for a short term business or pleasure trip to another country. Teaching 'mother tongues' and 'languages for business' are two extremes of a continuum of skills and knowledge, and there is every kind of language teaching in between.

At the same time, language teachers are concerned with values, for values are inherent in any kind of teaching whether teachers and learners are aware of them or not. The teachers of 'mother tongue' have to reflect on what the language means for those who speak another language at home. They have to think about how their teaching is not only focused on practical skills but also creates a sense of living in a specific time and place, in a specific country, in a specific nation-state; language and identity are inseparable. Those who teach second and foreign languages have to think about how the language is offering a new perspective, a challenge to the primary language of identity, and a different vision of the culture(s) in which they live and have hitherto taken for granted.

Language teaching has both practical purposes and challenging values, and it is this complex relationship that the teachers mentioned earlier wanted to think about in the midst of their career.

Language teachers can expect a career of 30–40 years and half way through this they may begin to feel that the vision they had as young teachers needs renewal. At the beginning of their careers, teachers are full of enthusiasm and visions – which may be indeterminate and not yet well formed – and to give shape to their enthusiasm they undertake initial teacher training.[1] This however tends to focus on the everyday issues of methods, classroom discipline and the problems that all new teachers face. It is important to temper this with engagement with the significance of language teaching for individuals, for societies, for teachers themselves. They need to maintain the knowledge that they are doing something worthwhile, even in the midst of their daily, often stressful work.

By mid-career, teachers have established a routine for dealing with discipline and similar issues even though it is in the nature of such things that they are never totally resolved. Mid-career teachers have different priorities and they are usually offered short in-service courses or sometimes they can attend Masters courses. Short courses may keep them up to date with new methods and recent policy changes but hardly give them the opportunity to renew their enthusiasm and vision. Longer courses should allow them to see their work in a wider educational context, but unfortunately longer courses are not offered to everyone.

This book is written for all who wish to think about their teaching in the wider context, to see the bigger picture, clarify or renew their vision and their work in the classroom.

The book is also written from a personal perspective. I have partisan views of language learning and teaching after 50 years of being involved in languages as learner and teacher, and I accept Hobsbawm's admonition that partisanship should bring change and progress. What constitutes 'progress' is not always obvious and depends on circumstances, on the historical moment. Progress in language teaching was defined differently in 1945 than it was in 1989, to take but two dates that are significant not only in world-historical terms but also for language teaching. For it is one of the themes of this book that language teaching is a social and political activity. I hope that these essays will inspire readers to think about what progress might mean and to be involved in change. This has been one of my own pre-occupations as a teacher and researcher, through my own work and that of my students. My professional life has been largely, though not exclusively, in Europe and this affects my perspective. All teachers will have their own personal picture within which their language teaching vision exists. They should be aware of this and of the way it impacts on their own thinking and practice.

The European situation is, however, a particularly interesting one and offers food for thought for other parts of the world. The 'European project' in which some kind of co-operation among nation states is taking place is an experiment in economics, identities, social policies and politics that may be followed elsewhere in the world.[2] Languages and language teaching have been an integral part of the evolution of nation states and this new situation has implications for language teaching in a post-nation-state world. One small indication of this is the plan to develop a parallel to the *Common European Framework of Reference* for languages in Asia, or the use of the *Framework* and related work in North America and elsewhere. I hope therefore that my European perspective will not be dismissed as parochial.

This is a book of essays. They can be read independently and in any order. This means that there is some repetition to ensure each can stand alone, and I have provided some notes between chapters that will help readers to locate them in the book as a whole. The essays can also be read in order, because there is a gradual move from the vision of language teaching that I think most teachers would share to a proposal for language teaching as political action that many will not immediately identify with. The title of the book traces a development in the vision that I hope will persuade. The book is, like all writing, an illocutionary act and, if it stimulates a response, whatever that may be, I shall be more than satisfied, having met Hobsbawm's requirement.

Michael Byram
Durham, October 2007

Chapter 1

Foreign Language Education in Context

Three fundamental functions of all national education systems, and of compulsory education in particular, are to create the human capital required in a country's economy, to develop a sense of national identity and to promote equality or at least a sense of social inclusion. In various degrees and forms these have been educational aims since the foundation of national education systems in Western Europe and North America, and were exported, together with the forms of schooling, to other parts of the world by the colonial powers in the 19th and 20th centuries. The learning of a foreign language was in the early stages of this development, rather anomalous. It was not essential to the economy since it was colonial languages that were used in trade, supplemented by a few intermediaries with knowledge of local languages. It did not function in policies of equality or social inclusion but on the contrary was antithetical to these since only an elite learnt foreign languages. And it was, if anything, a potential threat to national identity because it introduced learners to different beliefs and values. In practice the threat was minimised by teaching methods based on translation, which by definition involves seeing another language and the values and beliefs it embodies through the framework of one's own language, and one's own beliefs and values.[3]

Some of the purposes and forms of education remain unaltered and are from time to time re-asserted,[4] but social changes of the late 20th and early 21st centuries which are encapsulated in the words 'globalisation' and 'internationalisation' have given new meaning and significance to foreign language learning. One example of this is to be found in Western Europe, and increasingly in Central and Eastern Europe. The creation of a single market by the European Union is a microcosm of globalisation and has led to increased mobility and frequent interactions among people of different languages. This in turn has led to a political will to develop a new concept of identity, a European identity, which is fostered by increased foreign language learning. A second example is China, where entry into the World Trade Organisation is creating a demand for language learning on a massive scale but where access to international communication, particularly through the Internet, is perceived as sufficiently threatening to national values and beliefs to lead to censorship.

Foreign language education is thus no exception to the need to locate all education in its social, economic and political context. There are factors to be considered in the educational purposes as sketched above (and developed in detail in Chapter 2), but there are also factors to be taken into account in the definition of 'foreign' language education.

Defining Foreign Language Education

From a psychological perspective on the processes of language learning, there may be no useful distinction between 'second' and 'foreign' languages, since it can be argued that the acquisition processes are identical. In an educational and political context, however, the status of a language in a given society is important, and the distinction significant. Consider the case of French. In the anglophone provinces of Canada, French is taught as a Second Language, being one of the two official languages of the country. Across the border in the USA it is a foreign language with no official status but considerable prestige. In Australia, too, it is a foreign language but its prestige is being threatened by other foreign languages from countries such as Japan, which are geo-politically more important to Australia than to France. In India, French is present in the curriculum of the Central Institute of English and Foreign Languages, the major university for languages, but with the exception of Pondicherry is not otherwise a significant language in India. On the other hand, in some African countries it is an official language. Yet in both India and Africa, French is clearly a non-indigenous language, in one 'foreign' in the other 'official'. Finally, in France, Belgium and Switzerland, French is taught as the or a national language and assumed to be school pupils' 'mother tongue', even though there are many French, Belgian or Swiss citizens for whom it is chronologically their 'second' language since they have learnt, for example, Arabic in the home. Furthermore, it may not be perceived by some French citizens as their 'national' language because they accord this status to Breton or another language of an indigenous minority.

Secondly, it is important to distinguish 'learning' from 'education'. In most countries, people learn more than one language in the course of their lives. They do so in many settings, of which educational institutions are only one; they learn in many ways, of which being taught in a classroom is only one. What distinguishes foreign language education from learning is that it has social and political purposes reflected in the formalities of an educational institution and embodied more or less explicitly in the learning aims and objectives attributed to the institution by governments at local or national level.

As a consequence of globalisation and internationalisation, these educational policies and aims have changed, or more accurately the emphasis has changed. Although there was a famous call for change in aims in the late 19th century, when in the 'Reform Movement', Viëtor said *'Der Sprachunterricht muß umkehren'* ('Language teaching must start afresh'), the fresh start took almost a hundred years to be accepted. The change required was from aims of acquiring a foreign language for purposes of understanding the high culture of great civilisations to aims of being able to use a language for daily communication and interaction with people from another country. As this change became accepted, ultimately under the banner of 'Communicative Language Teaching', the aims of language teaching in educational institutions began to coincide with the aims of people who learn languages in many other ways and locations. Foreign language *education* is now largely focused on the purposes of language *learning* and these seem self-evident to learners – and to politicians – and thus foreign language education has to meet the expectations of success in foreign language *learning*. Those expectations are high because parents and politicians see people around them, especially young children, apparently learning languages quickly and successfully in non-educational settings, through interaction with other children, through exposure to mass media. To what extent their expectations are justified and how often they are fulfilled varies from country to country and is an issue to which I shall return below.

To what extent the shift of focus in foreign language aims is satisfactory is still under debate. The shift within compulsory education seems to be almost complete, even if the practice lags behind the policy at times. For example, in Japan in 1993, a Government Commission on *Foreign Language Policy Revision for the Twenty-First Century* (see Koike & Tanaka, 1995), proposed fundamental structural change in syllabus, teacher training, public examinations, exchange programmes and so on, to improve learners' communication skills. In the USA, the publication in 1996 of *Standards for Foreign Language Learning: Preparing for the 21st Century* (NSFLEP, 1996) moved away from a framework of four skills (listening, speaking, reading and writing) where the focus is on language as a system to be acquired, and substituted goal areas (communication, cultures, connections, comparisons and communities) where the focus is on what can be accomplished through a foreign language. The underlying principles are provided by three modes of communication – interpersonal, interactive and presentational – which describe the ways of functioning in a language. Similarly, the *Common European Framework of Reference for Languages: Learning, Teaching,*

Assessment (Council of Europe, 2001) developed by the Council of Europe in the 1980s and 1990s proposes an approach based on an analysis of how languages are used in communication, on the 'functions' people use them for, the 'notions' they use them to express and the 'tasks' they wish to accomplish with them, instead of an analysis of the grammatical system.

All of these are influential documents on which new curricula and teaching methods are being constructed in the new century throughout the first world. The second world of the former Soviet bloc is also quickly moving from traditions of language learning based on linguistic analysis and is in fact overtaking many first-world countries by moving more quickly to this new position without passing through intermediary phases of language teaching methods such as the audio-lingual method. Changes in the third world are however much slower. Communication-skills methods require hardware and teaching materials, which are costly. Methods that rely on minimal equipment and which can be used in large classes, with emphasis on grammatical analysis, are still widespread. On the other hand, 'new' methods of developing communication skills by using a language as a medium of instruction in other subjects, which are currently being (re)discovered in Western Europe and imported from immersion programmes in North America, have been current in Eastern European countries for decades. In many African countries too, bilingual education is common. Here it is a necessity rather than a choice because foreign, i.e. non-indigenous, languages (English and French above all) are the official languages of many African countries and therefore automatically the languages of instruction. Children acquire them as a consequence of attending school.

The shift of emphasis to communication aims goes unchallenged in compulsory schooling and vocational education but is disputed in university education. Language teaching in universities for non-majors is following the shift in emphasis on aims and methods with little hesitation and the formation of an association to support this kind of teaching in Europe (the Confédération Européenne des Centres de Langues dans l'Enseignement Supérieur) is a symptom of the recognition of this function of university education. On the other hand, 'study' of languages, as opposed to language learning, for language majors and their lecturers, seems to be caught between the poles of language as 'a means to an end' and language as 'an end in itself'. When language is a means to an end, the purpose has traditionally followed that of the study of classical languages – Chinese, Greek, Latin, Sanskrit, Arabic – i.e. to gain access to great texts, often literary but not exclusively so. In some countries, the literary canon has been expanded to include, or given way absolutely to, the study of cultures and societies, drawing on a range of disciplines such as anthropology, sociology, economics and history, and not just literary history and criticism. A striking example of this is the growth in interest in British/ American/Canadian Studies – the study of life in Britain/USA/Canada from many disciplinary perspectives – in departments of English where previously the study of English literature was the norm, the literature of the 'native' anglophone countries or in more recent times all literature written in English whatever the country of origin of the author. Similar developments are taking place in other language 'disciplines' and have for example fostered a debate in German Studies in the USA about what should be taught and which are the reference disciplines (Schulz *et al.*, 2005). One of the issues is precisely whether language study is a 'discipline' with a clear definition of an object of study, a methodology and an epistemology, or whether it is an 'area' whose boundaries are in fact 'fuzzy' and, in the contemporary post-modern world, appropriately so (Di Napoli *et al.*, 2001). In this environment, people also ask whether language study develops 'criticality' in students in higher education, because criticality is a crucial characteristic of university education. That it is possible to develop criticality even in beginners courses at university has been shown in the teaching of Japanese at a British University (Yamada, 2008). If language study were to be found wanting in this respect, questions might be raised as to its appropriateness as a university 'discipline' (Brumfit *et al.*, 2004).

Foreign Language Education Policies

As foreign language learning has become more important for societies responding to globalisation and internationalisation, governments have paid more attention to policy-making. In many cases, the focus is on the teaching and learning of English, and in many countries, particularly in East Asia, English as a Foreign Language (EFL) is almost synonymous with Foreign Language Learning. This is a consequence of British colonialism continued by American dominance of world affairs.

The role of English thus often dominates the development of language education policies and the teaching of English has been a major influence on the methods of teaching all foreign languages. The most significant factor in policy-making for EFL is the relationship English has with native-speaker communities. As an 'international language', there should in principle be no priority accorded to British or US English, or in fact any other country where English is the national or official language. Yet there is still a strong tendency in many countries to pay allegiance by accepting British or US norms of language use, of pronunciation, of grammatical correctness and of dictionary definitions of meanings. Despite the special circumstances of English being spoken by many more non-native than native speakers, native speaker norms are still taken as international norms, in spite of the questioning of the whole concept of 'nativeness' in this sense, and in spite of the potential for an international English with its own norms of pronunciation and grammar (Jenkins, 2000; Seidlhofer, 2003; Davies, 2003). For example, in Singapore, the government has formulated an explicit policy of maintaining external norms against the development of Singaporean English, not least for fear of Singaporeans losing competence in the major medium of international trade.

Native speakers, and the governments and cultural institutes of native speaker countries, have a vested interest in promoting attitudes of deference to native-speaker norms in that they thereby continue to dominate communication and gain advantage in negotiation. There has been much debate about the argument that there is both conscious and unconscious 'linguistic imperialism' (Phillipson, 1992; Phillipson & Davies, 1997) beneath these processes. On the other hand there is growing evidence that the dominance of native speakers, for example as teachers setting and embodying linguistic and cultural norms, is being challenged (Medgyes, 1994), and international users of English are taking ownership of it for their own purposes (Canagarajah, 1999).

Other languages and their native-speaker communities have not been criticised as vehemently as English. Nonetheless the institutionalisation and promotion of French, German, Italian and Spanish (in the Alliance Française, the Goethe-Institut, the Istituto Italiana di Cultura and the Cervantes Institute) is an indicator of the significance of the teaching of their languages in the foreign policies of the countries in question. The Cervantes Institute, for example, was founded in 1991, embracing the aims of language teaching for communication, and the significance of Spanish continues to grow in the commercial development of South America and as the second language of the USA. The Goethe-Institut plays a crucial role in the teaching of German because in many countries German does not have a substantial place in school-level education, but is learnt by adults, and adult education is seldom a priority for governments. The Goethe-Institut thus offers a systematic base for the learning of German and it too has embraced communicative aims for language learning.

Policy responses to the evolving significance of language learning, and in particular the dominance of English, are mainly based on acceptance of the trend towards English. A very striking example of this was presented in Japan in a 'Report of the Prime Minister's Commission on Japan's Goals in the 21st Century' (Kawai, 2007):

It is necessary to set the concrete objective of all citizens acquiring a working knowledge of English by the time they take their place in society as adults, organise English classes according to level of achievement, improve training and objective assessment of English teachers, expand the number of foreign teachers of English, contract language schools to handle English classes, and other general materials. In addition, the central government, local governments, and other public institutions must be required to produce their publications, home pages, and so on in both Japanese and English. ... In the long term, a national debate on whether to make English an official second language will be needed. (Commission of Japan's Goals in the 21st Century, 2000: 10)

The final statement caused uproar. The threat to national identity that has in principle always been present in the teaching of foreign languages but never in practice, suddenly loomed very large.

Politicians in democratic societies, at whatever level they operate, follow the perceived demands and needs of their publics, who seek every opportunity to learn English, to have English introduced to their children at an early age, to use English for work and leisure. These perceptions may not be as well-founded as they seem and the future of English may be less dominant, evolving simply as one of a number of languages an individual speaks (Graddol, 1997, 2006). Furthermore, as the case of education in France demonstrates, the choice of foreign language by parents for their children can sometimes support languages other than English since the choice of a 'difficult' or 'less widely used' language ensures a pupil is placed in a good learning environment and among an elite. Nonetheless, here too, the tendency is for a reduction of diversity as most parents 'play safe' and choose English (Puren, 2000).

Policies to encourage diversity of language learning in non-anglophone countries thus run against the trend and are difficult to sustain in a democracy. In Eastern and Central Europe, memories of the obligatory learning of Russian, which people counteracted by deliberately forgetting all they had been taught, are a strong barrier to enforced language policies in the new democratic era. On the other hand, there is some recognition in policy-making that language teaching is a necessary but not sufficient response to change, and needs to be accompanied by 'internationalisation' of the whole curriculum in compulsory education. Examples include Japan, South Korea, Sweden and Denmark where such a policy has been formulated by national ministries of education. This typically means that teachers of all subjects are expected to make explicit the international dimension; science teachers might draw attention to the nationality of well-known scientists and the places and circumstances in which their discoveries were made, or mathematics teachers might draw out the historical origins of mathematics in the Arabic-speaking world. Visits and exchanges with other countries are seen not simply as an opportunity to practise foreign languages but as occasions for cross-curricular projects and comparative studies.

Policies are made by national governments and sometimes by subnational entities. The European Union is the only example of a supranational polity that believes that it needs to develop a language education policy. As a political entity with, at the time of writing, 23 'official and working languages' functioning in its institutions, it formulated ten years earlier a policy that all citizens of its member states should learn three of these languages, their own national language and two foreign languages of the European Community (European Commission, 1995). This was seen as crucial to the development of the economy and a sense of identity, not unlike the policies of nation states:

> Proficiency in several Community languages has become a precondition if citizens of the European Union are to *benefit from the occupational and personal opportunities open to them in the border-free single market*. This language proficiency must be backed up by the ability to adapt to working and living environments characterised by different cultures.
>
> Languages are also the key to knowing other people. Proficiency in languages *helps to build up the feeling of being European* with all its cultural wealth and diversity and of understanding between the citizens of Europe. (European Commission, 1995: 67; emphasis added)

However, in more recent documents the simple and attractive 'one plus two languages' policy has been emphasised less than the importance of diversification in language learning in a European Union that has almost doubled in the number of member states since the 1995 document.

The Council of Europe is similarly a supra-national body, but focused on cultural co-operation. It embraces 46 member states at the time of writing, almost twice as many as the 25 of the European Union, and has also formulated a policy to promote linguistic diversity. It has not committed itself to a specific number of languages but recognised that diversity is a function of each particular situation and should be pursued as an over-arching principle:

> Council of Europe language education policies aim to promote:
>
> * *Plurilingualism*: all are entitled to develop a degree of communicative ability in a number of languages over their lifetime in accordance with their needs.

- _Linguistic diversity_: Europe is multilingual and all its languages are equally valuable modes of communication and expressions of identity; the right to use and to learn one's language(s) is protected in Council of Europe Conventions.
- _Mutual understanding_: the opportunity to learn other languages is an essential condition for intercultural communication and acceptance of cultural differences.
- _Democratic citizenship_: participation in democratic and social processes in multilingual societies is facilitated by the plurilingual competence of individuals.
- _Social cohesion_: equality of opportunity for personal development, education, employment, mobility, access to information and cultural enrichment depends on access to language learning throughout life. (Council of Europe, 2005: 4)

In both cases, the wish to promote diversity stems partly from a recognition of the economic value of plurilingual individuals able to move freely in a multilingual market-place, and partly from a concern to sustain the culturally diverse heritage of European countries.

A comparable policy in nation states would promote continuing cultural, and not only commercial, relations with a wide range of countries, not just those where English is the native or official language. Understanding of other cultures, for example of China or of Arabic-speaking countries, presupposes acquisition of Chinese or Arabic in order to have access to significant texts. A policy that encourages diversity in language learning for these reasons would be a revival of earlier aims of language learning for cultural purposes. Although it would be perceived as incompatible with communication aims and emphasis on major languages, above all English, it has in fact a complementary function since political and economic affairs often founder not on a lack of linguistic competence but on a lack of cultural understanding.

The policy dilemmas in anglophone countries are different. Despite what might appear to be the advantages of 'linguistic imperialism', the US President's Commission on language learning was established in 1978 and found 'a serious deterioration in this country's language and research capacity at a time when an increasingly hazardous international military, political and economic environment is making unprecedented demands on America's resources, intellectual capacity and public sensitivity' (President's Commission, 1979: 1). Language education policy is a matter of national capacity and a response to danger. After the attacks of 11 September 2001, this sentiment became more urgent and increasing amounts of money were channelled into language learning for purposes of 'national security':

> President Bush today launched the National Security Language Initiative (NSLI), a plan to further strengthen national security and prosperity in the 21st century through education, especially in developing foreign language skills. The NSLI will dramatically increase the number of Americans learning critical need foreign languages such as Arabic, Chinese, Russian, Hindi, Farsi, and others through new and expanded programs from kindergarten through university and into the workforce. The President will request $114 million in 2007 to fund this effort. (Press release, 5 January 2006. Online at www.actfl.org/i4a/pages/Index .cfm?pageID=4249. Accessed 16.02.08.)

Language teaching and learning is part of foreign policy and the reference to 'critical need foreign languages' could be a euphemism for 'knowing the languages of the enemy' or of competitors or, hopefully, of co-operation. This is complemented by another formulation in the same document where the concept, more familiar from other policy documents, of 'respect for other cultures' is used. The third element is the reference to providing 'an opportunity to learn more about our country', a purpose also found in such disparate countries as those of the Gulf States and Japan, but not in the countries of Western Europe:

> An essential component of U.S. national security in the post-9/11 world is the ability to engage foreign governments and peoples, especially in critical regions, to encourage reform, promote understanding, convey respect for other cultures and provide an opportunity to learn more about our country and its citizens. To do this, we must be able to communicate in other languages, a challenge for which we are unprepared. (Press release, 5 January 2006. Online at www.actfl.org/i4a/pages/ Index.cfm?pageID=4249. Accessed 16.02.08.)

British governments have reacted much more slowly and it was necessary for a privately-sponsored commission to be formed in the late 1990s before a substantial policy review could be inaugurated (*Languages: The Next Generation*, 2000). Terrorist attacks in London in 2005 did not however lead to the same association of language teaching with national security.

The case of another anglophone country, Australia, is different in that foreign language education policy there has developed within a broader national language policy, stemming from recognition of the multilingual composition of the Australian population itself, comprising people of aboriginal origins and languages, and others of European and East Asian emigration from non-anglophone countries. Language policy from the 1970s encouraged multiculturalism rather than assimilation to an anglophone norm, including provision of opportunity to learn second and foreign languages. In the 1990s increased emphasis was placed on the relevance of some languages more than others to the competitiveness of the business community; these were particularly Japanese, Chinese, Korean and Indonesian (LoBianco, 2003). Thus, despite the different policy content, the significance of languages in foreign policy is again evident.

Evaluation and Planning of Foreign Language Education

The growing importance of foreign language education in social, political and economic terms leads to more attention being paid to its efficiency. Investment of time in the formal curriculum of compulsory education and of money in the materials to support it, particularly the use of information and communication technology, calls for evaluation. Decisions about which languages to teach, how many, at which points in education both compulsory and post-compulsory, and in particular a general policy to encourage linguistic and cultural diversity lead to more conscious planning of foreign language education.

As we saw above, planning and policies for language education are being taken seriously by politicians, but evaluation of the success of policies is still rare at national and international level and tends to be limited to the collection of statistics (for an example at an international level see Eurobarometer, 2001–5). An exception to this are the studies carried out by the International Association for the Evaluation of Educational Advancement (IEA) in the 1970s. These considered policies, human and material resources and institutions in English teaching in ten countries and French teaching in seven countries. Rather than comparisons among countries, which are almost impossible because of the variations and complexities of different systems, these studies allowed insight into such factors as the length of time spent on learning, the intensity of courses, and the identification of important independent variables. The amount of time spent on learning is crucial, but the starting age is not. Exposure to a foreign language outside the classroom leads to higher achievement than when a foreign language is a school-based subject (Cumming, 1996: 1, 5). Further studies of this kind planned during the 1990s were not completed and international evaluation has therefore not been brought up to date.[6]

Evaluation studies on a smaller scale are more frequent and methods have been developed as part of a wider concern with educational evaluation. Important distinctions are made between formative and summative evaluation, between quantitative and qualitative techniques of data-collection and among the different foci for evaluation: teaching methods, teacher qualifications, materials. The inclusion of language teaching in the development of quality management and the use of 'benchmarks' as part of public accountability for financial investment is evident in Western countries and will doubtless spread. In Hong Kong, for example, teachers of English have been required to take tests to establish if their competences meet pre-determined benchmarks. In Britain, the definitions of what levels students of languages in schools and universities can be expected to reach are defined in a 'Language Ladder' of six levels each with descriptions of what learners 'can do' if deemed to be at that level (www.dfes.gov.uk/languages; accessed 31.01.06).

In all cases it is clear but not always acknowledged that the level of achievement expected should be a function of the time devoted to language learning. Statements about what might be expected at the end of a given period are rare, and sometimes invidious comparisons are made of outcomes without comparing the period of study or the conditions of learning such as the number of learners in a class.

Policies for Plurilingual Learners in Multilingual Environments

Foreign language education cannot be separated from language education in general. The difficulty of defining a *foreign* language that we saw earlier is an indication of this. The interest of *Second* Language Acquisition researchers in the relationship between processes of acquisition of first and subsequent languages is a further indication. Educationists have argued that learners' understanding of languages and of themselves as language people requires an integrative approach to teaching all languages (Hawkins, 1987; van Lier, 1995). 'Awareness of language', as this perspective is called, or in French '*éveil aux langues*', also helps learners to become more effective because they are conscious of how languages can be learned and skills transferred from one language to another. Policymaking should also take this into account in order to ensure more return on investment in time and other resources.

What 'language awareness' thinking also reveals is that many, perhaps most, language learners are not monolingual people meeting another language for the first time when they have foreign language teaching. They are plurilingual people who have acquired different language varieties in their environment. Many policies and practices have yet to recognise this and continue to assume implicitly that learners compartmentalise their languages, and that teachers should compartmentalise their teaching so that in a 'French' lesson in an English school there should be no reference to German, let alone English, as if the learners were not able to profit from their inevitable mixing and comparison of their languages.[7]

The ability to learn languages, to become a plurilingual 'language person' with a range of competences to different levels in different languages, needs to be the focus of language teaching just as much as the ability in a particular language being taught at a particular time.

Foreign language education must also be seen in its social environment. Internationalisation and globalisation are forces that are not yet fully understood and the evolution of English as a world language is also unclear (Graddol, 2006), but there is no doubt that both the ability to use several languages for various purposes and the capacity for empathy and understanding are crucial. People are interacting with each other face to face or at a distance, they are being told about, and shown to, each other by mass media, but neither real-time experience of others, nor increased exposure to information, necessarily lead to empathy and understanding. All learners are thus experiencing an environment in which many languages are spoken: a multilingual environment.

Finally, language education needs to take note of the political environment, to develop in the future towards a greater conscious inclusion of political and social purposes. What was seen in the second half of the 20th century as a training in skills should not shun concern with values and critical understanding of others, ourselves and how we interact together as individuals and groups. Language teachers of all kinds are under-prepared for this task because so much emphasis has been placed on technical matters of selection of content, theory of learning, and options for 'delivery' of teaching through old and new technologies. These remain significant because the problems are yet to be solved, but the task for language educators is above all to educate, to promote an ability to change perspective and to challenge what is taken for granted. The great German educator Wilhelm von Humboldt had already described this in the early 19th century:

> By the same act whereby (man) spins language out of himself, he spins himself into it, and every language draws about the people that possess it a circle whence it is possible to exit only over at once into the circle of another one. To learn a foreign language should therefore be to acquire a new standpoint in the world-view hitherto possessed, and in fact to a certain extent is so, since every language contains the whole conceptual fabric and mode of presentation of a portion of mankind. But because we always carry over, more or less, our own world-view, and even our own

language-view, this outcome is not purely and completely experienced. (von Humboldt, 1836/1988: 60)[8]

We can never escape our own languages – whether we have just one or several when starting a new language – but in taking a different perspective, language learners of any age or disposition can be brought to a greater critical awareness of themselves and others and thereby become more adequately educated for an international world. This is the real challenge for all language education.

Chapter 1

Chapter 1 shows that foreign language teaching needs to be seen in a broad context. There is always an obvious educational context, the place of languages in schools and post-school institutions, and what this means for the individual learner. Just as important is the role of foreign language teaching in foreign policy. Nation states project themselves through supporting the teaching of their languages in other countries. They also decide which languages need to be learnt at home for strategic purposes. And finally foreign language education policy needs to be seen as part of policy for languages of all kinds whether they are deemed to be national, regional, minority or foreign.

Chapter 2

Chapter 2 deals more specifically with what foreign language education can offer the individual within the wider purposes of compulsory schooling, a phenomenon that is still relatively new, and a consequence of industrialisation and the evolution of nation states. As the world changes, nation states are having to respond to internationalisation and the chapter argues that this requires a shift in focus from simply 'linguistic' competence as the aim of language teaching to a richer vision of intercultural competence. To what extent this vision can be seen in policies is traced by analysing documents from three countries: France, Japan and England.

Chapter 2

Purposes for Foreign Language Education

Aims of education

Education systems in industrial and post-industrial countries have three main purposes. Firstly, from their beginnings in the 19th century they have socialised young people into the nation state society into which they are born. Socialisation involves acquiring knowledge about one's society and knowing how to behave and act within it, but it also involves emotional attachment:

> Naturally states would use the increasingly powerful machinery for communicating with their inhabitants, above all primary schools, to spread the image and heritage of the 'nation' and to inculcate attachment to it and to attach all to country and flag, often 'inventing traditions' or even nations for this purpose. (Hobsbawm, 1992: 91–2)

Kedourie states this in even stronger terms:

> In nationalist theory (...) the purpose of education is not to transmit knowledge, traditional wisdom (...) its purpose rather is wholly political, to bend the will of the young to the will of the nation. Schools are instruments of state policy, like the army, the police, and the exchequer. (Kedourie,1966: 84)

One very important aspect of this was, and is, the acquisition of the language (or in some cases, languages) of the state.[9] Geography is also a part of this. Children learn geography not only as a discipline, for it inculcates into them certain images with which they can identify. For French children, France is presented as a hexagon, all the easier to visualise. Chinese children learn that China has the shape of a cockerel. History is also a crucial subject because 'we' learn 'our history' even if we forget most of it afterwards and have a garbled version, parodied brilliantly in *1066 And All That* for the English (Sellar & Yeatman, 1993). And of course the teaching of history is tightly controlled, especially when some of it does not bear scrutiny by young people, as is the case in Japan where some of the actions of the Japanese army in the Second World War are not included in history books. Literature also plays its part. The vigorous debate in England in the

1980s over the requirement that all young people should read at least one play by Shakespeare, owed as much to nationalism as to the supposed benefits of great literature, which after all can also be acquired from other giants of the literary world. Literature for Goethe was 'world-literature' but for the English nationalists, it was a mark of English identity: you can be English only if you have read Shakespeare.

The second purpose for an education system has always been present but has become the main focus in post-industrial societies. This is the idea of 'human capital' (Woodhall, 1997; CERI, 1998). Even though schools of the 19th and early 20th century developed literacy and numeracy in pupils, it was to ensure that they could manipulate the machinery that created society's wealth. Thereafter they could and should leave school and find their place in industrial society. In a post-industrial society and a 'knowledge economy', this is not enough, and the focus must shift from investing in machinery to 'investing in people', to cite a scheme started in Britain in the 1980s. The idea that human beings are the source of economic development and society's wealth is encapsulated in the notion of human capital developed during the second half of the 20th century. The success of the 'Asian tigers' was attributed to investment in human capital, and the place to invest seemed to be in the education system.

Traces of this way of thinking can be found in education policy documents, as politicians introduced the terminology and the ideology into their rationales for changing and developing education systems. It is encapsulated in the British Prime Minister's claim that 'Education is our best economic policy' (DfEE, 1998)

The benefits are expected to be for the state and population as a whole as well as for the individual, and yet it is not entirely clear that this is the case and certainly not proven that investment in education is sufficient even if necessary (Levin & Kelly, 1997). Furthermore, it seems that investment is likely to be much more effective if placed in the early years of schooling than in higher education, and the increasing expectation that states cannot finance higher education is a symptom of the doubts about limitless investment.

The third purpose of education is not necessarily present in all education systems. The use of schooling as a means of creating equality, or at least equality of opportunity, is an idea more evident in some countries than in others. In Europe it is a common theme. The debates about comprehensive schools in Britain and Germany, for example, have gone on since the 1960s. Both societies were, and are, divided by social class, and both had secondary school systems that reflected and reinforced this. The reproduction of societal structures by education systems was theorised by Bourdieu in the

1960s and later (1970), but experienced earlier, and in Britain attacked by Halsey and other sociologists (1980).

In Britain, where central government could exert pressure on but could not control the local authorities responsible for education, the comprehensive school was introduced gradually but almost everywhere. All children from the same neighbourhood should go to the same secondary school, and secondary education is the crucial location for social mobility. Even if Bourdieu is right that the higher strata always manage to manipulate the system to their advantage, the devastation of not even getting a place in a grammar school was removed by the comprehensive school system, in both England and France.

In Germany, education is under the control of the federal states and the introduction of comprehensive schools was and is a direct reflection of the political colour of the state government. Comprehensive schools and the creation of equality of opportunity through them are still the small minority, but the replacement of an examination system for selection to the highest secondary school, the gymnasium, by a combination of teacher advice and parental choice has reduced at least the appearance of inequity, and provided more equality of opportunity.

A new dimension of this third purpose for education has emerged as countries in the industrial and post-industrial world have seen a drop in their birth-rate and a need for immigration to supplement the labour force. Their populations have become ever more heterogeneous and the question of equality more complex. In this the 'old countries' such as Japan are following the 'immigration countries' such as the USA and Australia, with the same need to offer the children of these new populations equality or at least equality of opportunity. It is coloured by the need to ensure, as a precondition of social mobility, that these children feel 'included'. So 'equality' and 'inclusion' are related, and one might expect that the first purpose of education, to socialise young people into the national society would make the children of immigration feel included, but this is far from the case. The 19th century mode of creating attachment to the state was building on a potential, a sense of belonging together already present in the population (Hobsbawm, 1992). This is not evident in a multicultural society and the tension between 'national' and 'multicultural' education is a consequence that is still being resolved.

The Benefits of Foreign Language Education

Why are these three purposes of education important to those who teach foreign languages? If they see their task as teaching knowledge of the grammatical system of another language and/or the skills of using it to transfer information, to 'bridge an information gap', then the three purposes of education have little if any importance. There are however few such teachers. The majority know that teaching linguistic knowledge and skills is an important part of their task, but especially those teachers who work in general education, i.e. in compulsory schooling or in universities, are committed to something more. There is plenty of evidence for this, anecdotally among all teachers and teacher trainers and in research on teacher thinking (Byram & Risager, 1999; Sercu *et al.* 2005).

We should therefore consider foreign language education within this broader perspective and ask how it contributes to the purposes of education. From the perspective of the state and its education authorities, it is important to analyse and understand foreign language education because it has a rather ambiguous position. In times of crisis and conflict between states, foreign languages are treated with suspicion and teachers suspected of a lack of loyalty. This was the case for example in the USA during and after the First World War. On the other hand, languages are often seen as crucial to economic achievement, as is the case in Japan and in many other trading countries in the contemporary world. In China, entering into the World Trade Organisation, preparing for the Olympic Games in 2008 and the general opening up to capitalism and interaction with Western countries, caused a boom in language learning, encouraged by government. The fact that language learning is often simplistically equated with learning English is another reason why education authorities should better understand foreign language education and the three purposes of education.

It is also important to look at the issues from the viewpoint of the individual, of the pupil in school and the student in university. Foreign languages are usually presented to learners from an instrumental viewpoint: they will be able to use the languages for work or leisure, to find work in another country or to travel in the real or virtual world. Teachers also say that language learning 'broadens the horizons', although learners do not usually understand this until afterwards. Furthermore, even the instrumental value of language learning, unless it is English, is not obvious to learners, and even for English, the value has become evident only since the advent of the Internet. Before that, not many of the millions of learners of English or other languages could realistically envisage travelling abroad or meeting travellers from other countries. Indeed, this was not even a realistic hope for most teachers of languages, particularly outside rich Western countries. The reason for language learning in such circumstances seems obscure to learners if they are told it will be 'useful'.

The relationship of foreign language teaching and learning to equality of opportunity has attracted very little if any attention even from writers concerned with the politics of language learning and the hegemony of English. Analyses of achievement in language learning seldom inquire into the relationship with socio-economic status, although the issues are gradually being recognised. For example in a policy document on *Languages for All: Languages For Life* from the English ministry of education it is noted that 'there are issues of pupil motivation and relative lack of success of lower income groups and boys' (DfES, 2002: 11), and this implies that boys from lower income groups are particularly unlikely to succeed. The lack of success for children of lower income groups has again been recognised in a review in 2007 (DfES, 2007: 4), and in a more recent survey in Germany it is concluded that:

the following family background variables are the most relevant predictors of competence development in the German component of DESI:
* the cultural capital of the family;
* the socio-economic status of the family;
* the migration background (negative in German L1, positive in English L2);[10]
* a German-speaking family. (Nold, 2006: 12)

At first sight, it might be argued that foreign language learning requires a new beginning for all learners, and this allows the disadvantaged to start on the same footing as others. On the other hand, the evidence that those with cultural capital acquired from the home are more successful in their educational attainments in general appears to apply to language learning too. There is no obvious reason why it should be otherwise. The boy who told me, his French teacher, that his father wanted him to opt out of learning French in order to start learning metalwork and prepare for a job in the shipyards, is a single but telling case. Children whose parents have learnt a foreign language themselves are more likely to find encouragement, understanding and practical help with their homework, and the evidence from Germany suggests that children with a migration background – and therefore experience of other languages and cultures – also have some advantages.

The question of the social inclusion of the children of immigrants, particularly in the rich Western countries, is more readily addressed than the question of social class. Education authorities often seek to include their languages of origin in the curriculum. If this is considered too complex or costly, they offer the opportunity to learn the languages outside normal school hours, or at least the opportunity to take examinations and acquire a formal qualification. At first sight, this is generous, but there are questions and doubts. Does the teaching use foreign language methods when it is in fact children's first language? Is it really their first language, or is it the official language of their country whereas they themselves speak a regional variety or a different language, as they are from a minority within their country of origin (speakers of Berber in Algeria and Morocco for example)? Does it replace, for these children, the usual foreign languages and thus their opportunity to learn a foreign language in the sense this has for their peers? Is the language also taught to their peers for whom it is a foreign language, or treated as relevant only to immigrant children? Are these children being denied the same learning opportunities as their peers, and therefore being excluded from some aspects of social equality and mobility offered to others? These questions, like those related to socio-economic status and equality of opportunity, are not yet answered by empirical research or even by conceptual analysis.

What we can conclude is that foreign language learning – and first/ foreign language learning for minority children – has a complex relationship with equality of opportunity. It has perhaps not attracted much attention because those who write about equality of opportunity and education policy do not see foreign language learning as a significant issue. For example, Hargreaves, a leading writer on education in Britain, in his seminal book, *The Challenge for the Comprehensive School* (1982) has no substantial comment on foreign language education, perhaps because his focus is on 'community' which is a local and implicitly monocultural entity. (The need for a more complex conceptualisation of communities is the subject of Chapter 10.) On the other hand, those who research and write on language teaching are usually more concerned with methodology or with which languages should be taught and why. It is likely that language learning is in a dependent relationship with socio-economic status, and that policy for immigrant languages teaching is problematic in terms of equality of opportunity even whilst it is attempting to be socially inclusive. Education authorities need to devise policies that compensate for disadvantage in this as in all aspects of education.

For individuals, the effort to overcome this dependency relationship is more difficult. It is difficult to acquire the cultural capital that will help them because foreign languages are by their nature external to the society in which they live. Opportunities for acquiring the cultural capital of foreign language learning outside the home are restricted, unless the family is sufficiently rich to buy private language lessons. On the other hand, English is now omni-present in many societies and far more freely accessible, and may become the door to greater access to language learning of all kinds, a door that was opened only recently.

The position of English as a world language means there is a more obvious relationship between language learning and the economic purpose of education. Education authorities readily see the importance of investing in the teaching of English for economic benefit, as do learners, and especially the parents of young learners. The rise of private schools of English, the investment by education authorities in innovative teaching methods such as bilingual education or content based instruction, the introduction of English at ever earlier stages of education, are all indicators of the conviction that language learning leads to economic benefit. Furthermore, this is not confined to English, since even in Britain and the USA, the same phenomena are appearing if at a slower pace and pursued by a smaller proportion of people, be they education authorities or parents. Both believe that learning a foreign language – usually European but with increasing interest in Asian languages – is bound to be beneficial. Are they justified?

It would be difficult for education authorities to point to evidence of a causal relationship between investment in language teaching and the GNP or economic benefits in trade with other countries. Nonetheless, surveys of industrialists and traders directly involved usually indicate that they believe language competence is important. The continuing increase in interest from them for training in cross-cultural competence is another indicator, and a sign that they know that linguistic competence must be complemented by cultural competence. Some even believe that linguistic competence can be replaced by cross-cultural competence if personnel do not have linguistic competence or time to acquire it.

It would be equally difficult to demonstrate empirically that language learning benefits individuals economically, because language learning cannot be separated out from other aspects of investment in education and human capital. There is nonetheless the strong conviction amongst those whose parents invested in their education, that they too should invest in their children's education and ensure their children learn languages, especially English. The continuing high status of English medium schools in Hong Kong is one example of this, despite government attempts, backed by academic research, to persuade the population that learning through the medium of Chinese is better (Chan, 2007). It remains, however, an open question what proportion of the millions of learners of English in the world, will in fact benefit economically. How many mainland Chinese learners of English, for example, will do so?

The relationship of foreign language learning with the third purpose of education, socialisation into the nation state and affective attachment to it, brings out the specific nature of foreign language education particularly strongly. The importance of language in the evolution of nationalism and the nation state is argued by Hobsbawm. He shows that there was a potential for nationalism among populations at the end of the 19th century as they began to identify with the state and to acquire democratic rights in their relationship with the state. This does not explain the rise of nationalism in itself, the creation of identification with nation and not just with state, and Hobsbawm argues that the 'identification of nation with language' was crucial in this, not for reasons of communication but as symbolism:

> Languages become more conscious exercises in social engineering in proportion as their symbolic significance prevails over their actual use, as witness the various movements to 'indigenise' or make more truly 'national' their vocabulary, of which the struggle of French governments against 'franglais' is the best known recent example. (Hobsbawm, 1992: 112)

Language in its written form and when spoken in public is a powerful symbol of the imagined community of nation (Anderson, 1991) and, in its practical use for communication, presupposes that all members of the community have acquired the written language at school. If this pattern is repeated in every nation state, there will be as many national languages as states. In some cases, the distinctions created in newly formed states *a posteriori* – evident in the former Yugoslavia – between one language and another are a further indicator of the significance of the symbolism.

Nationalism is thus inward-looking and exclusive about language, a symptom of the isolationism and nationalism, indeed fascism, that contributed to the Second World War, but was criticised by Dewey already in 1916, as we shall see below. Since 1945, nation states have become more open and international. This is the effect of economic globalisation and cultural internationalisation, the latter often caused by the former, and confused with it. Education policies are formulated as responses to globalisation, and usually suggest an increase in language learning as the best way to operationalise the policy. This is particularly evident in East Asian countries where the operationalisation of such policy means more learning of English from an earlier age, and more innovative approaches such as bilingual methods for older pupils, as in Taiwan. When this happens, it is a realisation of the relationship of foreign language learning with the second purpose of education, the investment in human capital for economic gain, rather than with internationalisation.

In fact, as we shall see below, if language learning is taken in a narrow sense then it does not and cannot lead to a reduction in isolationism and an increase in internationalisation. To cite just one example here, a policy 'to cultivate "Japanese with English abilities"' is not a policy of internationalisation but of globalisation. Its aims are to give Japanese people the skills they need for economic purposes – investment in human capital – but not an international perspective that overcomes an underlying isolationism. The title of the policy describes precisely what is intended. In other countries, notably in Scandinavia, internationalisation policies spring from a different source: not from economic analysis but from analysis of the relationship of one country with others, of the ideal of mutual understanding, and of the social responsibility of rich countries towards poor countries. In these circumstances it is more evident that language learning is only part of the realisation of the policy, that other subjects in the curriculum also have a role.

If language learning is to be part of a policy of internationalisation, it has to be more than the acquisition of linguistic competence, for such policy needs to counterbalance the socialisation into national identity which underpins national education and national curricula. Foreign language education has the potential to make a major contribution if it offers learners experience of 'tertiary socialisation', a concept invented to emphasise the ways in which learning a foreign language can take learners beyond a focus on their own society, into experience of otherness, or other cultural beliefs, values and behaviours. That experience can and should give them a better purchase on their previous culturally determined assumptions.

The term 'tertiary socialisation' was used, in passing, in an article reporting on empirical research into children's perceptions of other cultures and what this told of their awareness *inter alia* of politics and political nationalist rivalries among European countries:

> Foreign language teaching can be a major factor in what might be called – as an extension of the notions of primary and secondary socialisation – the process of tertiary socialisation, in which young people acquire an intercultural communicative competence: the ability to establish a community of meanings across cultural boundaries. [...] this involves both cognitive and affective processes. These are, of course, not easily assessable as objectives but they are fundamental to the contribution of foreign language teaching to learners' education. (Byram, 1989b: 5)

The concept was subsequently pursued by Doyé (1992, 2008) who developed the allusion to Berger and Luckmann's (1966) account of primary and secondary socialisation and combined this with the insights of Piaget and, in particular, Kohlberg into cognitive and moral development. The most significant point Doyé makes is that the patterns of thinking and living, the schemata and the behaviours, learned in early childhood as given and natural are challenged by a multicultural world. This requires the acquisition of new patterns and modification of those that already exist. Acquiring new ones, he argues, is easier than developing the existing because this 'requires rethinking and unlearning of familiar patterns acquired in primary and secondary socialisation' (Doyé, 2008: 29). He then goes on to discuss how this happens in the cognitive, moral and behavioural domains, and how education – including foreign language education – can and should promote such psychological changes.

Doyé's focus on the classic authors provides the baseline, which now needs further refinement. Berger and Luckmann's account does not fit easily with descriptions of fluidity and hybridity in contemporary societies, since they assume a society that is static, made up of different strata or classes and they describe mobility in terms of moving from one stratum to another. Their insights are still valid, but need to be applied differently. Similarly Kohlberg's work has been portrayed as biased and not cognisant of female moral development (Gilligan, 1982), and the implied universalism and defined sequential stages are no longer to be accepted without question. Wringe (2007) demonstrates that the question of moral education, when discussed from a psychological theory perspective, is more complex than can be accounted for by work in the Kohlberg tradition and, furthermore, needs to be completed by philosophical perspectives.

Risager (2007: 226) argues that the distinction between primary and secondary socialisation is false, that the two 'mesh' with each other and 'primary socialisation in the family is influenced by socialisation via children's institutions and the media'. Similarly, tertiary and secondary socialisation 'mesh' and 'global development means, then, that many children and young people around the world get impulses and signals that contribute to a tertiary socialisation process, from the early childhood years' (Risager, 2007: 226). She also argues that the concept of tertiary socialisation is problematic because it is based on a national paradigm – i.e. it takes place when people engage with people from another nation state. 'Tertiary socialisation' therefore is not useful, and can be dispensed with. Only primary socialisation, 'the basic, personality-forming socialisation, which can quite well take place in a multilingual and multicultural environment' and secondary socialisation which 'comes later' and 'can also take place – and to an increasing extent will take place – in multilingual and multicultural environments' are necessary.

The criticism of the separation of stages that actually 'mesh' may be too crude. Doyé says the usefulness in pedagogy is that *inter alia* the concept 'describes the third stage in the development of the individual, which in an age of multiple intercultural encounters presents a necessary extension of the first two without implying the idea of a succession of clearly separable phases' (Doyé, 2008: 31). What is crucial to this 'extension' is the challenge and the need to rethink and unlearn, which Risager – in fact basing her critique on Byram (1995) – does not consider. Doyé's point is that the concept is useful 'for our purposes' (i.e. in pedagogy and didactics), because it 'focuses attention' on 'cognitive, evaluative and behavioural socialisation' and provides a 'sound basis for the planning of teaching in various fields and subjects, language teaching in particular' (Doyé, 2008: 230).

We thus find ourselves back with the pedagogical and didactic purposes. The psychological reality of tertiary socialisation needs empirical research but, even if this were not to support the concept, its usefulness in planning teaching and assessment would not necessarily be undermined. It provides teachers with a guide to thinking about offering learners the challenge that will make them rethink and unlearn.

In the cognitive, moral and behavioural changes of tertiary socialisation there is a process of reassessment of assumptions and conventions stimulated by juxtaposition and comparison of familiar experience and concepts with those of other cultures and societies. The purpose is not to replace the familiar with the new, nor to encourage identification with another culture, but to de-familiarise and de-centre, so that questions can be raised about one's own culturally-determined assumptions and about the society in which one lives.

This can, and should, take place within a society where the presence of the cultures of other social groups, both indigenous and immigrant, is a stimulus. This is multicultural education. It can, and should, also take place through juxtaposition of the dominant culture in one's own society with that of other societies and nation states. This is international or intercultural education. The two are related and language education that encourages learners to learn the language and culture of a group in their own society is at one with language education focused on another society.

Juxtaposition and comparison can lead to a questioning and critical attitude towards what hitherto has been accepted without question. This applies equally to the mundane matters of what is considered edible and inedible and to the abstract questions of value and morality. It is a pedagogical decision about what to introduce at which stage in language learning, depending in part on the age of the learners. It is a political decision as to whether the questioning and critical attitude should be encouraged in learners.

Internationalisation may mean no more than 'making the strange familiar' and facilitating interaction with people of other cultures, perhaps with a view to trading with them. This is a weak form of internationalisation and one that is easily conflated with globalisation and the economic purposes of language learning. The strong form of internationalisation is a different matter. It deliberately provokes a questioning attitude both towards other societies and towards one's own, what elsewhere I have called 'critical cultural awareness' (1997) and, in a further step, the teacher takes the role of 'transformative intellectual' (Giroux, 1992; Guilherme, 2002) encouraging learners to involve themselves in changing the world around them.

John Dewey captured the contrast between isolationism and education for democracy at a point in history when the nation states were at war and internationalisation at its lowest ebb. For him obstacles to education for democracy come from any group that:

> ... has interests 'of its own' which shut it out from full interaction with other groups, so that its prevailing purpose is the protection of what it has got, instead of reorganisation and progress through wider relationships. [...] It *marks nations in their isolation from one another*; families which seclude their domestic concerns as if they had no connection with a larger life; schools when separated from the interest of home and community; the divisions of rich and poor; learned and unlearned. (Dewey 1916/1985: 87; emphasis added)

The breadth of Dewey's vision, which castigates all types of isolationism, places internationalisation within a wider concept of democratic education. It shows how foreign language education, which Dewey unfortunately ignores, has a role in the mission of education as a civilising influence and a liberating, empowering force in people's lives.

Purposes and Policies: Three Cases

If, as argued here, foreign language education is potentially an integral part of the purpose of a general education, and brings to it a specific contribution, is this recognised amongst those responsible for education systems? As mentioned earlier, curriculum theorists and philosophers on education have tended to ignore foreign language education. What about policy makers? They certainly pay attention to the contribution that foreign language education can make to the economic purpose of education systems, increasingly as globalisation dominates their thinking about economic development at national level. Do they also recognise the importance of language learning and internationalisation in its strong form? They certainly readily use the word 'internationalisation', but do they recognise what distinguishes it from globalisation and the relationship to the socialisation purpose of education? Do they consider the question of equality of opportunity and social inclusion?

I have chosen the policies of three countries to explore these questions: France, Japan and England. France and Japan are countries with a strong national identity where the national language has a significant symbolic role, but they differ in their response to globalisation and the dominance of English as a world language. Secondly, France is part of the European Union, of the first supra-national polity, which has significance for education as socialisation. England is also part of the European Union, being an integral part of the United Kingdom, and faces similar questions but from a different perspective; English identity is much less well defined and conscious than French or Japanese. England is also different from the other two because of the position of English in the world and the impact this has on beliefs about foreign language learning. I shall first consider if and how the countries' respective policies reveal a view about language education and its relation to the three general purposes of education.

In Japan, the strategic plan of 2002 to cultivate 'Japanese with English abilities', mentioned above, links language teaching and learning only to the economic purpose of education. It uses the discourse of human capital investment, and the plan is presented as part of a larger 'strategy to enhance human potential'. The motivation is explicitly 'the progress of globalisation' with which 'skills in English' are automatically associated. The spread of English as an international lingua franca is not related to internationalisation in education, and there are no indications that anything other than linguistic skills are required; there is no reference to cultural competence:

> With the progress of globalisation in the economy and in society, it is essential that our children acquire communication skills in English, which has become a common international language, in order for living in the 21st century (*sic*). This has become an extremely important issue both in terms of the future of our children and the further development of Japan as a nation. (http://www.mext.go.jp/english/news/2002/07/020901.htm; accessed 12.7.02)

Investment in human capital, the final sentence implies, is important for both individual and national economic gain.

When this general policy is formulated as a 'course of study' for lower secondary school, there is no evidence of a link with internationalisation, nor is there any indication of an awareness that in pursuing economic ends, linguistic competence is necessary but not sufficient. The emphasis is confined to the four traditional skills: 'to accustom and familiarise students with listening/speaking/reading/writing ...'.

At upper secondary level, there are three aims:

> To develop students' practical communication abilities such as understanding information and the speaker's or writer's intentions, and expressing their own ideas, deepening the understanding of language and culture, and fostering a positive attitude toward communication through foreign languages.

'Communication' is understood as exchanging 'information, ideas, etc.' and is clearly influenced by the rhetoric of communicative language teaching which stresses 'bridging information gaps'. The attitudinal dimension is also focused on communication, whereas in many other countries the point is to encourage positive attitudes towards people of other countries rather than communication *per se*. What is expected of teachers is that they should propose topics that interest learners and are related to 'the daily lives, manners and customs, stories, geography, history etc. of Japanese people and the peoples of the world, focusing on countries that use the foreign languages'. Here is the first indication of an interest in internationalisation, but it cannot be without significance that the foreign language lessons should be used to deal with Japanese people first and then other cultures. International understanding is also defined in these terms. Teachers are expected to treat:

> Materials that are useful in deepening international understanding from a broad perspective, heightening students' awareness of being Japanese citizens living in a global community, and cultivating a spirit of international co-operation.

The final phrase is the only one that suggests the view of internationalisation as defined earlier, but it is not explained or expanded.

A comparison with the English national curriculum makes the limitations of the Japanese statement more evident. In the statement of aims for the early years of lower secondary school the notion of 'developing cultural awareness' is formulated as follows:

(1) working with authentic materials in the target language, including some from ICT-based sources (for example, handwritten texts, newspapers, magazines, books, video, satellite television, texts from the Internet)

(2) communicating with native speakers (for example, in person, by correspondence)

(3) considering their own culture and comparing it with the cultures of the countries and communities where the target language is spoken
(4) considering the experiences and perspectives of people in these countries and communities. (http://www.nc.uk.net/nc/contents/MFL-3–POS.html#N182DB; accessed 20.2.08)

It is more explicit here that learners should be able to take up other perspectives and that a comparative juxtaposition of own and other should be pursued. On the other hand there is also an automatic assumption that the purpose of learning a foreign language is only to communicate with native speakers, whereas the Japanese document suggests that learners should meet materials which make them reflect on 'peoples of the world' even if the focus is still on native speakers.

In England, there is no document for upper secondary, nor even the second half of lower secondary, since foreign language learning is no longer obligatory after the third year of lower secondary. It may be inappropriate to criticise the English statement for lack of a concept of critical cultural awareness (*savoir s'engager* in Byram, 1997 and Chapter 4 below) but, if it is not developed at this stage, there is no further opportunity to do so. This same lack of criticality is absent from the Japanese document too.

The English document is more ambitious and specific in relating foreign language learning to other parts of the curriculum, and to learners' general development. It also makes important claims about how learning a particular language in school has wider implications for the understanding of self, of one's position as a citizen and of the nature of language:

Through the study of a foreign language, pupils understand and appreciate different countries, cultures, people and communities – and as they do so begin to think of themselves as citizens of the world as well as of the United Kingdom. Pupils also learn about the basic structures of language. They explore the similarities and differences between the foreign language they are learning and English or another language, and learn how language can be manipulated and applied in different ways. Their listening, reading and memory skills improve, and their speaking and writing become more accurate. The development of these skills, together with pupils' knowledge and understanding of the structure of language, lay the foundations for future study of other languages. (*The National Curriculum for England: Modern Foreign Languages:* 14. Online at http://www.nc.uk.net/nc/contents/MFL-3–POS.html#N182DB; accessed 20.2.08)

Foreign language learning is, like all subjects in the curriculum, expected to promote pupils' 'spiritual, moral, social and cultural development'. There is potential here for language teachers to relate their work to the overall purposes of education and of the concept of tertiary socialisation. As Doyé (1992) points out, most people in a society act according to what Kohlberg describes as 'conventional' norms, the norms of their own society, but intercultural education should attempt to lead them into the 'post-conventional' stage of being freed from these norms and into open-mindedness about other cultures. The English national curriculum is not formulated in these terms. It simply says language teaching 'provides opportunities to promote (...) moral development, through helping pupils formulate and express opinions in the target language about issues of right and wrong'. The concept of 'social development' is also formulated simply in terms of being sympathetic and tolerant, of a spirit of co-operation when communicating. There is nonetheless potential here for language teachers to take a broader view of their work.

Yet there is no attempt to articulate the notion of internationalisation, or to explain and expand the phrase 'begin to think of themselves as citizens of the world as well as of the United Kingdom' which is found in the introductory statement quoted above. There are a number of quotations from well-known national figures, including sportsmen and actors, about the importance of learning languages, but these are cliché-ridden and the only substantial comment on internationalisation is in an anonymous quotation in French, presumably from a pupil, who says:

> *Les langues permettent de voyager à l'étranger sans avoir de difficultés de communication. Si on sait parler la langue du pays, les vacances sont plus amusantes. On peut faire de nouvelles connaissances, rencontrer des amis et généralement c'est plus facile d'obtenir des informations. C'est essentiel pour encourager de bonnes relations internationales, surtout de nos jours quand il y a beaucoup de conflits.* (*The National Curriculum for England: Modern Foreign Languages*: 15. Online at http://www.nc.uk.net/nc/contents/MFL-3 – POS.html#N182DB; accessed 20.2.08)
> [Languages allow you to travel abroad without difficulties in communication. If you know the language of the country the holidays are more fun. You can make new acquaintances, meet friends, and generally it is easier to obtain information. It's essential for encouraging good international relations, especially today when there are many conflicts.]

The final phrase about conflict is the only reference to the political significance of language teaching and learning, and there is nothing else in the document to encourage teachers and learners to think seriously about themselves as 'citizens of the world' in language learning lessons.

Similarly, there is very little concern with these matters in the French education system. Despite the fact that it is recognised that English is spoken as the first language in anglophone countries and as second language *'dans de nombreux pays du monde'* [in many countries of the world], the focus quickly moves to a variety of English widely used in Britain. There is only passing reference to an international context or to the concept of internationalisation. Just one comment in the final sentence of the policy document links language learning with the notion of social inclusion and its importance in a multicultural society:

> *L'apprentissage d'une langue étrangère étant connaissance d'une ou de plusieurs autres cultures, il donne accès à d'autres usages, à d'autres modes de pensée, à d'autres valeurs. Apprendre une langue étrangère, c'est apprendre à respecter l'autre dans sa différence, c'est acquérir le sens du relatif et l'esprit de tolérance, valeurs d'autant plus nécessaires aujourd'hui que la communauté du collège tend de plus en plus à devenir une communauté multiculturelle.* (www.cndp.fr/archivage Ministère de la jeunesse, de l'éducation nationale et de la recherche. Les langues vivantes au college ; accessed 01.01.05)
>
> [As the learning of a foreign language is the knowledge of one or more other cultures, it gives access to other customs, other ways of thinking, other values. To learn a foreign language is to learn to respect the other in his/her difference, it is to acquire the sense of the relative, and the spirit of tolerance, values which are all the more necessary today as the school community is tending to become a multicultural community.]

Other comments refer to the importance of developing tolerance in young people, and here the child is seen as the future citizen:

> *Plus que jamais, il apparaît nécessaire que les langues vivantes contribuent à développer chez l'enfant, c'est-à-dire chez le futur citoyen, le sens du relatif et de la tolérance. C'est la raison pour laquelle ce nouveau programme fait une place non négligeable aux contenus culturels.*
>
> [It appears to be more than ever necessary that foreign languages contribute to developing in children, that is in future citizens, the sense of the relative and of tolerance. This is the reason why this new programme puts significant emphasis on cultural contents.]

Above all, however, it is stressed repeatedly that the principal aim of language teaching should be to inculcate the ability to communicate, that knowledge of other cultures is subservient to this, even where there is a hint that language learning also requires the ability to decentre:

> *Parler une langue étrangère, c'est savoir parfois se mettre à la place de l'autre,*

penser comme lui, se représenter le monde de l'autre. La méconnaissance des référents culturels peut être une entrave à la communication.

[To speak a foreign language means to be able sometimes to put oneself in someone else's position, think like them, and imagine the world of the other. Lack of knowledge of cultural references can impede communication.]

The French authorities are perhaps afraid that teaching a cultural dimension might be misunderstood as the need to give lectures on facts about anglophone countries – a fear about a methodology. Despite this the emphasis is on learners being able to recognise, name, describe and relate knowledge of other countries to their own culture. The question of attitudes and moral development is referred to only in the phrase 'the sense of the relative and of tolerance' (a concept that will be examined in more detail in Chapter 10), but there is no connection with psychological and moral development which could be related to the concept of tertiary socialisation; and even the emphasis on acquisition of knowledge does not present this as an enlargement of or challenge to existing cognitive structures. It is only at the final stage of compulsory education that there is a statement that learners should be encouraged to decentre in order to contribute, in undefined ways, to education for citizenship:

De plus, à chaque fois que cela sera possible, on commencera à initier l'élève à la prise de distance nécessaire dans la lecture de tout document, contribuant ainsi à son éducation à la citoyenneté

[Furthermore, whenever possible, one should begin to initiate pupils into establishing a sense of distance necessary when reading any document, thus contributing to their education for citizenship.]

It is not clear whether this means French or international citizenship, and there is no suggestion that there might be some form of critical cultural awareness, of critical questioning of assumptions in one's own society. It seems that the French authorities do not consider 'children', as they are described in this document, as mature enough at age 16 to take a critical perspective on documents, and by extension on their own experience.

Not surprisingly, none of the documents from these three countries makes any allusion to equality of opportunity and the relationship of language learning to social origins. Only the French documents refer briefly to the question of inclusion of diverse groups in a multicultural society. More surprising perhaps is that only in Japan is there an emphasis on the economic purpose of education, on investment in human capital. This may be because, in contrast to France, English in Japan is presented as an international language and linked with the concept of globalisation. In England, there is more emphasis on future study of language based on a better understanding of the nature of language. This is related to the fact that there is no one foreign language that is the most obviously 'useful' for anglophone learners, and language learning at school is an apprenticeship for learning throughout life.

Most disappointing is that in none of these countries is there more than a cursory and superficial consideration of how language learning can be crucial in the internationalisation of education. There is continuous emphasis on communication with people of other countries and, in the French documents in particular, communication is properly defined as more than exchanging information and bridging information gaps. However, the concept of decentring is linked only with the improvement this will bring in communication, not with taking another, critical and liberating perspective. The potential for tertiary socialisation – irrespective of use of this or other terminology – is not envisaged in any fully developed sense.

The influence of policies on the practices of teachers in their classrooms varies from country to country, and within countries. The more centralised the system, the more likely it is that there will be a strong relationship between policy and practice, but the implementation of policies even in centralised systems is notoriously difficult.

The presence of a strong inspectorate may help to ensure implementation but even then teachers will make their own decisions in subtle ways not visible to inspectors. This is a source of hope when there is absence of the educational values of internationalisation in the policy documents, as many teachers doubtless have their own views (see Byram & Risager, 1999). On the other hand, policy documents reveal the general atmosphere and ethos in which languages are taught, and the weaknesses of the three policies analysed above are indicative of the way in which language teaching is practised.

There is, in fine, much still to be done if foreign language teaching is to take its place in contemporary education. Teachers need understanding of these complex issues, and those who write the guidelines and documents that form the framework for teaching and learning need to provide a richer vision in which the place of foreign language education in an internationalised world is described in depth, and the consequences for the purposes and methods of teaching and learning are discussed.

Chapter 2

Chapter 2 locates foreign language education within the three main purposes of compulsory schooling: to create a sense of belonging to a nation state, to ensure the continuing existence of the 'human capital' on which a state's economy depends and to promote equality of opportunity and equity for all members of the nation state. The reasons for teaching and learning foreign languages have changed as more emphasis has been put on human capital in post-industrial countries; language learning is seen as important to the economy. Internationalisation, however, is not just a matter of economic change but of new relationships with people of other countries, and it is argued that this should lead to an enriched view of language teaching that goes beyond linguistic competence to include 'tertiary socialisation', i.e. acquiring perspectives that challenge those of the nation state and prepare young people for a different sense of belonging in the world. When three countries are examined, however, it becomes evident that their policies and curriculum documents do not yet include such an enriched vision; there is still much to be done.

Chapter 3

Chapter 3 focuses on the current emphasis on linguistic competence. Is it possible to acquire the kinds of linguistic competence that states seem to expect in their requirement for human capital with foreign language capacity? The analysis of two countries (Norway and Japan) and their policies shows that expectations must be defined carefully. What is possible in one situation may not be possible in another. Norwegian school pupils have a quite different learning context from that of Japanese pupils and the question of 'successful' teaching and learning cannot be decided in an impressionistic way. It is too simplistic to say the Norwegians or any other country are 'good language learners' and the Japanese or other nations are 'poor language learners'. Policy makers must provide the conditions for success, but must also realise that there are factors outside schooling that are sometimes more significant than those over which they have control.

Chapter 3

Is Language Learning Possible at School?

Some countries are famous for their success in language learning and others are notorious for their failures. In Europe, the Scandinavian countries, the Netherlands and Germany are among those in the first group and Britain immediately springs to mind for the second group. In East Asia, comparisons are made between South Korea and Japan, to the disadvantage of the latter, especially when the commentators are Japanese. Yet, these impressions are often misleading, as recent research in Germany has shown, where 40% of learners do not reach a score of 500 on the Test of English as a Foreign Language (TOEFL) after nine years of study. Furthermore, it is those who spend some time in study abroad who are far more likely to reach this level, i.e. those whose learning is substantially complemented by learning outside school (Köller & Baumert, 2003). Learning outside school is, as we shall see below, a crucial factor.

Whatever the situation, schools and teachers are made responsible, and it seems obvious to politicians, industrialists and other pundits, that the blame (and occasionally the praise) should be laid at the door of language teachers. The question that is never asked is what is meant by 'success' in language teaching and learning, and whether 'success' can be reasonably expected from language learning in schools, for there is much more to be said than is contained in a TOEFL score. What is assumed is that in the reputedly successful countries, the teaching must be better, or the learners more gifted for languages. In the latter case this leads to unjustifiable generalisations about the British or the Japanese being poor language learners, and the Dutch or Scandinavians being 'natural' learners.

To understand all this better we need to ask the questions that are usually not asked. What is 'success' and 'failure'? Who is responsible? Is success, once defined, a realistic aim for teachers and learners in mainstream, compulsory schooling? What are the sources of success when it occurs? These are questions that interest language professionals but are also drawing attention from politicians and the general public because the economic significance of English as an international language means that language learning is no longer just a matter for teachers. I will therefore focus on English, but the arguments could be pursued for the teaching of other foreign languages in schools.

The Ambitions of Policy-makers

It seems self-evident to politicians and others in non-anglophone countries that the learning of English is essential. Success in English is thought to be crucial for every country in a globalised economy where English is the lingua franca. In anglophone countries, the argument is turned on its head and it is said, that because English is the lingua franca, speakers of English must learn other languages. This is a more difficult argument to understand and has been ignored in Britain until recently. Here I will focus on the intuitively simpler question of why schools should teach English as a foreign language. I will take Norway and Japan as examples since both consider English essential and are similar in that respect.[11] They also differ in many ways and the contrast and comparison are equally informative.

A definition of 'success' could be derived from the examinations and syllabuses in each country, but can also be deduced from the policy statements on the purposes of English learning. The introduction to the Norwegian curriculum for English begins as follows:

> For a small language community like the Norwegian, good language abilities are of decisive importance for contact between peoples and co-operation with others, both in a European and a global perspective. [...] The need to communicate in English is steadily increasing in private life, in education and in working life. [...]

> By learning languages, pupils have the opportunity to become familiar with other cultures. Such insight provides the basis for respect and increased tolerance, and contributes to other ways of thinking and broadens pupils' understanding of their own cultural belonging. In this way pupils' own identity is strengthened. (http://www.utdannings direktoratet.no/dav/78FB8D6918.PDF; accessed 01/05)

What is noteworthy here is that 'co-operation' and communication are not limited to the economic sphere but are equally important in private life and education. There is also explicit reference to 'tolerance', and language learning is considered to be the means of becoming more aware of one's own culture and identity. There are thus three factors: co-operation/communication, tolerance, and enhanced self-understanding/strengthened identity.

There are similarities but also important differences in a Japanese policy statement from 2002, the basis for a major revision of the teaching of English, which includes the following:

With the progress of globalisation in the economy and in society, it is essential that our children acquire communication skills in English [...].

At present, though, the English-speaking abilities of a large percentage of the population are inadequate, and this imposes restrictions on exchanges with foreigners and creates occasions when the ideas and opinions of Japanese people are not appropriately evaluated. However, it is not possible to state that Japanese people have sufficient ability to express their opinions based on a firm grasp of their own language. (http://www.mext.go.jp/english/news/2002/07/020901.htm; accessed 12.02)

What we see here is the same concern with global perspectives but more explicitly and exclusively focused on the economy and society. The private sphere of life is not mentioned. As in Norway, there is a concern with the strengthening of identity, but here it is put in terms of the Japanese nation rather than the identity of individuals. What is not present in the Norwegian statement is the Japanese emphasis on using English as an international language to present Japanese ideas and opinions during co-operation and exchanges with others. The title of the new strategy plan 'Japanese with English abilities' reflects the emphasis on Japaneseness and the absence of reference to tolerance and other ways of thinking that are present in the Norwegian policy.[12]

This might be attributed to Japan being a 'collectivist' society, but a later statement on how this plan can be realised pays more attention to the oppor-tunities for the individual: 'It has become possible for anyone to become active on a world level'; and to the impact on daily life: 'a wide range of activ-ities, from daily life to economic activities, are being influenced by the move-ment to a knowledge-based society driven by the forces of knowledge and information'. The emphasis on presentation of a Japanese perspective is repeated 'English abilities are important in terms of linking our country with the rest of the world, obtaining the world's understanding and trust, enhancing our international presence and further developing our nation', as is the emphasis on Japanese language, which is seen to be the basis for learning English: 'It is also necessary for Japanese to develop their ability to clearly express their own opinions in Japanese first in order to learn English'. (http://www.mext.go.jp/english/topics/03072801.htm; accessed 29.2.08)

In both Norway and Japan, the relationship between foreign language learning and education in the national language – the 'mother tongue' for most but not all pupils in both countries – is emphasised. In the Norwegian document, the relationship is a matter not only of linguistic competence, but also of the educational purposes of both kinds of language teaching:

The work to strengthen pupils' total language competence is a common task for teaching in all language subjects. Therefore the aims and approaches in language subjects are seen as coherent. Thus mother tongue and foreign languages build on a common vision of language where language learning is not only a training in skills, but also education, socialisation and development of awareness of language and culture.

In the Japanese case, the focus is only on the improvement of language skills, in both Japanese and English. Given the belief that current English skills are insufficient, this is not surprising, but the concern about Japanese language is also limited: 'to cultivate Japanese language abilities for appropriate expression and accurate comprehension'. A similar formulation is found in the curriculum for the subject Japanese:

To develop the ability to express the national language properly and understand it accurately, to heighten the ability to communicate, to cultivate thinking power and imaginative power, to enrich language perception, and to deepen awareness of the national language and develop an attitude of respect for the national language. (Monbukagakusho, 2003b: 7, quoted in Parmenter, 2006: 148)

One final similarity and difference between Norway and Japan is worth noting. In both countries, there is an unquestioned assumption that English shall be the dominant foreign language. In Norway, the rationale is that English is 'a major world language' and also 'represents the language area with which we have the closest links in terms of geography, culture and language history'. In Japan the rationale is based on the fact that 'English has played a central role as the common international language in linking people who have different mother tongues. For children living in the 21st century, it is essential for them to acquire communication abilities in English as a common international language'. The close relationship between Norway and the anglophone world, especially linguistically, is a point to which we shall return. What differs noticeably in the two countries is that the Norwegian curriculum sees learning English as 'a good basis for learning several foreign languages', whereas in Japan other languages are not mentioned.[13]

Defining and Comparing 'Success'

Extrapolating from these documents, 'success' in learning English can be characterised as follows:

Norway:

- ability to use English to co-operate and communicate in private, educational and working spheres of life;
- tolerant attitudes and respect for others;
- understanding of own cultural belonging;
- better self-understanding and strengthened identity;
- becoming educated, and socialised and more aware of language and culture.

Japan:

- ability to use English in situations related to international economy and society;
- ability to communicate a Japanese perspective, ideas and opinions
- improved skills in Japanese language.

The advantage of defining success on the basis of policy documents rather than on tests such as TOEFL now becomes clear. Tests attempt only to measure some of the characteristics of success. They do not measure a Norwegian's tolerant attitudes and respect for others, nor the ability of a Japanese to communicate a Japanese perspective, ideas and opinions.

Tests focus on skills of communication primarily in terms of linguistic competence, even though success in communication and co-operation also depends on non-verbal competence, on personality factors, on inter-cultural competence. These may well be taught and learnt but are seldom, if ever, assessed. Despite the importance of non-verbal communication and intercultural competence, familiar enough to linguists, those who claim that language teaching is not successful – the politicians and others in countries like Japan and Britain – are more likely to be thinking of linguistic skills than of the other components of communicative success, not least because they remember what they themselves were tested on when they were language learners. They are less likely to be aware of the other characteristics of successful learning such as tolerance and promoting Japanese ideas and opinions. If we followed this layman approach, we could narrow our focus to test results and, if there is a common standard, to comparison of results in different countries. This is however not an easy matter. International comparisons of educational achievement are difficult and complex. The IEA and OECD have the best reputation in this field but there has been no analysis since 1996 when a study remained incomplete (www.iea.nl/languages; accessed 29.2.08).[14]

Instead of comparing the incomparable, we can continue the analysis of documents, which has the advantage of taking the context of language learning into account. This will allow us to see whether levels expected of teachers and learners under the conditions of general education, where language learning is just one of many subjects, are realistic.

Continuing the comparison of Japan and Norway, it is important first of all to note that Norwegian is in the same language family as English, unlike Japanese. Japanese learners have to deal with a language in a different family, with no cognates to help them, and with a different writing system.

Secondly, it is important to remember how much exposure to English in their own environment young people in Norway have. English is learnt 'for free', as some students put it, because it is so dominant in the media and other aspects of Norwegian society (*Language Education Policy Profile: Norway* http://www.coe.int/lang; accessed 29.2.08) and they acquire their fluency and interest outside the education system. A survey of 10th grade students showed that they think that only half of the English they know is learned at school, and those who do not think of school as their main source of English input are the ones to get the high marks in examinations (Bonnet, 2002: 146). This must be seen in the context of the strong position of English in the curriculum, where it is taught from the first year of schooling at the age of 6/7, and implies that Norwegian students are learning a large amount of English incidentally, outside school.

Expectations at the End of Compulsory Education

Norway

It is not unrealistic therefore that, by the age of 16/17, Norwegian students' attainment in English is expected to be high. This extract from the curriculum makes this explicit, describing what it is hoped students will do during the final year of compulsory education:

Use of the language
During the course of study, students shall:
* work with authentic texts from different periods, *inter alia* short stories, for example by John Steinbeck, young people's novels, extracts from novels (for example by Charlotte Bronte, Lewis Carroll, Sir Arthur Conan Doyle and Agatha Christie), poetry (for example by Emily Dickinson, Rupert Brooke and Langton Hughes), songs (for example by the Beatles), jazz, blues, negro spirituals, biographies, articles, expository and argumentation texts, information material, extracts of plays (for example by William Shakespeare and Tennessee Williams), extracts from films, dramatisations of novels and plays, musicals, films, texts taken from media such as radio and television, newspapers and magazines;

- produce oral and written texts, discuss and argue, have training in the exposition of their own thoughts and deal with contemporary issues;
- explain technical matters in English, for example by giving a lecture or writing reports;
- read at least one novel or simplified text they choose themselves, and a short story they choose themselves or a non-fictional text, and discuss their impressions and understanding of what they have read.

If students are able to do such work – and of course some will be more successful than others – they obviously have a high level of competence in English. A comparison with the global descriptions of levels in the *Common European Framework* shows that descriptions of the highest level, Level C, are similar to what the Norwegian document says:

C2 Can understand with ease virtually everything heard or read. Can summarise information from different spoken and written sources, reconstructing arguments and accounts in a coherent presentation. Can express him/herself spontaneously, very fluently and precisely, differentiating finer shades of meaning even in more complex situations.

C1 Can understand a wide range of demanding, longer texts, and recognise implicit meaning. Can express him/herself fluently and spontaneously without much obvious searching for expressions. Can use language flexibly and effectively for social, academic and professional purposes. Can produce clear, well-structured, detailed text on complex subjects, showing controlled use of organisational patterns, connectors and cohesive devices. (Council of Europe, 2001: 24)

The Norwegian document then also specifies what knowledge of English language culture and their own learning processes students should have by this stage:

During the course of study, students shall:

- learn about various types of sentence construction, sentence links, word classes, their conjugation and function in language, linguistic means to become familiar with different varieties of the English language;
- work on culture and societal conditions in English-speaking countries, *inter alia* human relationships, preservation of nature, the environment and culture, international co-operation, the rights of indigenous peoples, *inter alia* 'the Sami', war and peace, through international contact and extended knowledge of the literature in different English-speaking countries;

- resolve problems they meet in working with the language by using a wide range of aids, experience how information which is useful in the subject English can be stored, organised and made accessible in the classroom and in the library;
- discuss and evaluate learning materials and modes of working with respect to the aims of English teaching and make choices that are useful for their own learning.

Here too it is clear that much is expected.

What time is available for reaching this high level of language and culture knowledge and use? Table 3.1 shows the total number of hours in October 2004, which included a slight increase on previous years. The totals for some other subjects are given in order to see the proportion of students' learning time allocated to languages, both English and the second foreign language, the latter being an optional subject in the final three years of compulsory education.

Table 3.1 Norway: hours of learning

Total in obligatory education	9994
Norwegian*	2261
English	741
Second foreign language	304
Mathematics	1501
Social studies	855

* students have to learn the two varieties of Norwegian
Source: Proposals for the allocation of lessons October 2004[15]

Japan

The situation in Japan is quite different (Table 3.2). Here English is normally learnt form the beginning of lower secondary, in the final three years of compulsory education. Although the vast majority of students in fact stay at school beyond this age and continue their learning of English, this also applies to Norway. In both countries students have a basis for further learning at the end of compulsory education as they move into upper secondary, but in Japan they have had far less time on language learning.

Table 3.2 Japan: hours of learning

	Total lessons in obligatory education	Elementary School	Junior High School**
Total hours of instruction	8307	5367	2940
Japanese	1727	1377	350
English/foreign language	315	None*	315
Mathematics	1184	869	315
Social studies	640	345	295

* No other language instruction (except in experimental projects)
** There are also optional hours in Junior High School, which may be used by some schools or some pupils in schools for extra Japanese or English: 1st year 0–30; 2nd year 50–85; 3rd year 105–165 hours).

This comparison makes explicit that not only is English learnt in Norway from a young age – which may be a better starting point, although this is a disputed issue (Singleton & Lengyel, 1995) – but twice as much time is devoted to it, and we must not forget that students learn it 'for free' outside school.

What are learners in Japan expected to know and be able to do with their English at the end of a relatively limited amount of time devoted to the subject during three years in Junior High School? Whereas the Norwegian document describes what learners are expected to do (learner outcomes), the Japanese documentation focuses on what the teacher should do, what instruction should be given (teacher input):

Language activities

The following language activities should be conducted over three years in order to develop students' abilities to understand and express themselves in English.

Listening – instruction mainly on the following items should be given:
- to follow the basic characteristics of English sounds such as stress, intonation and pauses, and understand the meaning of utterances;
- to listen to English, spoken and read in a natural tone, and understand specific content and important parts;
- to listen to questions and requests, and respond appropriately;
- to understand content correctly by asking speakers to repeat, etc.

Speaking – instruction mainly on the following items should be given:
- to become familiar with the basic characteristics of English sounds such as stress, intonation and pauses, and pronounce English sounds correctly;
- to speak correctly about one's thoughts and feelings to the listener;
- to carry on a dialogue and to exchange views regarding what has been listened to or read.;
- to speak extensively by utilising various techniques such as using linking words, etc.

Reading – instruction mainly on the following items should be given:
- to distinguish between different letters and symbols, and read correctly;
- to read silently, thinking about the content written, and to read out aloud so that the meaning of the content is expressed;
- to read and understand the general outline and pick out the important parts of stories, descriptive texts, etc;
- to understand the writer's intentions in messages, letters, etc. and respond appropriately.

Writing – instruction mainly on the following items should be given:
- to distinguish between different letters and symbols, and write correctly with due attention to the spaces between words, etc;
- to take notes and write impressions, opinions, etc. about what has been listened to or read;
- to write correctly about one's thoughts and feelings to the reader;
- to write messages, letters, etc. that correctly transmit the writer's intentions to the reader. (http://www.mext.go.jp/english/shotou/ 030301.htm; accessed 29.2.08)

Because of the way this is formulated it is difficult to compare it with the global descriptions of Levels in the *Common European Framework,* but there seems to be some correspondence with the levels designated as 'Basic User':

A1 Can understand and use familiar everyday expressions and very basic phrases aimed at the satisfaction of needs of a concrete type. Can introduce him/herself and others and can ask and answer questions about personal details such as where he/she lives, people he/she knows and things he/she has. Can interact in a simple way provided the other person talks slowly and clearly and is prepared to help.

A2 Can understand sentences and frequently used expressions related to areas of most immediate relevance (e.g. very basic personal and family information, shopping, local geography, employment). Can communicate in simple and routine tasks requiring a simple and direct exchange of information on familiar and routine matters. Can describe in simple terms aspects of his/her background, immediate environment and matters in areas of immediate need. (Council of Europe, 2001: 24)

This seems to be a realistic aim for the time available, but it means that a Norwegian student at the end of compulsory education is far more advanced than a Japanese student. Although in practice the great majority in both countries then go on to further studies, it is unlikely that students in Japan will catch up with their Norwegian peers, who often continue to study English, although not compulsorily.

Yet, as we saw above, the policy-makers of both countries are conscious of the need for international English, and in Japan are so concerned that they have developed a strategic plan to improve the situation. Given the greater difficulty for Japanese students with a language of another language family and writing system, and their lack of 'for free' input from the environment,[16] the logical conclusion is to increase the hours for teaching and learning, together with many other actions to improve methods of teaching learning and assessment.

Matching Policies with Possibilities

My purpose is not to make policy proposals for Japan, but to ask whether language learning is possible in schools, using these two cases as starting points. The simple answer is that many learners in both education systems reach the expected levels, and in that sense language learning in schools is possible (albeit with the help of a favourable environment in Norway). It is also noteworthy that teachers are doing what is expected of them by curriculum planners, although teachers in Norway get a lot of help from the environment. Nonetheless in Japan the dissatisfaction remains, and this is not surprising given the low level expected in curriculum planning.[17] The question that follows from this is not only whether 'success' is being achieved in an education system but also what level it is reasonable to define as success in different circumstances.

It is evident from my analysis of the Norwegian and Japanese policy statements – which are not dissimilar to policies in other countries – that policy-makers make heavy demands on schools with respect to the level of English they see as necessary in the globalised economy and internationalised world. In Norway, there is coherence between policy and curriculum planning, and the policy expectations correspond to the curriculum outcomes and the levels of use of English at the end of compulsory education.

Since many students pass the Norwegian examinations, English learning in Norway is successful, and on the whole Norwegian politicians seem to be satisfied, although they may not be aware of the amount of help schools get from extra-school learning. Attention now focuses on the teaching of a second foreign language where the situation is unsatisfactory and much more comparable with the teaching of English in Japan. It is a moot question whether Norwegian students can attain the same levels in French or German or other second foreign language for which they do not have the 'for free' input they have in English.

In Japan in contrast, there is a clear mis-match between the needs for international English as presented in the policy statements on the one hand and the curriculum documents on the other. Although the levels expected by curriculum planners are realistic for the time available, and although learners may attain them, they will not be able to use English to express themselves in complex ways, to represent Japanese views, to enhance Japan's presence in the world as policy-makers hope.

The conclusion I draw is that my original question, and the title of this chapter, is too simple. I started from that question, however, because it is the kind of question policy-makers, parents, employers and others ask. They do not realise that questions of this kind have to be related to a specific context and to specific policy ambitions. If the expectations of a society are to be fulfilled, then the appropriate conditions have to be provided.

There are not only conditions of time available as analysed here. Questions of teacher qualifications, teaching and assessment methods are important too, and are a problem under discussion in Norway just as much as in Japan, despite the apparent success of Norwegian teachers. Nonetheless, however good the teachers, materials, examinations and other matters, policy expectations and curriculum demands of learners need to be matched by time allocations and a realistic analysis of the whole societal environment in which language learning takes place.

Chapter 3

Chapter 3 started with the question of whether it is possible to learn foreign languages at school and concluded that this is far too simple a question, even though it is one that underlies much policy making and the expectations of the general public. By analysing what is expected by the end of compulsory schooling in Japan and Norway – two quite different teaching and learning contexts – it is possible to understand in more detail what 'success' might mean, what can be reasonably expected and what teaching and learning conditions need to be provided. Like the vast majority of countries in the world, it is a matter of acquiring English because of its importance as perceived by politicians and parents. Policy makers and people in general often assume that what is involved is striving to acquire the linguistic competence of a native speaker or someone who is 'near-native'. If this is to be possible in practice – and it is not evident that it is possibility in theory – then a more radical approach to curriculum planning needs to be taken.

Chapter 4

Chapter 4 introduces an alternative to the native speaker as a model for the learner. The intercultural speaker is not simply someone with linguistic competence. Whatever the level of linguistic competence possible in a given set of learning conditions, it is just as important to consider what cultural competences should be acquired. This chapter explains the rationale for the concept of the intercultural speaker and describes what is involved by comparing the intercultural person with the bicultural. Being bicultural is different from acting interculturally because the former is largely a matter of where and how people are brought up, whereas the latter is a consequence of formal education, the creation in learners of a potential to act in small or major ways as people mediating between cultures.

The Intercultural Speaker: Acting Interculturally or Being Bicultural

The phrase 'intercultural speaker' was coined in the mid-1990s in the course of writing a paper (Byram & Zarate, 1997) on the assessment of socio-cultural competence as defined in the work of the Council of Europe (van Ek, 1986). The purpose was to suggest how levels of socio-cultural competence might be defined and assessed in a way similar to the levels of linguistic competence that were later published in the *Common European Framework of Reference* (Council of Europe, 2001).

There were a number of problems. The first was that the definition of socio-cultural competence assumed that language learners should learn the language spoken by native speakers, that understanding and using the language required the learner to be familiar with the native context, and by implication that there was just one native context:

> Every language is situated in a socio-cultural context and implies the use of a particular reference frame which is partly different from that of the foreign language learner; socio-cultural competence presupposes a certain degree of familiarity with that context. (van Ek, 1986: 41)

In the definition of linguistic or 'grammatical' competence, it had already been stated that this involves the production and interpretation of 'conventional meaning [...] that meaning which native speakers would normally attach to an utterance when used in isolation' (van Ek, 1986: 39). The subordination of the language learner to the native speaker has been a well established and unquestioned assumption since the beginning of the modern phase of language teaching in Europe and the USA, in the late 19th century. For example, Gouin's methodology (1892) was predicated on the assumption that learners could acquire a language in a way that systematised what children acquiring it in natural surroundings do, and with the same results.

Since the 1980s the dominance of the native speaker as a model for learners has been much challenged, not only as an unattainable ideal, but also because it is difficult to define. Native speakers are multifarious, have competences that differ from each other and vary over a lifetime and are often multilingual. The notion is also politically suspect because of the hegemonic imposition of an unattainable model on learners who cannot resist (Pennycook, 1994). Furthermore, whereas van Ek implied that there is just one context of use for any given language, this is clearly not the case for many languages that are used in different societies as the official or dominant vernacular. Some of these criticisms have been challenged; for example the notion that learners are not able to resist the hegemony of the native speaker model (Canagarajah, 1999). It can also be argued that there is a need for a linguistic norm, especially for English (Davies, 2003), as otherwise a number of mutually incomprehensible Englishes will develop, with a loss of the advantages of speaking an international language. Trying to anticipate this problem, the government of Singapore encourages citizens to speak standard English – largely modelled on British English – and to avoid the Singlish, which may be becoming a variety that gives Singaporeans a linguistic identity, but which is not accessible to other speakers of English.

Whatever the arguments with respect to linguistic competence, there is a serious problem with the model of the native speaker for language learning. Our focus on socio-cultural competence made this particularly evident. The native speaker, perhaps in some idealised form, can be the model in one competence but need not be in all. For if the native speaker were taken as the model for socio-cultural competence, then the ultimate consequence would be an identification with a particular 'context', the acquisition of the 'conventional meanings' of native speakers in that context, and the complete familiarisation with the use of those conventional meanings in that context. This is not what van Ek suggests, but his definition implies the subordination of learners' knowledge and use of a language to the way it is used by native speakers in a given context. We wished to re-assess this position.

Our view was that a learner should be conceived as a 'complete' individual, not as one who is 'almost' a native speaker. We were not alone in this since other authors of Council of Europe documents stressed the concept of the autonomous learner, and in the final version of the *Common European Framework of Reference* (CEFR) learners and other users of a language are viewed 'primarily as "social agents"' (Council of Europe, 2001: 9). We saw the learner as someone who, as a social actor,[18] inhabits a space between their own conventional meanings and context on the one hand, and those of *some* native speakers of the language on the other. We did not at that stage consider the use of a language as a lingua franca nor the relationships among social actors using a lingua franca.

It was important to find a designation that would draw attention to this in-between position and simultaneously contrast with the model of the native speaker. Hence the term 'intercultural speaker', and a redefinition of the cultural competence involved, which we labelled intercultural competence to distinguish it from socio-cultural competence.

The goal of our paper, to suggest levels of intercultural competence and modes of assessment, proved to be too difficult in the time available, although other attempts have been made since, as discussed Chapter 14.

The process of further conceptualisation of the intercultural speaker and the difference from the native speaker was pursued by Kramsch (1998), and the question of whether the concept is too embroiled in assumptions deriving from European philosophy was addressed by Parmenter (2003). Kramsch points out that the idealised model of the native speaker should be replaced by an account much closer to reality, where 'speakers (acquire) over their lifetime a whole range of various rules of interpretation that they use knowingly and judiciously according to the various social contexts in which they live and with which they make sense of the world around them' (Kramsch. 1998: 27). When they do this they are operating like the intercultural speaker who is also 'operating at the border between several languages or language varieties, manoeuvring his/her way through the troubled waters of cross-cultural misunderstandings' (Kramsch. 1998: 27). Parmenter's contribution is to identify tendencies in the assumptions and concepts in the definition of intercultural (communicative) competence that are a consequence of its origins in a Euro-American context. She points out how some elements of the concept would fit easily with assumptions and concepts in Asia, and others not. There needs to be for example 'an awareness that there are alternative concepts of self, communication and education' (Parmenter, 2003: 142) that would enrich the European-American way of thinking about the intercultural speaker. More empirical work is needed to pursue this line of thought in the practice of pedagogy.

Here, I propose to take another perspective in order to refine the concept. I will compare and contrast being intercultural with being bicultural.

It needs to be said immediately that there is an important general difference. People become bicultural in a natural way, as a consequence of living in certain situations, through which, as Kramsch says, they negotiate and steer their pathway. On the other hand, people become intercultural in the sense defined here, as a consequence of being the learner under the direction of a teacher. The teacher has certain hopes and intentions for the learner that contribute to the learner's education as personal development.

The difference can be formulated through the contrast between 'describing' and 'prescribing'. I will first describe what being bicultural *is*, and then define what being intercultural *ought to be*. In the second case there is a specific role for teachers and education systems, and I shall suggest what needs to be done to ensure that language education, and/or other dimensions of education, provides intercultural experience and develops intercultural competence. The main question I am interested in elucidating is whether becoming intercultural involves a change in one's relationship to the culture(s) into which one has been socialised, i.e. some change in cultural identity, as well as some change in attitudes towards other cultures and one's own. In this context, the definition of 'culture' I shall use is the 'shared beliefs, values and behaviours' of a social group, where 'social group' can refer to any collectivity of people, from those in a social institution such as a university, a golf club, a family, to those organised in large-scale groups such as a nation, or even a 'civilisation' such as 'European'. The beliefs in question are the 'shared meanings' (Taylor, 1971) which justify and underpin their behaviours and the 'social representations' (Farr & Moscovici, 1984) they hold in common. There are also shared 'values' that include the values attached to their beliefs and behaviours, and the attitudes they have towards their shared social representations.

Being Bicultural

Social identity theory (Tajfel, 1981) suggests that individuals interact on two levels: in interpersonal and in intergroup behaviour. When circumstances are such that group characteristics are prominent – the presence of another language is one indicator of group difference and therefore accentuates the presence of group characteristics – individuals categorise themselves and others in terms of their belonging to groups, i.e. they act at the second level. The empirical work in social identity theory shows how individuals can be influenced by groups, and their individuality, their personal identity, dominated by their group identity; how individuals respond to other individuals in terms of such categorisation; how this leads to comparison and competition which is in turn a basis for self-esteem. When a person's group is successful in competition with others, the person's self-esteem is increased. Group membership can be created artificially, as experiments have shown (Tajfel, 1981; Sherif & Sherif, 1969), but it is usually a result of the process of socialisation.

Through the processes of primary and secondary socialisation (Berger & Luckmann, 1966), individuals become members of many social groups. Becoming a member of a social group involves incorporating its culture (cf. Bourdieu's concept of 'habitus' 1977) but also being accepted by others in the group and defining oneself as a member of the group (Tajfel, 1981).[19]

Being a member of a group is thus a consequence of self-ascription, but it is also reinforced by other-ascription, by being categorised by others as a member of a group (Barth, 1969). Most of the groups to which an individual belongs complement each other: one can be a member of a golf club and a football club, of a school and a family, although there may be some degree of conflict in the cultures involved (some families do not accept all the beliefs, values and behaviours that a school expects of its children). Others are mutually exclusive: one cannot be a member of two rival football clubs, or at least not openly so. Where one is a member of rival groups, for example someone with two nationalities, there will be situations in which one needs to keep silent about membership of one whilst acknowledging membership of the other.

When one group is dominant, it can force individuals into the category of a low-status minority group and this can have a detrimental effect on the self-esteem of the individuals if they accept the dominant group's definition of them. This is one of the worst effects of colonialism in the past and in the present.

Where people from two social groups interact and are in competition, they force each other to act in terms of their identification with one or the other group. This is problematic for people who would like to belong to more than one group but are forced to choose by other people who perceive the groups as mutually exclusive, and therefore the identities associated with them as mutually exclusive. This is very evident when football teams and their supporting groups meet, or when the groups are nation states at war.

There are thus mutually exclusive identities where membership of national/ethnic groups is concerned. With Edwards (1985), I distinguish between ethnic groups which focus on membership by descent and shared culture, and national groups which are ethnic groups with political ambitions. This is different again from the notion of a state, although nations often wish to realise their political ambitions in the form of a homogeneous nation state. The most recent European example is in Yugoslavia, but it was also the case in the 19th century in Wales, and still today in Ireland (Hobsbawm, 1992). On the other hand, the drive towards political representation and independence as a nation state is not a necessary development, as Oommen argues:

> a nation is essentially a cultural entity and it is not natural for a nation to establish its own state, as is widely believed. Such theories and experiences are European and do not fit the reality of South Asia. (Oommen, 1999: 2–3)

In fine, membership of ethnic national groups has to be either mutually exclusive or, if an individual wishes to be in two (or more) groups, he or she has to manage this carefully, since most members of an ethnic group are mono-ethnic and tolerate poorly the presence of 'hybrids'. Being bicultural is often a difficult state of being, as we shall see.[20]

My illustrations are taken from South Tyrol, Italy, where young people who are bilingual, born of one parent from the German minority and one from the Italian majority, have difficulty because the assumption is that people are either German or Italian, with both parents from the same ethnic group, and that 'mixed' parentage is problematic and best avoided.

The first quotation shows the power of other-ascription: other children will not allow someone to be both German and Italian, and it is the language that is seen as the symbol of ethnicity:

Was it difficult to become bilingual?

I would say that I haven't had any particular problems in the languages, but with the (other) children. Because I was in the German school, they looked on me as if I was an Italian, and in the Italian school they considered me to be German. (Egger, 1985: 178; my translation)

So the tactic for the person with adequate linguistic competence is to pass as a member of the group with whom one is interacting at a given moment:

Because I was always quite good in both languages, if I was in German groups, I spoke German, and they didn't notice that I was an Italian, and have an Italian mother, and if I was among Italians, they always thought that I'm Italian. So I never had difficulties. (Egger, 1985: 178; my translation)

But how does the individual experience this process of ascription by self and others, this acceptance of the common assumption that one must be either one thing or the other? What is the effect upon identity? Unfortunately there is only a little systematic and theoretically well-founded research that tells us what is involved in being bicultural. There is nothing analogous to Second Language Acquisition research, which describes the process of acquisition, or to discourse analysis which analyses the language processes of interaction between people of different languages and cultures (Scollon & Scollon, 1995). Norton (2000) has studied women immigrants in Canada, and Miller (1999) has analysed the changing identities of young immigrants in Australia. Both focus on issues of power in the community, of developing new social identities, and the significance of language learning in this context, but do not pursue the psychological impact of being obliged to learn another language and the effect on the individual's existing social identities. Pavlenko has analysed autobiographical narratives of people who have experienced several cultures to theorise about their acquisition of language and culture (Pavlenko & Lantolf, 2000). He, a Chinese researcher, has traced in three articles the cross-cultural lives of herself and two other Chinese women teachers as they experienced change within China – the Cultural Revolution – and as they moved to Canada. She uses narrative analysis to document their construction of new identities as teachers (He, 2002a, 2002b, 2002c) but this approach does not provide a basis for theorising about other people's experience.

Another area of research that has attempted to theorise bicultural identity comes from counselling and psychotherapy (Valdez, 2000; Poston, 1990; Herring, 1995). This research attempts to explain how people have to deal with choice between two cultural identities that they could accept but which are seen as mutually exclusive by the cultural groups in question. The conflict is experienced particularly by young people with biracial (Afro-American and Euro-American) identities but also by Hispanic-Americans with parents from Hispanic and Euro-American ethnic groups. The focus here is on the problems experienced and on how therapists can help their clients to overcome the problems, but the existence of such problems is perhaps more widespread than is often realised, as shown by the following extract from an interview with Italian immigrants to Belgium:

Do you feel Belgian or still Italian?

Well let's say it's difficult. We have taken on all the customs here, but it's difficult to say we're Belgian because of that, just as it's difficult to say that we're not Belgians, either. Since all our children are here ... so we're neither one nor the other...Here we're foreigners, and at home we're foreigners too ... All the people of our age, a whole generation, left Italy ... so when we go back to Italy, we're treated like foreigners, since the new generation doesn't know us ... Personally, I'm alright wherever I am earning a living ... I don't have anything against the Belgians or against the Italians ...

[...] In the final analysis, we feel just as foreign over there. We go there, and we are foreign too, so when we go back, they say 'Ah the immigrants are here'. We're foreigners here and there, really. We have nowhere really. Well we're used to the Belgian rhythm, I think. We don't even pay attention any more to the word 'foreigner', but from time to time, it gets to us, you know. (Byram, 1990: 90)

Despite having lived for more than 20 years in Belgium, the sense of anomie is strong, and the power of other-ascription very evident. Wherever they go they are 'foreigners' and though they no longer pay attention to people calling them foreigners, the final line reveals hidden and suppressed emotions created by others, by people who do not allow them to belong.

These people had moved from their original home to their new one in adulthood, but it is important to distinguish this experience from becoming bicultural through primary socialisation. Studies of this phenomenon include the acquisition of deaf bicultural identity (Holcomb, 1997) and the biculturalism of 'kikokushijo', children of Japanese expatriates. Kanno concluded from four case studies of teenage kikokushijo that:

> Although the four individuals were of diverse personalities and attitudes, their stories all reflect a bicultural self that made it difficult to fit comfortably and naturally in any one society. (Kanno, 2000: 378)

The difficulty was blamed on the host societies and in some cases on individuals' lack of will to participate in those societies, and there is a tendency for the literature to identify problem cases. On the other hand one study shows how, though there may be stages of 'denial or confusion', it is possible for a bicultural to arrive at a stage of 'integration' (Garrett, 1996). The narrative of the life of a member of the Eastern Band of Cherokee Indians is analysed in terms of a five-stage model of bicultural identity, leading ultimately to 'integration', defined as follows:

> a secure, integrated identity with the ability to function effectively in both cultures. In addition, they understand the meanings behind various cultural values, beliefs, expectations, and practices of which they are a part. (Garrett, 1996: 18)

The description that the interviewee offers in his own words suggests very explicitly that a person can hold within himself two cultural, ethnic identities and, because he gained acceptance by both groups (as a highly regarded medical doctor) it seems that being two people is not difficult for him:

> I think who I am, is that I truly am two people, matter of fact. Doc Amoneeta Sequoyah used to call me 'Gagoyoti' in other words 'two people'. In Cherokee, that's a way of saying, well you're this and you're that. For me a lot of my conflicts in earlier years were because I wasn't sure who I was. Was I Indian, was I white, you know, what was a mixture of person, where did I belong? I knew deep down inside, I didn't belong with that class of people who felt they were better than

others. And I knew that the people I came from, the Cherokees, there was something very special. (Garrett, 1996: 18)

Despite the successful outcome, this person too had experienced conflict and a sense of not knowing where he belonged. Again this is bound up with how other people, especially the dominant majority group, attribute an identity to the individual whether the individual wishes it or not.

A particular striking instance of this is caught by Eva Hoffmann in her account of becoming a resident of Canada, and ultimately a Canadian. She and her sister have just been given new versions of their Polish names that are easier to pronounce for the teacher:

We make our way to a bench at the back of the room; nothing much has happened, except a small, seismic mental shift. The twist in our names takes them a tiny distance from us – but it's a gap into which the infinite hobgoblin of abstraction enters. Our Polish names didn't refer to us; they were as surely us as our eyes and hands. These new appellations, which we ourselves can't yet pronounce, are not us. They are identification tags, disembodied signs pointing to objects that happen to be my sister and myself. We walk to our seats, into a roomful of unknown faces, with names that make us strangers to ourselves. (Hoffman, 1989: 105)

Hoffman's experience as described in the rest of her book suggests that she never felt quite at ease with the new set of values, beliefs and behaviours despite spending most of her life in North America. She had moved from Poland to Canada about the age of 12 and in some respects she has the same experience as the Italian migrants. The power of primary socialisation in one cultural environment may be such that 'late' acquisition of another cultural identity is not entirely successful, but it is unlikely that a specific age can be identified as crucial, given the complexity of being bicultural.

Another example of this complexity is found in the account by Christina Bratt Paulston of her own bicultural experience. Her primary socialisation was into a monocultural Swedish environment and later she moved to the USA. She draws on a particular model of culture that identifies three dimensions: cognition, affection and action. Under cognition, she suggests that a characteristic of being bicultural is to be 'able to interpret what the same phenomenon means from the viewpoint of two cultures' – also a characteristic, I shall argue, of the interculturally competent person. It is however when she talks about the affective dimension that there is an implicit link with the notion of socialisation:

Under the Affection domain, Kleinjans posits the following levels:

perception, appreciation, re-evaluation, reorientation, identification. Perception and appreciation simply refer to the coming to know and to like aspects of another culture, like food and music as well as aesthetic and moral values. [...] Re-evaluation is the process of changing one's values. 'It might mean a shift in priorities, the giving up of certain values for new ones, or an enlargement of one's value system.' Reorientation means changing the direction of one's life, 'spurred by values he has adopted from the second culture.' Identification is becoming one with the people of the other culture; 'A person changes citizenship'. (Paulston, 1992: 124)

The final phases of reorientation and identification are very reminiscent of Berger and Luckmann's (1966: 176ff) discussion of re-socialisation. In the extreme case this becomes 'alternation' where, as in religious conversion, an individual abandons one set of beliefs and values for another. They argue, however, that there are degrees of transformation of beliefs and values lying between the extreme of alternation and the normal process of secondary socialisation. As long as there are no abrupt discontinuities in the individual's subjective biography and new beliefs and values are not incompatible with existing ones, then re-socialisation of the extreme kind does not take place.

Paulston is a professional linguist who has no trouble with being bilingual, but finds it difficult to be bicultural. It is not her bi/multilingualism that is the most important issue. Degrees of competence in two or more languages are only relevant, as we saw in the South Tyrolean example, in as far as they allow people to hide one of their identities; it is not the degree of competence itself that makes someone more or less bicultural. Since the monolingual members of one group cannot usually evaluate the competence of someone speaking the language of the other group, it is simply the fact that they do so which is important. If they decide that the person's competence in their own language is not that of a native speaker, then they ascribe that person to membership of another group, just as children in Japan assume that anyone who is obviously not Japanese and speaks English must be American.[21]

Paulston suggests that also from the point of view of the bicultural individual, there are levels of incompatibility in the experience of conflicting cultural values:

At these levels I don't believe it is possible to be bicultural. When I took out US citizenship, I had to give up my Swedish citizenship; I could not have both. And so it is with conflicting cultural values; in the same way as one just can't believe in the overriding importance of consensus and conciliation of group interests at the same time as one believes in confrontation and the overriding rights of the individual in solving problems. (Paulston, 1992: 129)

The analogy with citizenship is misleading since some states allow people to have two citizenships, but Paulston's point is that some aspects of the two identities that are potentially available to her are incompatible and she has to choose. Choice is not in this case forced on people by the other-ascription of their peers. At the deepest level, it is an inevitability. At the deepest level, beliefs and values – such as confrontation versus conciliation – are unalterable and incompatible and there is no alternation possible. At other levels, it is possible to choose behaviours – 'learning to be late' – to suit the circumstance, i.e. there is deliberate alternation:

So what happens, I think, is that the individual picks and chooses. Some aspects of culture are beyond modification. Many Americans comment on my frankness, but Swedes never do. Now I wouldn't want to claim that Swedes lie less than Americans, but I do think there is more emphasis on the value of always telling the truth (or saying nothing) in the socialisation process of Swedish children. I know some people dislike me for it, and still I don't change because I simply cannot. But many aspects of culture are within the bounds of modification; one can learn to be half an hour late and not consider it moral slackness; one can learn to eat with one's fingers and still feel like an adult. But such modifications mainly concern surface behaviour, behaviour one can switch back and forth. (Paulston, 1992: 129)

Paulston also points out that when individuals have conflicting values imposed on them, the result may be some form of psychopathology, and we saw earlier that there is research that springs from therapeutic work. The experience of the young people in South Tyrol is fortunately not so extreme, but there are certainly indications of living with constant pressure, being drawn in two directions, and Paulston refers to cases where mental break-down has taken place.

This is where Paulston's account coincides with the literature from psychotherapy and counselling, but she makes a useful distinction between levels: the ability to adapt in behaviour without necessarily changing in values and beliefs. In behaviour where there are no conflicts present, it is possible to be bicultural, but where there are conflicting values at other 'deeper' levels, it is not. She remains convinced that at the levels of reorientation and identification, the individual cannot accommodate conflicting values and meanings.

Acting Interculturally

As Genevieve Zarate and I said in our first paper on intercultural competence (Byram & Zarate, 1997), to act interculturally is to bring into a relationship two cultures. At the time we were thinking of the cultures of nations and in particular of nation states since we were developing the concept in the context of foreign/modern language learning.[22] One of the outcomes of teaching languages (and cultures) should be the ability to see how different cultures relate to each other – in terms of similarities and differences – and to act as mediator between them, or more precisely between people socialised into them. This also includes 'mediating' between oneself and others, i.e. being able to take an 'external' perspective on oneself as one interacts with others and to analyse and, where desirable, adapt one's behaviour and underlying values and beliefs. Thus at any given point in time, the individual is bringing into contact through their own self, two sets of values, beliefs and behaviours. Moreover, any individual may have a range of experiences and competences that allow them to relate a variety of combinations of cultures so that the relationships are not just binary but plural.

So the phrase 'intercultural *speaker*' can be paraphrased as an 'intercultural mediator', although the emphasis on speaker is useful because it reminds us of the importance of language, and the implication that mediation pre-supposes some linguistic competence. The relationship between language and the shared values, beliefs and behaviours in a social group is complex and much debated, but it is undoubtedly close, as shown for example by Wierzbicka's work on richly connoted keywords (1997), or by Agar's concept of 'languaculture' (Agar, 1994a, 1994b; Risager 2007). As a consequence, the best mediators are those who have an understanding of the relationship between, on the one hand, their own language and language varieties and their own culture and cultures of different social groups in their society and, on the other hand, the language (varieties) and culture(s) of others, between (inter) which they find themselves acting as mediators.

The phrase 'acting as mediator' is important. It distinguishes 'intercultural' from 'bicultural' since the latter need not involve the act of mediating. In most case, bicultural people simply live with others through whichever of their cultural identities is appropriate. They might also be asked to mediate, to explain the relationships between two cultures they know, but this is an extra demand for them to become intercultural, and one they may not be able to meet.

'Acting interculturally' pre-supposes certain attitudes, knowledge and skills that need to be learnt. Being bicultural, as Paulston argues, can mean changing behaviour at a surface level without changing values at a deeper level. Being bicultural, she says, is not possible at the deepest level of values acquired in early socialisation. To act interculturally, however, requires a willingness to suspend those deeper values, at least temporarily, in order to be able to understand and empathise with the values of others that are incompatible with one's own. To take Paulston's example, if a Swedish person is to act interculturally between someone who is always frank and someone who seeks to avoid embarrassment and hurt, then she must suspend her frankness. This might be difficult because it was acquired in early socialisation and she may need the help of a teacher to raise to consciousness the assumption that being frank is the only way to act, in order then to act differently

Since being intercultural is an activity, I have tried to describe what should be the behaviours involved (Byram, 1997). I have done so in 'behavioural objectives' terms since the description also served the purpose of proposing an approach to curriculum design. However, I do not want to imply by the term 'behavioural objectives' that what is involved is some simple adoption of surface behaviour, or a simple adoption of classic behavioural approaches to curriculum design. The issues involved are affective and cognitive as well as behavioural, as the following extracts from a definition of intercultural communicative competence (Byam, 1997) indicate:

- *Attitudes*: curiosity and openness, readiness to suspend disbelief about other cultures and belief about one's own (*savoir être*).
- *Knowledge:* of social groups and their products and practices in one's own and in one's interlocutor's country, and of the general processes of societal and individual interaction (*savoirs*).
- *Skills of interpreting and relating*: ability to interpret a document or event from another culture, to explain it and relate it to documents from one's own (*savoir comprendre*).
- *Skills of discovery and interaction*: ability to acquire new knowledge of a culture and cultural practices and the ability to operate knowledge, attitudes and skills under the constraints of real-time communication and interaction (*savoir apprendre/faire*).
- *Critical cultural awareness/political education*: an ability to evaluate critically and on the basis of explicit criteria perspectives, practices and products in one's own and other cultures and countries (*savoir s'engager*).

Acting interculturally can be something very simple or very complex. On one occasion at Malaga airport in Spain, a favourite destination for people from the North East of England, I saw a boy of lower secondary school age, who had apparently studied Spanish at school, explaining to his parents what the signs meant, where they had to go and how to find their luggage. On another occasion in a negotiation about a salary for a Portuguese person in a British university, I had to explain to the Dean what 'the thirteenth month' of salary is in Portugal, which I did not know existed in Portugal but had come across in Germany: an 'extra' month which is part of what in Britain would be an 'annual salary'. There was no linguistic problem here, but a taken-for-granted understanding on both sides of what is a 'normal salary'. An ability to decentre was crucial in both situations, and an ability to transfer previous experience was important in the second.

Let me now turn to the issue of the relationship between being intercultural and social identity. The link is again provided by socialisation theory, taking the concepts of primary and secondary socialisation one step further in language learning.

It has been argued that, when children are introduced to foreign language learning in schools, they undergo a further, tertiary, stage of socialisation (Doyé, 1992; see Chapter 2 of this volume). In its simplest version, this occurs essentially in two ways. First, the children are required to re-live some of their primary and secondary socialisation in a new way. For example they have to re-learn how to count, or what the names of colours are, and this usually means a new way of linking language to reality because the names of colours and numbers do not have a one-to-one relationship with the apparent equivalent in their first language. At a more advanced stage, they learn that their concepts of 'freedom', of 'friendship' and of 'homeland' are not universal and are understood differently elsewhere (Wierzbicka, 1997). Second, their experience of the world is extended, as it is constantly in schooling, but with a different set of beliefs, values and behaviours implicit in the new world they encounter. Whereas most of the rest of the curriculum is founded on secondary socialisation, simply extending experience of the society into which children were born, language teaching has the potential to introduce new cultures from other societies. This includes the possibility of introducing children to the culture of a new social group with a different national identity, contrasting with their own.[23] Should language teachers therefore try to make their learners bicultural?

The analysis of biculturalism shows that the experience may be a painful and confusing one. In the extreme case, it could mean 'alternation' as described earlier, with the implication that it means learners abandoning their existing national identity, but such a case is very unlikely. In a less extreme version, there can be a fear that secondary socialisation is 'contaminated' by the values, behaviours and beliefs of another culture, for example when the foreign language is of a higher status than the learners' own. Learners may as a consequence be tempted to reject their own national/ethnic identity and imitate that of the dominant language group. The teaching of (American) English in some countries may be a case in point, and is much discussed in South Korea and Taiwan (Ho, 1997; Hsieh, forthcoming). In the European situation, professional experience and intuition suggests that language learning in the classroom is not usually sufficient to create a desire to pass into another national group, to take on another national identity, and experimentation with students in upper secondary in Germany (Meyer, 1991; Kordes, 1991) suggests that they cannot reach a very advanced stage of being an intercultural speaker/ mediator.

A Comparison of Being Bicultural and Acting Interculturally

I started with the question as to whether an analysis of what it is to be bicultural can help in being more precise about what teaching intercultural competence means. It is also interesting to consider whether an analysis of acting interculturally throws more light on the experience of being bicultural.

It has become clear that to become bicultural can be difficult and depends on how different the two cultures are as well as on the degree of acceptance by other people. Analyses may exaggerate the difficulties because the literature is largely focused on people who find the experience problematic and need help. More analyses of 'success stories' (e.g. DeKorne et al., 2007) are needed, and it may then become clear that biculturals find some aspects of their experience less difficult to deal with than others. As Jackson argues, the complexity of contemporary societies allows young people to act creatively:

> In late modern pluralistic societies, individuals might identify with aspects of a cultural tradition, argue with other aspects and also draw creatively on new resources in reshaping their own cultural identities. (Jackson, 2004: 90)

What is remarkable for its absence from the discussion of biculturalism is any examination of if and how biculturals act as intercultural speakers/ mediators between their two cultures. Nor is there any discussion of biculturals' attitudes to third cultures. Research on bilinguals – and most biculturals are bilingual – suggests that they have a greater meta-awareness of language and an ability to decentre, but this has not led to research on attitudes to other cultures. It is possible that biculturals are 'ethnocentric in two cultures', just as monoculturals can be ethnocentric in one. If this were the case, then it would be necessary to teach biculturals to decentre from their dual ethnocentricity, but the ways in which this would be done would differ from the methods used with monoculturals to encourage them to decentre from one single ethnocentricity

What makes acting interculturally different from being bicultural is the issue of conscious awareness. The literature on biculturals who need therapeutic help suggests that part of the treatment is to make them aware:

> The therapeutic approach to work with these bicultural clients needs to focus on helping clients become aware of the complex process that occurs in the development of their self-identity and how this complex development affects their everyday interaction with the environment. (Valdez, 2000: 242)

The pedagogical literature, both theoretical (e.g. Zarate, 1993; Kramsch, 1993) and practical (e.g. Byram et al., 2001), focuses on making learners aware of the relationships between cultures, and promotes methods of comparative study to do so.

It is more important to change attitudes. Whether learners are monocultural or bicultural, they share certain social representations of other cultures with those in their own group(s). They also share attitudes towards those representations. For example they may believe with others in their group that another group's customs include arranging marriages for their children, and they are likely to share their own group's attitudes of approval or disapproval of the custom. It is possible, first, that the shared representations are inaccurate or incomplete and one task of the teacher is to ensure that learners understand the custom in full, as it is understood by those who practise it. This may already change disapproval to approval, or even vice versa, but then the teacher must decide whether they wish to influence the attitudes or simply make learners aware of their own basis for approval/disapproval, i.e. their own culturally specific values. One option for the teacher is to refer learners to internationally agreed human rights as a basis for making a decision, rather than attempting to impose their own views from their position as teacher (Byram, 1997: 44–46). Even this is not simple, since human rights is a much debated area where it can be argued that human rights too are culturally relative, but teachers and learners always need at least a starting point, even if it is a simplification that has to be constantly problematised and refined. The introduction to a second culture for monoculturals, or to a third for biculturals, is only a first step in this educational process.

Chapter 4

Chapter 4 presents the concept of the intercultural speaker which is the 'outcome' of teaching for intercultural competence. The intercultural speaker is someone who is aware of cultural similarities and differences, and is able to act as mediator between two or more cultures, two or more sets of beliefs, values and behaviours. The intercultural speaker is not someone who is bicultural, someone who can pass as belonging to two cultural groups. This is a matter of circumstances, of being brought up in a situation where identifying with the values, beliefs and behaviours of two groups is an option or even a necessity. Bicultural people are not necessarily able to act interculturally as they may not be conscious of the two cultures in which they live and the relationships between them. Acting interculturally presupposes that one is aware of difference and similarity and can decentre in order to help others to act together – or indeed to act oneself with others – in ways that overcome obstacles of difference.

Chapter 5

Chapter 5 takes the question of teaching for intercultural competence – which is often conceived as a focus in secondary and post-secondary education – into the primary school. Primary school children are still very much in the process of acquiring their understanding of the world – their own world as defined by the education system and that of other countries – and it is a moot question as to whether they can or should be taught intercultural competence. Yet language teaching – especially the teaching of English as a foreign language – is increasingly present in primary and even pre-primary schooling, and it is necessary to consider if and how intercultural competence rather than mere linguistic competence can be part of the intended outcomes of primary school language teaching.

Chapter 5

Intercultural Competence and Foreign Language Learning in the Primary School[24]

In the vast majority of industrial and post-industrial countries in the world, the presence of one or more foreign languages in the primary school is taken for granted; this almost always includes English as a foreign language. The reasons are not all educational, and indeed from an educational and psychological perspective, the arguments for early language learning are not without challenge. There are nonetheless strong political arguments present in the discussion in many countries, and pressures from employers and parents.

Employers see language learning as one of the essential skills in international trade – and almost all trade is now international – and parents see the acquisition of languages, particularly English, as sn important way of investing in their children and giving them the social and cultural capital they will carry forward into future generations. As well as ballet lessons, piano lessons and horse-riding – a common combination to maintain cultural capital in Britain (Lareau, 1997) with similar processes existing in other countries – young children must now learn English.[25] In these circumstances it is some notion of English as an International Language (EIL) that probably underpins the desires of most parents and employers. If they think about the cultural dimension, it will be in the context of interacting with other non-native speakers. The oft-noted tension appears here too between language learning for instrumental reasons as part of the investment that society makes in human capital and the educational purposes embodied in the cultural dimension in language teaching. Of course it might be argued that at primary school age there would be no sense in introducing a cultural dimension that was directly connected to EIL and business, and the vision of young children being trained for international business is hopefully too bizarre to be entertained. However language learning without a cultural dimension risks other dangers.

One such danger is that children learn a foreign language – notably English – as a means of encoding their own world through some assumed simple relationship between their own and the foreign language. In this case, it is unlikely that young learners will have the experience of 'otherness' that should be a fundamental characteristic of language learning in schools.

Let us assume then that the basic rationale for early language learning has been accepted, although as Johnstone (2002) points out, the conditions must be right. What approach to the cultural dimension should we take?

Context and Content

It is easy to forget, in the activities of daily routine in the school and classroom, that all education functions in a given society at a given time, that the choice of what is taught and how it is taught is partly determined by the social, political and economic position of the society that the education system serves. Language teaching is no exception (see Chapter 1). The impact of the globalisation of the economy and the internationalisation of social life are increasingly evident. Mobility in employment is likely to increase, from east to west, from south to north especially in those parts of economies that are labour-intensive and need a new, and cheap, labour force. Mobility in the opposite directions is already evident in the sectors of economies that require skilled workers and above all managers of global companies. On the other hand, there is increased tourism for some sectors of the global population, and much language teaching has used this as a rationale and introduced it into textbooks. But the linguistic and cultural competence required for work and residence in another country is quite different from that required for leisure and tourism. The theories and methods that have provided the guidelines for language teaching hitherto are inadequate for the new task, and require refining and developing.

For we must also bear in mind that, in addition to the social, political and economic context, there is another: the disciplinary context which determines what happens in the classroom on a day-to-day basis. It is theories of language (what a language is and how it works), of language learning (how people acquire a foreign language and how this may vary with age) and of social interaction (how people of different language origins relate to each other when they meet) that determine classroom methods. Although such theories often seem remote from practice, even a cursory analysis of the history of language teaching in the last hundred years would reveal how changes in theory have visible effects on classroom practice.

The most recent theories have stressed that when a foreign language is used for oral communication between living individuals in real time, linguistic competence (knowledge of the grammar and of the dictionary meanings of vocabulary) is insufficient. Learners need both linguistic competence in order to produce grammatically correct and meaningful speech and also the ability to speak appropriately, to choose the language that suits the occasion, the topic and the person with whom one is speaking. Thus the aims of language teaching have become more complex, but not complex enough. There still remains the problem that this description of 'communicative competence' is based on an analysis of how native speakers interact with each other (Hymes, 1971), but does not take into consideration the special nature of speaking in a foreign language, either to a native speaker of that language or to another foreign speaker with whom the only common means of communication is the foreign language, i.e. the lingua franca situation. The theory of communicative competence has to be changed and developed to take into consideration what happens when people move to and reside in another country with a different language and different ways of behaving, different beliefs and different shared understanding of the world, i.e. a different culture.

An enriched model of 'intercultural communicative competence' has been presented in an earlier chapter (Chapter 4) and it is with this in mind that we can turn to the more specific questions of language teaching in the primary school.

Learning Foreign Languages and Cultures in Primary Education[26]

Like everyone else, young learners (at least in developed countries) find themselves in a world of close-knit internationalism and of increasing mobility. They meet people of other cultures and origins in their own environment, and they are as mobile as their parents. So the encounter with otherness is not simply somewhere in their future but also in their present. There is a need to include in the aims of primary foreign language teaching the development of intercultural competence. However, there is also the widespread fear that such an inclusion might go beyond the capacities of most primary school children, and may threaten their acquisition of a firm identity. In particular, language learning is perceived in some situations as a threat to children's 'national identity', although there is a dearth of evidence to support this fear.

On the question of the general capacity of primary school children for intercultural competence, Barrett's (2007) authoritative analysis of empirical research and contemporary theories is crucial, and the issues he identifies that have direct relevance to teaching for intercultural competence are the following:

- children have geographical knowledge from early primary age – about their own country from 5–6 and about other countries a little later; they exhibit preference for and pride in their own country from about age 7 and this strengthens through middle childhood; but levels of pride are variable across countries and with respect to gender;
- there seems to be no necessary relationship between knowledge about other countries and feelings about them; more knowledge does not necessarily lead to more positive feelings nor the opposite, despite the expectations of many language teachers and language education policy makers;
- school textbooks are often ethnocentrically biased and children may be strongly influenced by historical narratives about their own country, though such narratives may be resisted and rejected;
- stereotypes about a few countries are held by children from about age 5–6 but as they reach age 10–12 they not only demonstrate an ability to describe more countries but also increasingly acknowledge that there are variations around the stereotypes they hold;
- children aged about 5–6 exhibit in-group favouritism but not necessarily denigration of out-groups, unless with respect to traditional enemies; there is considerable variation in attitudes and feelings according to context;
- children acknowledge their own membership of one or more national or state groups from about age 5–6 but there is much variation in the strength of identification at that point and subsequently, depending on contextual and other factors.

Drawing conclusions from his analysis of these and other factors, Barrett argues that there is so much variability in children's acquisition of knowledge, beliefs and feelings about nations and national groups that a comprehensive theory has to be written as a description of the factors in the 'niche' in which children grow up. The multiplicity of factors will interact differently from one niche to another – for example from one country to another or in different environments within the same country – and will also vary over time in the same niche. Among the many factors that influence children's knowledge, beliefs and feelings, Barrett argues that significant others have a role to play, notably parents and teachers, although only the role of teachers has been empirically investigated. This implies that the primary school teacher must be aware of the emerging knowledge of and feelings about other countries, including the ones which may be associated with the specific language being taught, but should also be aware that there is no necessary and inevitable path of development, that s/he can also be influential. Barrett demonstrates that stage theories *inter alia* do not adequately explain empirical findings.

Bruner in his famous *Process of Education*, speaks in this spirit when he maintains that any subject can be taught effectively in some intellectually honest form to any child at any stage of development (Bruner, 1960: 33). He acknowledges that it is a bold hypothesis, but argues that, in most school subjects, learners and teachers are concerned with rather wide fields of learning and that in any case the selection and gradation of the concrete contents and objectives have to be carried out according to the capacities of the learners. 'Learner-appropriateness' is the key concept. For the intercultural education of primary school children, this means that the tasks given and the experiences offered must be selected in accordance with the learners' stage of development. They may be cognitively demanding as long as they are concrete; they may be emotionally complex as long as they are experiential; they may be practically exacting as long as they are systematically arranged, i.e. permit the progression from simple to difficult.

Several primary school theorists have dedicated themselves to the interaction of language and culture learning and the integration of linguistic and intercultural competence, and have convincingly shown how the integration can be achieved in a learner-appropriate manner. Curtain and Pesola (1994) identified seven cultural goals for primary foreign language teaching and gave excellent 'child-appropriate' examples for each of these goals. As Doyé says, citing Kubanek-German:

'Child appropriateness' does not mean that only the easily accessible contents are dealt with but that the educationally necessary subjects are treated in a manner that is adequate to the development of the children. (Doyé, 1999: 25)

Curtain and Pesola also make valuable proposals for the identification of cultural contents of an integrated curriculum. The common characteristic of these proposals is the fact that they locate the representations of other cultures in the environment of the children and use them as starting points for intercultural information and experience. The representations are grouped in three categories: *Cultural symbols* (such as flags and insignia), *cultural products* (stories and songs, coins and stamps) and *cultural practices* (habitual forms of greeting, gestures, eating and drinking practices) (Curtain & Pesola, 1994: 180–1). Similar suggestions come from Skender (1995: 108ff.). What she proposes for the teaching of French in Croatia is also applicable to primary foreign language teaching in general. She suggests four groups of techniques:

- identification of elements of the foreign culture in the children's environment;
- use of typical images;
- emphasis on the ludic dimension of learning through songs, games, rhymes, stories;
- creation of a 'French' atmosphere.

The most thorough approach is provided by Peter Doyé (1999). Doyé starts from an early discussion of intercultural competence (Byram & Zarate, 1997 – see Chapter 4) and from Bruner's work sketched above. He then presents a step-by-step approach to the identification of specific issues and aspects of intercultural competence:

- the selection of learner-appropriate contents;
- relativising the opposition of US vs. THEM (insider group and outsider group);
- taking perspectives and decentring;
- modifying stereotypes;
- unlearning prejudice;
- preventing discrimination;
- acquiring tolerance.

For each of these, which are drawn from theoretical positions such as the work of Allport (1954) on prejudice, or Lippmann on stereotype (1922), Doyé provides illustrative materials and methods, demonstrating his rare skill in combining theory and practice in accessible and thought-provoking ways.

Given that Doyé and others have shown the feasibility of the aims, we can consider how the objectives of intercultural competence can be met by relating them to the *savoirs* of the intercultural speaker, referred to in Chapter 4 (see also Appendix 1). Some aspects of intercultural competence are very appropriately pursued with children of primary school age. *Savoir-être*, the attitude of openness and curiosity, may be more easily encouraged in primary school than later partly because children in the earliest years of primary education have not yet fully absorbed the assumptions of their own cultural environment, and do not yet perceive the cultural as natural. This too is a *savoir* that is best developed through experiential learning where immersion in experience is followed by reflection upon it, under the guidance of the teacher.[27]

Young children also already have some knowledge (*savoirs*) about the practices of their own social groups, how to behave in specific situations, what is considered polite and what is not. They can be introduced to related practices in another language and culture and invited to think about similarities and differences, and what might be the problems and dysfunctions arising from one set of practices being inappropriately used in another language and environment. In the framework of primary education, one of whose tasks is to convey the fundamental techniques of learning (*savoir apprendre*), it is possible to promote the basic tools needed for intercultural competence. Primary school children can learn to ask relevant questions, analyse cultural phenomena, and carry out their own investigations. Realistic foreign language teachers who declare intercultural competence to be one of their central aims do so even though they are aware of the complexity of the task. They know that the road is long and strenuous. Intercultural competence is certainly not attainable in all its dimensions at the end of primary schooling, but the foundation for this important competence can be laid.

Teachers of Language and Culture in Primary Education

Language teaching with an intercultural competence dimension presupposes that teachers themselves will have acquired intercultural communicative competence to a reasonable level. It is tempting to argue that the level need not be very advanced, since the learners will not advance to complex levels of competence themselves. This temptation is all the stronger if the teacher is also to be responsible for other subjects in the curriculum, as is the case in many countries. For it is clear that there will be many demands on the inevitably limited time available for primary teachers' education and training. To some extent, the time constraints are eased if a more comprehensive view is taken and an integrated education and training at pre-service and in-service levels is planned. It could be argued, for example, that teachers of languages should be trained through in-service courses with a minimum of pre-service training with full qualification and the right to teach being attained only after in-service training. In most countries, this is probably at best a medium-term option.

In the short term, training is likely to be in-service, and it is important to resist the temptation to suggest that language teachers in primary education need only a limited degree of intercultural communicative competence. For it is clear that teachers have to make complex decisions about how and when to develop intercultural competence in their learners. In order to make these decisions they need a rich personal experience of the acquisition of intercultural competence themselves – the five *savoirs* – and a knowledge of developmental and social psychology.

These abilities can hardly be acquired by in-service training alone. Therefore, in the long term, primary foreign language teachers will have to gain their qualifications through a combination of initial studies and in-service training. As Felberbauer and Heindler argue:

The need is for teachers who are specialists both in primary education and foreign language pedagogy. As primary school experts they will be familiar with the conditions and the framework into which, as foreign language experts, they can integrate the language and culture of other countries. They have to gain their qualifications through initial studies at universities and colleges and through in-service studies. (Felberbauer & Heindler, 1995: 134)

Doyé (1999) proposes the 'Prague Model of Teacher Education', which would qualify specialist teachers of languages in primary schools. It consists of four elements:

- *education* – focused on the place of primary education in education systems as a whole, and the principles of integration of language and intercultural education;
- *foreign language pedagogy* dealing with aims, methods and materials – the central element in the model;
- *linguistic and cultural studies* in which students learn theory of language and theory of culture;
- *psychology,* including developmental and social psychology, theory of learning and psycholinguistics.

These would be the elements of a training course in higher education and would need to be complemented by experience in another country, 'fieldwork' (Byram, 1997: 68-9; Roberts *et al.* 2001)

It has long been recognised in British higher education that communicative competence at an advanced level is attainable only through fieldwork, and this applies all the more to intercultural competence. Thus it is as important that primary school language teachers should have an obligatory 'year abroad' as it is for future secondary school language teachers. This necessitates a proper attention to preparation and debriefing as well as appropriate tutoring, face to face or at a distance, during fieldwork to ensure that students develop and reflect upon their intercultural competence as much as possible during this unique experience (Roberts *et al.*, 2001).

This is very much a European perspective, where teachers can easily travel and reside in a country where their language is spoken, even if the country is distant (such as Japan or China) since there is financial support for this. In other continents, and where finance is a difficulty, the focus would have to be on fieldwork carried out in the home environment, the 'home ethnography' (Roberts *et al.*, 2001), where similar degrees of intercultural competence can be stimulated as people learn to 'make the familiar strange'. Where financial problems do not hinder travel, it is possible to give future teachers similar experience in intensive short periods of residence and fieldwork, as Jackson (2007) has shown.

The second dimension of teacher training involves the acquisition of methods and techniques for the classroom and fieldwork. Methods for introducing learners to fieldwork are particularly relevant where the geographical distance is not too great, and even young children can be taken to another country to experience a foreign reality for themselves. Choice of methods and techniques is in turn dependent on knowledge of developmental and social psychology as well as theory of language and language learning. The former will be part of the primary teacher's general training and need only be linked explicitly with discussion of intercultural competence. Language learning theory, too, can be linked with the teacher's training in first language acquisition theory and with training in the teaching of literacy in the first language. In this way, foreign language teaching can be integrated with other aspects of primary education with respect to general pedagogy.

The degree of integration of training in methods will depend on decisions about the place of foreign language learning in the curriculum. A full discussion of the question of 'integration' or 'separate subject' would take us beyond the limits of this chapter (see also Tost Planet, 1997), but it will have significance for the methods of developing intercultural as well as linguistic competence. I shall return to this issue in the next section.

Curriculum Planning and Teaching Materials

In one sense there is no problem about including an intercultural dimension in foreign language learning at primary school level since in their introductory statements most curriculum documents refer to the desirability of developing 'cultural awareness' or similar concepts.

For example, in the USA, the intercultural dimension has for a long time been recognised in a number of elementary school foreign language projects. Curtain and Pesola (1994: 419ff.) quote an excellent example of guidelines for the integration of culture instruction into the elementary school curriculum. It comes from Maryland (Montgomery County) and gives detailed recommendations for the introduction of cultural contents into the various subject areas of basic education. Examples can be found in Europe too and, in the curricula of some German Länder, the intercultural dimension is given prominence. There is a common consensus that, if culture is to be integrated into the language learning process, it must be planned for as carefully and in as great detail as are the language elements. Therefore, already in 1995, the *Didaktisch-methodischen Empfehlungen für das Fremd-sprachenlernen in der Grundschule* (Didactic-methodological Recommendations for Foreign Language Learning in the Primary School) in Niedersachsen not only argued the necessity for such integration, but for each recommended topic also made suggestions about ways in which *interkulturelles Lernen* could be promoted (Niedersächsisches Kultursministerium, 1995).

I mentioned earlier the question of integrated or separate subject teaching. Given that *savoir être* and *savoir apprendre* are most susceptible of development in the primary school, it is in a comparative methodology that integration might be best achieved. Wherever a topic can be planned to include a foreign perspective – one that can be explored through the foreign language – there is potential for arousing children's curiosity and allowing them to see a different perspective (*savoir être*). Older children particularly may be encouraged and provided with the resources for discovering parallel phenomena in another country (*savoir apprendre*) and even discover how other people perceive the children's own society and its practices and products. It is however crucial to ensure that children do not over-generalise from their discoveries, assuming that 'All French/Japanese ... people do this, believe that ...'. They must always have opportunities to discover a range of perspectives and experiences in other countries and one method of doing this is through direct contacts by visits, exchanges of materials, and electronic media.

Criteria for the analysis of teaching materials for primary education have been established by Balbi (1997). These are particularly useful where languages are taught as a separate subject. They identify above all the ways in which linguistic competence is served by different kinds of teaching materials. Criteria for the analysis of the cultural dimension of secondary school textbooks have also been established (Doyé, 1991; Byram, 1993). A similar task still needs to be carried out for primary education materials, taking into consideration the prioritisation of *savoir être* and *savoir apprendre*, identifying materials and techniques that provide a basis for the teacher's work on these *savoirs* in particular.

The criteria will also need to include consideration of developmental psychology. Even more than in secondary school, it is evident that materials for children beginning to learn a language at age 5 will differ radically from those starting at age 8, for example. The complexity of decisions that have to be taken in materials development and selection, as well as in curriculum planning in general, is immense. Adding a requirement of intercultural competence to the decisions about at what age and in what ways to promote linguistic competence creates a planning problem that individual teachers cannot be expected to resolve alone.

Conclusion

All this is only a continuation of the story of foreign language teaching as it has grown and changed over the last hundred years. We have recognised with the help of researchers and teachers that language learning is a complex activity. We have seen how the purposes and nature of that activity have also changed and become more complex in response to societal changes. If foreign language teaching in primary education is to contribute seriously to the international education of young people, it has to recognise the complexity of the task, to include intercultural competence among its aims, to seek relationships with other aspects of the curriculum in systematic ways and to demand properly trained teachers and appropriate teaching materials.

Chapter 5

Chapter 5 argued that it is both desirable and possible to extend the teaching of linguistic competence in the primary school to include intercultural competence. This is a matter of understanding the psychological development of children and their understanding of themselves and their world. It is also a matter of developing the appropriate materials and methods, but there are already examples of these available. Finally it is a matter of training teachers, not only in the methods and materials but also in their understanding of the purpose of teaching languages in the primary school, namely as part of the response of education systems to internationalisation in its various forms.

Chapter 6

Chapter 6 moves from discussion of teaching to discussion of types of research, some of which are closely related to teaching in that they too have clear educational purposes. Research is not only a question of disinterested investigation; it can and sometime should be targeted at certain problems and intended outcomes. In this chapter the focus is on research into the intercultural dimension of language teaching. It presents an overview of different kinds and purposes of research in general and uses this as a way of categorising and representing current research, that which is investigative and that which advocates a particular concept of language teaching and learning.

Chapter 6

Analysis and Advocacy: Researching the Cultural Dimensions of Foreign Language Education[28]

Analysis and Advocacy

Research in the sciences of education – to use a loan-translation taken from some other European traditions – can be broadly categorised under three headings: research that seeks to establish explanations in terms of cause and effect, research that seeks to understand the experience of people involved in education, and research that attempts to create change. The distinction between explanation and understanding was made by von Wright (1971) for the social sciences in general, but the sciences of education also often attempt to intervene and to change the phenomena which educationists study, for example modes of teaching and learning or the development and implementation of education policy.

Furthermore, educationists who wish to intervene and change do so from a particular standpoint, and with a particular outcome in mind. They have a view on what ought to be, and not just on what is. They may attempt to intervene in 'what is', and find ways of developing from 'what is' towards what they think 'ought to be'.[29] Or they may be content to let others undertake this task.

These various distinctions also apply to research on the cultural dimensions of second and foreign language learning. There is, for example, work that attempts to investigate the causal relationships assumed to exist between language learning and attitudes towards other people and cultural groups (Morgan, 1993), work that is looking for explanations. One can also establish hypotheses about causal relationships between perceptions of other cultures and motivations for learning, and much research has been carried out on motivation. Or one can look at possible causal relationships between teaching techniques/methodologies and knowledge about other cultures, or between learning about other cultures and understanding of one's own, or between vocabulary acquisition and culture learning. There is other work that attempts to understand, from the perspective of the learners, their experience of other cultures and groups, or of the teaching and learning process inside and beyond the classroom. The focus in all of this is on 'what is'. The two need not be mutually exclusive. Research that looks for cause and effect can also seek to interpret and understand how those involved, whether teachers or learners, experience the process and themselves theorise about it.

Then there is work that focuses on 'what ought to be', on the development of curricula and methods of teaching and assessment or on policies of teaching and assessment. This is undertaken in order to move contemporary practices towards new objectives that are deemed by those involved to be better than what already exists. It requires researchers to give reasons for their judgement and reveal their underlying beliefs about language teaching and education more generally. Some researchers will focus their efforts on establishing the reasoning for and the nature of potential changes. Others will also attempt to implement and evaluate their ideas.

The distinctions I am making are not focused on research methods or designs. I am not following the usual distinction made between quantitative and qualitative research, because this is a second-order distinction. Work that is explanatory in purpose can draw on quantitative and qualitative methods of collecting and analysing data, as can work that is searching for understanding or attempting to introduce new practices.

The first-order distinctions I shall call 'analytical research' and 'advocacy research', the former seeking for explanation or understanding of 'what is', the latter attempting to establish, and then to implement and evaluate, 'what ought to be'.

This distinction between analysis and advocacy corresponds *approximately* to empirical and conceptual work; advocacy involves reflection on theory, analysis of values and ideologies, determining purposes. Yet when advocates become involved in implementing change – in curriculum or policy development, for example – they also become empiricists. So the distinction, though conceptually clear, may be blurred in practice. For it is frequently the case that those who carry out research do so with an advocacy purpose, i.e. they have a standpoint that they hope to see vindicated. For example, an advocate who takes the view that language learning ought to lead to positive attitudes towards people of other cultural groups, and therefore posits this as a purpose, might undertake research to investigate whether or not, in existing classrooms, language learning does have a causal link to attitudes and, if so, whether it causes positive attitudes. If the advocate finds that there is no causal relationship, s/he might then get involved in producing, testing and evaluating new methods and materials which try to ensure a causal relationship. This is often in the form of action research, but it can be experimental with control groups. The advocate would in this case have moved from an 'armchair discussion' of purposes to empirical investigation of 'what is', and then to pro-active intervention to create 'what ought to be'.

Unfortunately advocates and analysts are sometimes not clear about their role and their work, precisely because advocacy and analysis can be merged in a specific project. It is equally unfortunate that the second-order distinction of 'qualitative' and 'quantitative' causes confusion by being presented as two research 'paradigms', which implies two ways of thinking, whereas they are just two ways of collecting and analysing data.

Analysis of Culture Learning and Language Learning

The analytical questions that can be asked about culture learning depend partly on whether the analyst is seeking explanation or understanding. From an explanation perspective, hypotheses about the relationships between culture learning and other aspects of learning and teaching can be quickly established, for example:

- the relationship between 'the' foreign culture, or perceptions of it, and the motivation for learning;
- the relationship between language learning and attitudes to, and/or perceptions of other cultures and peoples;
- the relationship between teaching techniques and methodologies and knowledge about other cultures;
- the relationship between learning (about) another culture and learners' perceptions of, and/or attitudes towards, their own culture;
- the relationship between culture teaching (or absence thereof) and vocabulary learning;
- the relationship between culture learning and the development of specific social identities, particularly national identity.

In many cases, a search for explanatory, causal relationships can be combined with an attempt to understand the learners' or teachers' experience of culture learning. An analyst might wish to understand learners' responses to and perceptions of being introduced to a culture that seems to threaten their own culture and identity. The case of learning English and being exposed to dominant anglophone cultures is the obvious one. Similarly, an analyst might wish to understand the, sometimes unconscious or inarticulate, rationale that teachers have for employing particular techniques and methodologies of culture teaching, and the origins of their beliefs.

The best-researched description of culture learning is undoubtedly the search for explanation of relationships between learners' understanding of other cultures and their motivation and achievement in language learning. This is too large an area to analyse here, but it is important to note that in early research by Gardner and Lambert (1972), the notion of 'integrative' motivation – the desire to learn a language to be in some sense closer to speakers of the language – was considered the best basis for success. Later research (Dörnyei, 1998) has shown that 'instrumental' motivation can be more important than 'integrative' motivation, depending on the social context in which languages are learnt. Later research has also shown that many other factors need to be taken into consideration, not least the impact of classroom conditions, if the causes of motivation are to be fully explained (Dörnyei, 2001), and then their effect on language learning. Where a language is dissociated in learners' perceptions from all links with native speakers – and in some circumstances this may be the case with English – then 'instrumental' or 'pragmatic' motivation will be the better concept for explaining achievement.

On the other hand, integrative motivation, expressed as a positive interest in peoples and cultures associated with a language, is still a significant area for analysis. This aspect of motivation is also related to analysis of attitudes. In both cases, assumptions that there are linear and uni-directional causal relationships between attitudes or motivation on the one hand and achievement in language learning on the other are mis-placed. It is for this reason that analysts have constructed complex models that attempt to show the inter-relationships between attitudes, motiva-tions, self-concepts, environmental factors and instructional factors. In the view of applied linguists and teachers, the complexity of such models may appear to limit severely their usefulness for teaching, and when Dörnyei and Csizer (1998) offer 'ten commandments for motivating language learners' based on research, these might appear intuitively self-evident. However, the significance of culture learning is reinforced by their including 'familiarise learners with the target language culture' as one of the ten.

The question of attitudes towards other cultures and perceptions of speakers of other languages has particular significance with respect to the educational aims of language teaching. Whatever the direction of the rela-tionship between attitudes and learning achievement in psychological models, the direction postulated in statements of educational aims is that learning languages should lead to positive attitudes and accurate percep-tions of other cultures, and the causal relationship between language teaching and culture learning in the form of insights and attitudes is one that has been analysed, albeit rarely. Byram *et al.* (1991) investigated the effects of different styles of language and culture teaching on learners' perceptions and understanding of a national culture. Their conclusions were disappointing in the sense that they could find no discernible effect of teaching, but a strong presence of other factors from outside the classroom and the school. More recently Australian analysts have investigated the relationship of teaching to attitude formation, which again is disappointing in that there seems to be no causal relationship between teaching and positive attitudes (Ingram & O'Neill, 2002). On the other hand, research in Japan suggests that there are causal relationships discernible, at least as teachers and learners perceive it; this is an example of searching for both explanation and understanding and subordinating explanation to understanding (Himeta, 2006).

There is also a major area of research on the relationships between teaching and understanding of and attitudes towards self and own cultures that needs much more analysis. Does teaching cause or create better self-understanding or reflection on one's own society?

Such analysis could be informed and enriched by another strand of work on culture learning, which is often comparative in methodology, comparing for example culture-specific views and reactions to communicative language teaching (e.g. in China and 'the West', Rao, 2002; in Colombia and the USA, Schulz, 2001). There is a particularly well-mined seam of analysis of vocabulary differences between, for example, English and Chinese (Cortazzi & Shen, 2001) or English and German (Olk, 2002) or French and English (Boers & Demecheleer, 2001). In most cases research which analyses speakers' understanding of apparently-similar vocabulary draws out implications for teaching and learning and is thus linked to advocacy which argues for particular aims and methods. Vocabulary teaching, as we shall see, is a particular focus in advocacy.

Research that is focused on understanding rather than explanation may not always appear to have immediate relevance to applied linguists and language teachers, particularly when it deals with phenomena outside the classroom. Explanation and identification of causal factors offers an obvious entry into how to make changes in practice and predict their outcomes. Research seeking understanding might not seem to offer such immediate applications, but is nonetheless an important area because it situates language and culture learning in social contexts. Lantolf (1999, 2000) has argued for a theoretical position that recognises the value of understanding processes of culture learning from the perspective of learners in informal learning contexts. Pavlenko and Lantolf (2000) have used personal stories as a basis for analysing 'second language learning as participation and the (re)construction of selves'. There are studies that analyse problems of 'identity loss' as children learn languages (Downes, 2001; Jo, 2001) or 'identity maintenance' for children of minority groups learning their heritage language (Mills, 2001). The particular role of the textbook in supporting learners' identity has also been analysed (Arbex, 2001).

The learners in some of these studies are from minority groups or find themselves in an identity-threatening situation. There is also a growing interest in the impact of language and culture learning on the cultural identities of learners in majority groups, especially when they spend time in another country to improve their learning (Crawshaw et al., 2001; Jordan, 2001). Related research analyses the interplay between social context, perceptions of self and language learning (Miller, 2003).

Advocating Directions for Culture Learning

Research that is advocacy, concerned with intervention in the status quo of language learning in order to develop it in a certain direction, is far more frequent than analysis. The quality of analysis research will be judged by criteria of clarity of concepts, validity and reliability of data, traceability in the interpretation and understanding of informants' experience, rigour in drawing conclusions from data, and so on. Advocacy research is often judged more by the power of the argument and the rhetoric which sustains it, by the relevance of the argument to a given time and place, and by the support cited from analytical research. Argument about 'what ought to be' may depend more or less closely on the analysis of 'what is'. Proposals for future directions may be judged, irrespective of analysis, as 'realistic' or 'unrealistic/ideal'. Advocacy reflects, more than analysis, the relationship of language learning and teaching to the social conditions in which it is located. As the contemporary world changes to a state of 'globalisation', arguments about culture learning have changed too.

In Germany, Kramer has argued for attention to a 'cultural studies' dimension to the teaching of English which has its roots in the critical social analysis of Raymond Williams and Stuart Hall in England (Kramer, 1997). Kramer argues that the study of English (Anglistik) needs to respond to the new ways in which people live their lives and engage in their culture in a time of rapid change. The study of language and culture should address questions of 'how we live' and also 'how we ought to live', thus introducing an explicitly-ethical dimension to teaching and learning. Starkey, too, introduces a strong ethical dimension by arguing that language and culture teaching should take note of and introduce human rights education into its aims and purposes (Starkey, 2002).

Changing social conditions are reflected in the work of Kramsch and Zarate. The former argues, like Kramer, for new purposes and re-definitions of language study to respond to 'epistemological shifts occurring in academia' (Kramsch, 1995: XIV). Her argument that language study creates 'a third place', a privileged and questioning location, where learners gain special insights into their own and others cultures, has become widely accepted. Zarate (2003a, 2003b) redefines the nature and purposes of language and culture learning, stressing the significance of in-between or border locations and the need for language teaching to respond to the particular challenges of European integration, as nation states and national identities fuse and change.

In her major work on the history and future directions of 'language and culture pedagogy', Risager shows that the focus on the cultures of a nation and the dominance of the nation state in the thinking of language teachers is a relatively recent phenomenon. She argues for a new direction that takes into account her analysis of the flows of language and culture through networks of a global nature. There can be no going back to the national paradigm (Risager, 2003, 2006, 2007).

Such authors present new perspectives and purposes. By doing so they open up new questions for analysis and advocacy. Analysts might explore the self-understanding of learners and teachers living in these newly-defined conditions, and advocates can find guidance for their planning in these new purposes, and the new teaching objectives that follow from them.

There are some signs of this in intervention and development work already, although the relationship of classroom practice to pedagogical aims and ethical questions is not considered frequently enough. Intervention and development work is often focused on the 'problems' of difference and distance, and how to overcome them. Culture learning is perceived as even less feasible if confined to the classroom than language learning. Culture learning needs to be experiential and experience of difference has to be at the centre of learners' and teachers' attention.

One example of this is work on teaching vocabulary, where teachers attempt to teach differences through 'culturally loaded' words (Galisson, 2000; Qi, 2001). Another is the use of language corpora to teach differences in pragmatics (Berrier, 2001).

Unsurprisingly, new communication technologies are promoted as a means of overcoming distance and giving learners experience of interacting with native speakers. Email contacts (Liaw & Johnson, 2001; Belz, 2001; Jogan *et al.*, 2001), electronic conferencing (Truscott & Morley, 2001) and the internet as a source of information (Herron et al., 2002; Gruber-Miller & Benton, 2001) are representative of this trend, which is analysed in more detail in O'Dowd (2007).

Tandem-learning, originally developed as a means of enhancing linguistic competence, is a means of creating opportunities for culture learning (Rohrbach & Winiger, 2001; Kötter, 2001). Where visits and exchanges are offered to learners for the same purposes, there are similar attempts to create culture learning (Gohard-Radenkovic, 2001; Harbon 2002; Breugnot, 2001).

Implicit in these approaches is the assumption that interaction with people who embody a culture, who are native speakers of a language, is crucial. This then leads to debate and argument for (and against) the use of native speakers as teachers, (Hinkel, 2001; Jiang, 2001). The debate about the advantages of non-native and native speakers with respect to teaching language (Medgyes, 1994) is thus extended to teaching culture, and the related question of the relationship between teachers' experience of other cultures and their introduction of a cultural dimension into their teaching is a focus of investigation (Aleksandrowicz-Pedich & Lazar, 2001).

Analysis of the cultural content of textbooks is a well-established area and, insofar as it has begun to develop theoretically well-founded criteria, might be better classified as research into the effects of teaching on learners' perceptions (Sercu, 2000). Reports on the difficulties of using textbooks written in one country when teaching in another (Yakhontova, 2001) are, however, similar to reports of difficulties of using Western communication technology in non-Western countries (Smith, 2001; Takagaki, 2001). Feng and Byram (2002) adopt an alternative, intercultural perspective in content analysis, and advocate intercultural representation in selecting textbook materials and analysis of intention and interpretation in handling authentic texts in the classroom.

In addition to all this, there is a wealth of doctoral research that often does not have a wider distribution especially when it is Action Research (see McNiff, 1988; Reason & Bradbury, 2000), and yet there is valuable experimentation.[30]

Some advocacy concentrates more on arguing for a particular didactic model to enhance culture learning: the vision of the classroom as a discursive space comparable to Kramsch's third place (Hallet, 2001); the introduction of techniques of participant observation in and beyond the classroom (Ilieva, 2001); the use of literature to explore otherness and develop intercultural understanding (Küster, 2000). The wider implications are addressed by seeing language and culture teaching from an interdisciplinary perspective (Ingram, 2001; Corbett, 2003), from the perspective of critical pedagogy (Guilherme, 2002; Phipps & Gonzales, 2004) or from a post-national, transnational perspective (Risager, 2007). These views are programmatic and still in the initial stages of implementation, but they are an invitation to experimentation. Unlike experimentation with new technologies, however, they also challenge the fundamentals of culture and language teaching.

Empirical research to analyse and evaluate the impact of such views should ensure that advocacy and analysis interact. This is not an easy task. The fact that there is a greater amount of writing that is advocacy argument and personal reports of activities in teaching and learning, is an indication that thorough and rigorous analytical research is much more difficult. There are practical difficulties – of funding, of time available, and of insufficient analysts – that need to be overcome, but there is also plenty of opportunity to identify worthwhile topics to research.

Finally, the relationship between analysis and advocacy can be found in the evaluation of change and development work. There are many views of what ought to be and there are many projects that implement new ideas, but they need to be evaluated, and here the investigation of the intended causal relationship between new teaching and what is learnt, and the interpretation and understanding that learners themselves put on their experience are the realm of analytical research.

A discussion of evaluation research would take this chapter too far, but what is common to evaluation and to searching for explanation or understanding, is the rigour of analytical methods. It is in the rigour of evaluation, and in the search for cause and effect and/or understanding of the innovation, that the analyst has a proper place, complementing that of the advocate and the teacher.

Chapter 6

Chapter 6 started with the distinction between research that seeks to explain and research that seeks to understand. This is a distinction that is familiar in all kinds of research in the social sciences, although it is often misinterpreted as being a distinction between quantitative and qualitative research. There is then a further distinction that is less familiar, between research which focuses on understanding or explaining what is and that which seeks to bring about what the researcher thinks ought to be. This is advocacy research and a particular example of the partisanship quoted from Hobsbawm at the beginning of this book. The chapter then presented an overview of current research to illustrate these different distinctions. The implications of this analysis are that researchers in language teaching and learning need to be very clear what kind of research they intend to carry out and if and how they intend to combine different kinds of research.

Chapter 7

Chapter 7 draws on research into the changing identities of language learners to discuss what the outcomes of language teaching ought to be. It starts with the question of how education systems have been devised to create a sense of national identity and the role of teaching 'national' and 'foreign' languages in this process. It then goes on to discuss how foreign language teaching ought to introduce a process of 'tertiary socialisation' if it is to fulfil its purpose of contributing to general education of young people in compulsory schooling. In order to clarify what tertiary socialisation means, the chapter introduces in more depth than in previous chapters the theories of socialisation and social identity and uses these to analyse data from interviews with language learners and young people in international schools

Chapter 7

Nationalism and Internationalism in Language Education

'Language Educators'

The phrase 'language teachers' in British English will evoke in most teachers' minds those colleagues who teach 'foreign' languages, and most frequently the languages in question are 'European' – French, German, Spanish and some others. 'Language instructors' in American English will have similar, but not identical, connotations, perhaps augmented by a wider range of languages in higher education, which is where many learners begin foreign language learning for the first time. In German, the word *'Fremdsprachenlehrer'* includes in the particle *'fremd'* the designation 'foreign', whereas the French phrase *'professeur de langues vivantes'* puts emphasis on contemporary as opposed to classical Greek and Latin languages, but nonetheless also implies 'foreign'.[31]

On the other hand, for those who teach the official language of instruction in a school, such as French in schools in France (*professeurs de lettres*), or 'English teacher' in Britain and *'Deutschlehrer'* in Germany, there is no specific reference to language and where, as in Japan, language is mentioned, there is an interesting explicit reference to its function in the nation: *'kokugo kyoushi'* ('national language teachers'). These teachers would not usually be included in the connotations of 'language teacher' and similar phrases. The separation of language teachers into two groups, those who teach foreign languages and those who teach national languages, is well established in educational discourse. Even where the language situation is complex, as in Belgium for example, where the teacher of French in French-speaking Belgium belongs to a different category from the teacher of French in Flemish-speaking Belgium. The underlying reason for this distinction between 'foreign' and 'national' language teachers lies in the function of languages in schools and in the society that schools reflect.

In a relatively simple case such as Japan, 'national' language teachers are developing their learners' capacities in a language that symbolises national identity, which is crucial to social integration, and is an essential tool for communication in their society. This applies in more complex but comparable ways in countries such as Belgium that have more than one official/ national language; but for the sake of clarity and simplicity, I will not discuss all the possible variations in different countries.

The national language has cognitive, affective and behavioural significance. Cognitively it is crucial for further learning within and beyond school. Affectively it symbolises national identity and is associated with iconic texts and national culture.[32] Behaviourally, it is a skill that has to be honed in order to acquire work and economic independence within the national society. In many countries, the third element – the emphasis on communicative skill in the national language – is a relatively recent concern and an emphasis that brings the interests of teachers of 'national language' into closer contact with teachers of 'foreign languages'. Nonetheless, the role of the 'national language' cognitively and affectively still makes a significant distinction.

Throughout this brief characterisation, I have used 'scare quotes' for 'national language' because it is not a usual designation, despite the Japanese case. It is not questioned but simply assumed that the language of instruction in schools will be the national language, or national languages in multilingual states such as Belgium. Similarly, the unifying and symbolic functions of teaching French in France, German in Germany, English in the USA and so on, are largely taken for granted, although the movement to make English the official language in the USA is an indication of fear that this function will be lost. Teachers of these languages would be surprised to be called 'national language teachers', whereas teachers of German, Spanish etc. in these countries, accept the designation of 'foreign language teacher' to cover all and any language other than the national language. Furthermore, it is clear that this characterisation is an abstraction from the complexity of reality. The United Kingdom is just one example, where the position of Welsh in Wales means that what I have said about national languages cannot be applied to English in Wales, but on the other hand the role of Welsh is similar to the role of English in other parts of Britain. Similarly, the position of a language such as Punjabi in Britain, where it is the chronological first language of many children, complicates the situation and Punjabi cannot be designated a 'foreign' language, even if it is quite clear that it is not a 'national' language. The position of Spanish in the USA is comparable.

It is only when non-paradigmatic cases are encountered that the function of the national language and its teachers emerges into consciousness. In Singapore, there are four official languages: Chinese, Malay, Tamil and English. The majority of the population speak one of the first three as their chronologically first language in childhood and in the home. Yet English is used as the language of instruction in schools, and the other languages have a different status as community languages. English is deliberately used as the language of instruction as a means of creating harmony and identification with Singaporean identity. It has cognitive, affective and behavioural functions as it does in other English-speaking countries but, because it is not the first language of most pupils, its symbolic and practical functions in Singaporean society are more evident and conscious, and clearly stated in national education policy. In British or American society, those same functions are present less obviously but just as importantly, and with a hitherto less explicit policy behind them.[33] National language teachers have a function as a major contributor to the socialisation of young people into national identity, but they usually take it for granted.

Foreign Language Educators

The function of the foreign language teacher is also usually taken for granted as being to provide skills for communication with people from other societies, to promote understanding and positive attitudes towards other societies and cultures, and to create an awareness of language as a personal and societal phenomenon. These aims for language teaching are to be found in many countries in statements about the purposes of language teaching. However, in contrast to national language teachers, foreign language teachers are not expected to promote an attachment to a society and culture, to have an influence on learners' identities and identification with a nation state and its culture.

Some of the functions of national language and foreign language teachers are thus fundamentally different. Yet, there are some aspects of their work that could bring them together, particularly those that focus on learners' linguistic, communicative skills. It has been argued for several decades in the anglophone educational world, in France and in Italy, that all teachers of language should develop their learners' awareness of all their languages, and of their existing and potential language repertoire. This viewpoint is encapsulated in the promotion of 'awareness of language' or '*éveil aux langues*', '*educazione linguistica*' (Hawkins, 1987; Donmall, 1985; James & Garrett, 1992; Costanzo, 2003; Candelier, 2004).

Furthermore, despite the responsibility for the relationship of language and national identity lying with national language teachers, there is still a potential for foreign language teaching to have a role in identity formation. If it is accepted that schools are or should be not only national but also international in their orientation, then foreign language teachers could be assigned the role of promoting an international identity and a sense of belonging to international communities of interest, such as those developing in the wake of globalisation.

Before I pursue this point, however, let me consider in some more detail how schools function as national institutions, not just through the teaching of the national language.

Education In and Beyond the Nation State

The increasing influence of the state in the lives of individuals through education and other social institutions was evident throughout the 20th century, not least in the wars started in Europe but affecting the wider world, and called 'World Wars'. In the case of the English, Taylor pinpoints, in a striking way, the precise date when the state became a defining factor:

> Until August 1914 a sensible, law-abiding Englishman (*sic*) could pass through life and hardly notice the existence of the state, beyond the post-office and the policeman. He could live where he liked and as he liked. He had no official number or identity card. He could travel abroad or leave his country forever without a passport or any sort of official permission. He could exchange his money for any other sort of currency without restriction or limit. He could buy goods from any country in the world on the same terms as he bought goods at home. For that matter a foreigner could spend his life in this country without permit and without informing the police. [...] All this was changed by the impact of the Great War. The mass of the people became, for the first time, active citizens. Their lives were shaped by orders from above; they were required to serve the state instead of pursuing exclusively their own affairs. (Taylor, 1965: 1)

By 1914 compulsory education was in place in England as in many other countries, and this was the main shaping influence 'from above'. What effect school had on women and children's experience of the Great War is difficult to guess, although tales of patriotism and maps of the advances on 'the front' were ever present in newspapers and in schoolrooms.[34] The effect of schooling on the Englishman's willingness to go to war, for at first men were not 'required' but volunteered to be soldiers, is difficult to estimate but doubtless significant. Hobsbawm (1992) argues that a proto-nationalism was evolving at the turn of the 20th century that was the basis for the emergence of the concept of the homogeneous nation state, and the emotions attached to it.

For Gellner the dominance of nationalism is intimately linked to the rise of industrialisation in European societies. Industrialisation required new job specifications, not the inherited occupations within a family or a limited world of village or similar community. Industrialisation also required mobility, both geographical and in terms of ability to change jobs. People could no longer educate their children themselves; there had to be state education and in particular the possibility of communication among strangers:

> a society has emerged based on a high-powered technology and the expectancy of sustained growth, which requires both a mobile division of labour, and sustained, frequent and precise communication between strangers involving a sharing of explicit meaning, transmitted in a standard idiom and in writing when required. For a number of converging reasons, this society must be exo-educational: each individual is trained by specialists, not just by his own local group, if indeed he has one. (Gellner, 1983: 34)

Nationalism, Gellner argues, is rooted in industrialisation and will continue to be a force in the industrialised society we inhabit; it is difficult to envisage a homogeneous global culture in reality despite what thought-experiments might suggest (Gellner, 1983: 118).[35] In this situation, the state needs to control education – needs to have 'the monopoly of legitimate education' – in order to ensure the continuing growth that is a fundamental characteristic of industrialisation. The significance of a common language is emphasised by Gellner and reinforces the arguments put by Anderson (1991) that nations become possible when a common language is sustained by the print media.

Hobsbawm takes this point further by arguing that it is through secondary education that social mobility is made possible; primary education provides for the minimal skills needed in industrial work, but secondary education is the gateway to new positions in society, in particular through some form of higher education, and often the first generation become teachers:

> The crucial moment in the creation of language as a potential asset is not its admission as a medium of primary education (though this automatically creates a large body of primary teachers and language indoctrinators) but its admission as a medium of secondary education [...] for it is this which [...] linked social mobility to the vernacular, and in turn to linguistic nationalism. (Hobsbawm, 1992: 118)

Hobsbawm argues that it is the very mention of language and the use of the census as a means of discovering which languages are spoken where within a state that leads to an awareness of the significance of language as a defining characteristic and marker of nationality, and to the emergence of linguistic nationalism and the emotional investment in language which became so familiar throughout the 20th century.

In contemporary times, the relationship of school and nation state is no less strong than in the early history of compulsory schooling (Reid, 2000). Examples can be found in any education system, but are particularly salient in Eastern Europe post-1990 where the need to reassert national identity after a long period of communism is strong. For example in Bulgaria children in Grade 1 have lessons about the 'Homeland' (*Roden Krai*) and there is a very clear statement of educational policy in the syllabus:

> One of the objectives of this school subject is to develop 'a positive emotional attitude towards one's place of origin and one's historical and cultural heritage'. It also defines how this positive attitude should be formed. Children should learn about 'the importance of family and their fellow country people'. They should be able to recognise the 'national symbols' and to describe the place they live in. They should also learn to recognise and position in time the 'official and family holidays in Bulgaria'. (www.helpdeskbg.org; accessed 6.06)

As the authors of the analysis of textbooks used for this subject point out:

> we infer the syllabus perceives the Bulgarian national identity as monolithic, uniform and invariable. However the syllabus suggests an opportunity to enrich this view of national identity through the contribution of individual children who can talk about events that are of personal importance to them and share experiences on various topics. (www.helpdeskbg.org; accessed 6.06)

They think that the risk of an imposed uniformity from such syllabuses can be avoided but the risk is real and can lead to a nationalist or even a jingoist curriculum.

Where this happens, education systems and educators are not immune to emotional influences, especially at times of national crises. Xenophobia is then embodied in a fear of other languages, and the treatment of German teaching and teachers during World War I in the USA is an example of this (Pavlenko, 2003). Even in times of peace, language education policy and the choice of language(s) of instruction is a sensitive issue especially where a state has ethno-linguistic minorities within its border – and there is scarcely a state that is not in this position. Other curriculum choices, particularly in the teaching of geography, history and religious studies, carry a potential for nationalism that is not challenged because the choices made seem self-evident and beyond question (Coulby & Jones, 2001).

It is not without significance that the moment in 20th century history that Taylor described as the turning point in the relationship of state and individual, the beginning of the First World War, coincided with the work of John Dewey on education and democracy. His work was published in the midst of a war of nation states, in 1916, and was _inter alia_ an argument for education that would liberate young people from all kinds of isolationism, including that of nations. Dewey argues for a significant political role for schooling, a role which provides change in a specific direction, rather than 'the perpetuation of [a society's] own customs'. The direction he wishes schools should pursue is towards 'democracy', by which he means not merely the forms of democratic government but above all the pursuit of co-operation, living together:

> A democracy is more than a form of government; it is primarily a mode of associated living, of conjoint communicated experience. The extension in space of the number of individuals who participate in an interest so that each has to refer his own action to that of others, and to consider the action of others to give point and direction to his own, is equivalent to the breaking down of those barriers of class, race and national territory which kept men from perceiving the full import of their activity. (Dewey, 1916/1985: 93)

Dewey refers explicitly to the barriers of nationhood. He sees the key in the notion of living and communicating together, although there is no discussion of how that communication shall be pursued or of the role of (foreign) language teaching and learning.

This spirit was taken up many years later by the Delors Report written for UNESCO, in which the principles of education in the contemporary world were described as four pillars, 'learning to know', 'learning to do', 'learning to live together, learning to live with others' and 'learning to be'. 'Living together' was presented thus:

> The task of education is to teach, at one and the same time, the diversity of the human race and an awareness of the similarities between, and the interdependence of, all humans. From early childhood, schools must therefore take every opportunity to teach these two things. Some subjects are particularly well suited for this task: human geography beginning with basic education, and foreign languages and literature slightly later on, for example. (UNESCO, 1996: 92–93)

'Living together' is seen by the UNESCO Commission as the most important of the four pillars because it is the means of responding to the tensions of contemporary life, tensions between 'the global and the local', 'the universal and the individual', 'tradition and modernity', 'long-term and short-term considerations', 'the need for competition and the concern for equality of opportunity', 'the extraordinary expansion of knowledge and human beings' capacity to assimilate it', 'the spiritual and the material'.

For Dewey and Delors, education is inevitably political, and participatory and co-operative (UNESCO, 1996: 93–94). I shall argue that education for democracy in a period of globalisation has to go beyond the isolationism of nationalism, and of national curricula, and that foreign language teaching has a distinctive role to play in this, but first we need to consider the socio-psychological processes involved in the relationship between education and national identity.

Socialisation and Social Identity

In their classic discussion of socialisation, Berger and Luckmann (1966) distinguish between primary and secondary socialisation. The former is closely associated with the family and the affective ties to 'significant others' and the latter with 'institutional functionaries', such as teachers, who are representatives of the society beyond the home. It is through the process of socialisation that children acquire their assumptions about the world, their values, beliefs and behaviours, and the role of language is crucial in this process. For it is through language that children encounter the assumptions that others present to them. Those others externalise their own assumptions in language, and language is the means by which children in turn internalise the assumptions of the group of people represented by significant others. In primary socialisation, the others are just 'there' and their representational function is not evident, but when children go beyond primary socialisation, notably through schooling, then the child:

> does apprehend his (*sic*) school teacher as an institutional functionary in a way he never did his parents, and he understands the teacher's role as representing institutionally specific meanings – such as those of the nation against the region, of the national middle-class world as against the lower-class ambience of his home, of the city as against the countryside. (Berger and Luckmann, 1966: 161–2)

Or, we might say, of this country as against others.

Berger and Luckmann thus provide an account of how people acquire their understanding of the society, and the sections of that society, in which they live. They also suggest that this is so strongly related to language that the acquisition of a new language has to build on the reality embodied in the 'mother tongue':

One learns a second language by building on the 'taken-for-granted' reality of one's mother tongue. For a long time, one continually retranslates into their original language whatever elements of the new language one is acquiring. Only in this way can the new language have any reality. As this reality becomes established in its own right, it slowly becomes possible to forego translation. One becomes capable of 'thinking in' the new language. Nevertheless, it is rare that a language learned in later life attains the inevitability of the first language learned in childhood. Hence derives, of course, the affective quality of the 'mother tongue'. (Berger & Luckmann 1966: 163)

What is important here is the close relationship between language and socialisation, and the shared perception of and thinking about the world, but there is a pre-supposition concerning the relationship of language and social reality. Searle (1995) discusses this at length and argues that 'institutional reality' is constituted by language. Searle also shows that there are language-independent facts, but those that are language-dependent 'must be communicable from one person to another [...]. Even in simple cases of institutional facts, this communicability requires a means of public communication, a language' (Searle, 1995: 77). It is this 'public communication' function that underpins the role of a shared language in the process of socialisation.

For it is in the shared language that there is a shared reality, and it is in the constant process of sharing language that the shared reality is maintained and transformed (Berger & Luckman, 1966: 172ff). By sharing a language, an individual shares a reality within a social group and is a member of that group, whether it is the small group of a school community or the large group that forms the population of a state, with all the complexities of over-laps and separations that link the two. Learning another language brings with it the potential to experience another reality. It also has the potential, not mentioned by Berger and Luckmann, to challenge what is taken for granted, even if there remains a strong emotional tie to the world embodied in the 'mother tongue'. Foreign language teachers can promote through their didactical methods a conscious processing of the differences between languages and the taken-for-granted realities they embody. They can also promote an identification with the social groups who speak the other language, a point to which we shall return later.

This relationship of individuals to the various groups with which they share internalised realities and maintain them through constant use of language, is further analysed by Tajfel (1981) in his account of social identity. Tajfel argues that individuals seek to acquire positive self-esteem, and that one way of doing this is through enhancing or valuing highly the groups to which they belong, since this augments their own significance *vis-à-vis* others in other groups. In other words, individuals tend towards in-group favouritism not least because it has implications for themselves as individuals. Tajfel's experimental work shows that favouritism towards the in-group is significant in differentiation of groups, and such group differentiation is part of the mechanism by which groups interact with each other. Tajfel is concerned with the relationships between groups where some sense of 'superiority/inferiority' is crucial to the relationship (he points out that these are not ideal terms) and with the process whereby individuals might wish to 'pass' from an inferior group into a superior group. What is important for us is that the tendency to group favouritism can be reinforced in secondary socialisation in schools, where the national in-group is given preference in the teaching of history, geography, litera-ture, language and explicitly patriotic events such as making a pledge to the national flag.[36]

After reviewing the research in depth and analysing his own data, Barrett develops a complex model of the relationships among the many factors that influence children's knowledge, feelings and beliefs about nations and states and summarises the role of the school as:

> a crucial agent for teaching children about the historical and cultural heritage of their nation and state. Firstly, the school provides children with explicit instruction about the heritage, values, emblems and symbolic imagery of their state and nation. [...] Secondly, the history textbooks which children use at school typically provide them with an officially approved narrative of the historical origins of their own nation and state which incorporates and prioritises the core collective values of their own country. [...] Thirdly, school practices may be modelled on the collective values on which the nation's civil culture rests, and through their participation in these school practices, children can internalise and appropriate the values, discourse and practices of their own nation's civil culture. [...] Fourthly, school textbooks are often skewed by ethnocentric biases [...] and children do report that these textbooks are a source of their knowledge about foreign peoples. (Barrett, 2007: 257)

The influence of the school is thus found in various forms in both the overt curricular input and by covert school practices, the hidden curriculum. It is reinforced in particular by the teaching of history, by the school prac-tices based on the nation's civil culture, and by textbooks, often skewed by ethnocentric biases. It is also reinforced by external factors such as national sport, and national television and press with its focus on national events and constant implicit reference to the assumption that the national is normal, with explicit reference being made only to the 'abnormal' of other countries (Billig, 1995). In order to go beyond these influences and what Dewey (1916/1985: 87) called the isolationist tendencies of nationalism, a third stage of socialisation can be promoted, one which challenges some of the taken-for-granted values, beliefs and behaviours implicit in national schooling, and I have invented the term 'tertiary socialisation' (Byram, 1989a).

The concept of 'tertiary socialisation' is prescriptive, suggesting purposes and objectives for education, rather than being descriptive as the concepts of primary and secondary socialisation are. For there is a problem to solve. The problem is that people of one social group draw on the values, beliefs and behaviours they acquired during socialisation when interacting with people of another social group. Berger and Luckmann describe how this happens within a society between people of different social classes. The same thing happens when people of different nation states interact, but the situation is made more complex by the fact that a different language is being used. In some cases, one person is using his/her first language and the other is using that same language as a foreign language. In other cases they may both be using a foreign language as a lingua franca. They then tend to invest the foreign language with meanings from their own language and society, and misunderstanding can easily take place. A simple example of this is a conversation about school. Should a French person and a Japanese be exchanging experiences of their *école* and *gakko*, by using the English word *school*, each may assume that they are talking about the same thing, whilst using the apparent translation of the word. The potential for misunderstanding is however significant since the three words do not refer to the same social institution or experience (Taylor, 2006)

Furthermore, interactions never take place in a vacuum and the social situation will have an effect on the success of communication. As Tajfel (1981) shows, social groups are often in conflict and in a relationship of tension, and where individuals are interacting against a background of conflict or competition, the achievement of mutual understanding is more complex because it is not simply a linguistic matter. Sometimes, as in the case of immigrants to a country, for example, the power lies with one group, the host group, and they expect immigrants to adopt the language and the culture it embodies, to become assimilated. The reaction from the less powerful is often antagonistic, and separatist. In other cases, there is goodwill and interest, but a lack of understanding continues to exist because neither can see what lies beneath the surface of communication.

The concept of 'tertiary socialisation' embodies the idea that teachers and others can help learners to understand new concepts (beliefs, values and behaviours) through the acquisition of a new language, new concepts which, being juxtaposed with those of the learners' other language(s), challenge the taken-for-granted nature of their existing concepts. Doyé (1992) has shown how this can be related to the psychological and moral development of young people, so that they can acquire a more mature way of making moral judgements (see Chapter 3). Risager (2003: 494–5) has rightly pointed out that all three stages of socialisation overlap, and criticised the focus on the national paradigm, the reference to the concepts acquired by others in socialisation into their national culture, saying that it is enough to describe the processes in terms of primary and secondary socialisation. This misses, however, the point that tertiary socialisation has a prescriptive purpose and is intended to guide teachers in their course and objectives planning.

Socialisation, we have said, involves the acquisition of social identities. Primary and secondary socialisation leads to the development of the repertoire of social identities individuals acquire as they become members of new social groups in a society. They acquire professional identities, social class and ethnic identities, identities as members of sports groups, and so on. Tertiary socialisation could also lead to the development of further social identities that are not constrained by language. People may acquire 'international' identities, a sense of belonging to one or more transnational social groups. Of course this is not the responsibility of language educators alone, and in some countries policies to internationalise the whole curriculum of compulsory schooling have been created. This might be expected to further support the process of tertiary socialisation and the acquisition of international identities, but this remains to be seen in practice.

The development of an international identity promoted through tertiary socialisation and an international curriculum can thus be posited as a desirable outcome from education in a period of globalisation/internationalisation. However, it is quite possible that an international identity will be in some respects in contrast and tension with a national identity as a consequence of the challenge to the taken-for-granted values that underpin national identity.

National and International Identities

In order to see the potential of language education in the development of international identities, we can consider those learners who are among the most advanced, who have taken their (foreign) language learning most seriously. Students of foreign languages at university have often been learning their language for ten years or more. They are 'language people' (Evans, 1988) who are dedicated to the language and the literature and culture associated with it. They often spend a long period in a country where the language is spoken with the intention of improving their linguistic competence and then they usually discover that other learning experiences become more important to them as they become interested in the way of life in which they participate.

Participation in a culture as a means of learning and understanding it was first developed systematically by anthropologist ethnographers. Participation is, however, tempered by observation and analysis, and the ethnographer who is a 'participant observer' usually maintains a metaphorical distance. To 'go native' is not the aim of ethnographers. Language people, on the other hand, do sometimes see this as the most desirable fulfilment of their study of another language, and this is encouraged by the tradition of attempting to imitate the native speaker in linguistic competence. It is a short step to imitating the native speaker in their identity too.

If this were to happen, it would not be an example of tertiary socialisation but of what Berger and Luckmann call alternation, i.e. a rejection of a previous identity and the socialisation out of which it evolved, and the acquisition of a new identity and the beliefs, values and behaviours it embodies. They suggest that this is in fact rare and akin to religious conversion (Berger & Luckmann, 1966: 176–7). It is a moot point whether alternation should be the aim of language teaching, since it implies a rejection of national identity, and that would for many people not be desirable. It is of course a debatable issue but not one that need hold us up here, for in practice it is very unlikely to happen. There is no empirical research that investigates this question in the 'classic' situation of a foreign language being taught as a subject for a few hours per week. It might be expected that being in an immersion class, with half or more of the school day being experienced in a foreign language, could have an effect on identity, but here again there is little research. Downes investigated whether such experience of English immersion for Japanese children would weaken their sense of being Japanese – a fear that Japanese parents articulated – and found that:

> the immersion students have a stronger attraction towards Western culture, a more positive attitude towards English, a stronger identity with Japan, and more awareness of Japanese culture. A possible implication here is that the immersion experience not only promotes positive attitudes toward another culture but also seems to foster a heightened sense of identity towards the child's own culture. (Downes, 2001: 12)

Research has otherwise focused on learners who are resident in a country where the language is spoken, and particularly on those who have a strong desire to 'invest' (Norton, 1995) in language learning (Armour, 2001; De Korne *et al.*, 2007).

Research on language learners who spend a period of residence in a country where their language is spoken brings a new dimension. Such learners have a different purpose for their residence. They are not economic migrants or asylum seekers, but neither are they like other students whose main purpose for residence in another country is to study a subject other than languages. In the following example, Lynn is a 'language person' who has learnt French for some 10 years, from the age of 11. She has just spent a year living in France and is speaking about the experience a few months after returning to England. She shows signs of wishing to 'convert' to a French identity, but also believes this is not possible because one has to be 'born' French. She has a theory of ethnic and national identity and socialisation that arises from her experience. Her theory coincides with some academic theories (Barth, 1969) and she has a notion of using boundary markers of physical appearance to indicate ethnicity – choice of hair style and of dress – and it has the desired effect. She also, however, shows signs of developing an international identity as a consequence of her tertiary socialisation, an identity she calls 'European':

> I would now say – I'm not sure now, but when I came back [i.e. from France some weeks earlier] – I would say I was European rather than English. [...] I would love to be French, but you can't. I can never be French because you have to be born French. I could be a European. I couldn't be French though. There's no way you can become French, but you'll never be French unless you're actually born French. [...] I've completely changed appearance, physical appearance. I've grown my hair. I used to have really short permed hair, very very curly, very very short. And I've grown it in the idea of becoming chic and French-like. I've changed my style of dressing, becoming much more conscious of what I'm wearing rather than just putting something on in the morning. But that's all obviously an influence of being in France. Because they do have this idea, you know, they are very conscious of what they are wearing and how they look. So I mean I have changed physically an awful lot and people didn't recognise me when I came back. People just walked straight past. (unpublished interview)

So, at best, Lynn believes she can 'pretend' to be French in terms of appearance but she cannot 'become French', or 'pass' from one ethnic group to another even though she would like to do so since she sees 'the French' as a superior group and would gain in self-esteem as a consequence (Tajfel, 1981). On the other hand, she has an as-yet-undeveloped concept of being European, which seems to have a different meaning, not comparable or in competition with being French or English. This is an indication of a new phenomenon, of creating an alternative, over-arching identity that includes some of the characteristics of being French and yet neither French nor English.

When interviewed 10 years later, Lynn was married to a Belgian, living in Belgium and had just had her first child, whose bicultural socialisation into two identities and languages is focusing her attention on her own identities too. Lynn describes learning from her parents-in-law something about the history of Belgium. which helps to 'put down roots': 'I haven't really got roots on that side but I'm putting down roots in that way by learning through them and I would like A (her daughter) as well to learn from them as well'. She is describing the creation of a sense of belonging, of ethnicity, in which historical awareness is crucial. Similarly, she and her husband renew the sense of belonging to England, by joining the National Trust,[37] by watching the BBC news.[38] Yet she does not have the right to vote in Belgium, and citizenship and identity do not coincide. In answer to the question of whether she feels she belongs in Belgium, Lynn says:

> As far as I can, yes. I will always not be Belgian, I will always be English but then there are so many other people who are in the same situation in Brussels. It's not a gaping difference.

So here the mutually exclusive nature of national identities is still present in Lynn's thinking but the notion of being European is no longer as strong as it was ten years before. The birth of her baby leads her to think about national identity, and the experience she will have of two national identities, a very common experience in a globalised world:

> Yes, but there are so many Europeans that it's hard to have an identity. I will always be English. Not that I have any great sort of sense of national pride or anything like that. I like coming back and we joined the National Trust this Easter. I think that is important for my daughter. I really want to do as much as possible to make her know, to have her learn her British side of her nationality so that she has roots there as well. It's obviously going to be different. She is never going to be English and she's never really going to be wholly Belgian. She's going to be a mixture of the two so there can be a different personality.

Lynn goes on to contrast a European identity with the need for roots and history. Yet being European has certain identifiable characteristics: being able to 'travel around freely', being part of diversity 'different languages and different cultures', being part of a strong economy ('the economy is improving') and being like other Europeans (and different from people of other continents like the Americans), whilst maintaining one's nationality:

You don't get so centred on the idea of being European, not particularly – obviously I am, and that's why I can work easily in Brussels and travel around very freely. [..]) I think being European is almost ... not negative, but you lose the differences and I think what is important about Europe is that there are all these different nationalities and different languages and different cultures. If you've all become one mishmash of something European, what does it mean/ You have to have the history, you have to have the roots and that means all the differences. If you just have European as one globular thing, I don't think so. I think it is good that Europe is becoming stronger and the economy is improving and we're defending ourselves a bit better against the Americans but as a whole entity I think it is hard. Everyone feels European, but that will never be your nationality.

This is an interesting case because 'being European' is the best contemporary example of an international identity in practice. It is encouraged by European Union institutions, through voting for a European parliament and other ways. Lynn's experience indicates that European identity is still not firmly formed, but her remark about the Americans also demonstrates that social identities are always clarified by contrast with others. For Lynn, European identity is defined by contrast with American identity, and the economic competition that is implied. However within Europe, European identity is not marked. If Lynn were to travel to Asia or South America, she would then be identified as – and therefore be influenced to identify with – being European and she would have an experience parallel to national identification that becomes apparent only when one leaves one's nation state.

Lynn anticipates a different situation for her daughter: 'she is never going to be English and she's never really going to be Belgian. She's going to be a mixture of the two so there can be a different personality.' Her daughter will be far from unique in her situation which is already very common and will become more so. Lynn is anxious that her daughter should have 'roots' in the national whilst experiencing the hybridity of the international and feels there will be an impact on personality.

This experience is felt particularly by some students in international schools. On the one hand there can be a definite sense of advantage, of opportunity to learn about and interact with people of other cultures and identities without being explicitly taught about them. It is part of the hidden curriculum; it leads to a greater awareness of the wider world, as they realise when they meet students from ordinary national schools.

Anna describes some of this in the following interview extract:[39]

Anna: I meet people from more different races and I can learn more about those races, their religions and stuff without really knowing it.

Interviewer: How does that happen?

Anna: Umm – I guess someone tells me that they're not coming to school on Friday because they have to go to a temple because it's this certain day that I've never heard about before so I'd be aware of that.

Interviewer: OK, how else has going to an international school affected your life?

Anna: Different – I guess I know more about the world in general now because topics don't centre on one country – it's like, how this country interacts with this country and what happens to the entire world because of those relationships.

Anna's examples include the overt signs of religious difference, and other students also stress that they have a strong sense of racial awareness, of consciously being anti-racist, but it is also very probable that they are acquiring a sense of belonging to 'the entire world' in less conscious ways. The teaching of contemporary history is not nationalist; it is focused on international relations.

On the other hand in the following extract, John is attempting to express some of the disadvantages of being international. By now in his mid-teens, he has already lived in three countries, in Switzerland, Hong Kong and Singapore, always attending international schools. He appears to share Lynn's theory that place of birth is a crucial factor in identity and seems to contrast this geographically-located national identity with being international, which he defines as living in different countries.

John: Well – if you live in a country forever you just feel that – one of the people in the country and you're – not – an alien, kinda alien to them – you have a place, you have a real home to live in – a place where you're born and a place where you live.

Interviewer: And that's different to the home that you have in Singapore?

John: Well – uhh – I was born in Sweden and then went to Singapore – well – [very long pause] – how can I say it? Just – different – you're born in Sweden and live in Singapore [...] Yeah, yeah in the back of your mind you just feel

that – well – it's not your real home and it's just a place –
it just feels different after you move a couple of times.

Interviewer: There's something about not having a place that bothers
you?

John: mmm – well – I'm just think that, trying to think about
how people think of you – differently – 'cause if you live
at home in a country that's where you're born you just
feel – people there accepted you for long time and as –
well – people think you're a smart kid or just teenagers
and people think they're stuck with you as one group –
aahh (sound of exasperation) – it's just how I feel and –
it's in the back of my mind.

The problem is how other people see you. Other people seem to have, in
John's view, an influence on how you are 'accepted' into a group. John thus
has a theory that social identity is in part dependent on other people, a
theory that is supported by Tajfel's (1981) work cited above. For John,
having an international identity is in contrast with a national identity, and
without a national identity he is not comfortable because not accepted.

John's experience is a further warning that educators must be careful not
to attempt to replace national identity with an international identity. The
theory of tertiary socialisation should not be interpreted in this way. For
Lynn, an international/European identity is not in competition with a
national identity. Being 'European' is a way of describing the change that
has taken place but it is not a change that destroys her national identity. In
her second interview she feels the tension more strongly and has also lost
interest in the European identity. John's experience also indicates the
importance in interpersonal interactions of national identity and belonging
to a known group. The theory of tertiary socialisation does not deny this
but provides a vantage point, a perspective, that allows people to understand and better engage in interpersonal interactions where national, and
ethnic, identities are involved.

Becoming international as a consequence of a process of tertiary socialisation is not an alternative, but complementary to a national identity and
the cultural beliefs, values and behaviours this implies. It can nonetheless
lead – and indeed should lead – to a re-appraisal of those beliefs, values and
behaviours. Re-appraisal may lead to re-assertion in some dimensions and
change in others. This is not a threat or an incitement to change national or
ethnic identity, and applies, *mutatis mutandis*, to religious identity too.

Given this basic position, we need to return to the question of language
education and the relationship between national and foreign languages.

Languages and Identities in the Curriculum

As well as being the embodiment of a shared reality, language is one of the strongest symbols of identity. This is apparent to members of ethnic minorities who often defend their right to use their language with much energy and, occasionally, the use of violence. For members of majority groups, language is taken for granted, not noticed, until they are confronted by other majority groups and find themselves in the position of a minority. This happens when people visit another country for the first time or when, as is happening in the USA, the balance of majority language and minority language changes. The strong reaction to the increase in Spanish in the USA is leading some English speakers to make the same claims for legal protection of their language as are made by speakers of minority languages in other countries.

Thus, even if members of linguistic majorities are not aware of it, their language is a symbol of their identity. The symbolic attachment begins with primary socialisation and when the same language is the national/official language and the language of schooling, the attachment is reinforced in secondary socialisation. Teachers of the national language are the main purveyors of this attachment throughout the period of schooling. As well as developing cognitive competence, they reinforce affective attachment, for example through the teaching of literature, and in particular poetry.

Both the affective and the cognitive dimensions of language use are evident in the denotative and connotative aspects of words and phrases. As young people acquire increasing sensitivity to their language throughout schooling, their understanding of their world – from the physical environment to the world of imagination – is fulfilled through their language and its denotative and connotative influence. This is not to say that they cannot escape that influence, nor is it a strong Whorfian position on language and thought, i.e. that language 'determines' thought (Bredella & Richter, 2000). It is simply to say that perceptions are influenced and accepted as givens as a consequence of denotations and connotations shared with people speaking the same language, people who have had the same educational experience.

However, the 'sameness' of educational experience, and in particular of national language learning experience, needs to be described, and in some education systems may be identifiable only at a high level of abstraction because of the variation in practice within schools and universities. On the other hand, in curricula that are very centralised and using teaching materials that have to be approved by central educational authorities, the sameness will be more quickly visible. The close relationship between education in the national language and the formation of identity, and the symbolic function of language as a marker of identity, will be all the more evident.

When a foreign language is learnt, denotations and connotations of the national language, which will be the only ones known to monolingual speakers of the language, are challenged. The naturalness of the national language disappears and the arbitrary nature of the linguistic sign is revealed, provided that the language is not taught as if it were simply an encoding of the learners' first language. What is also revealed is that, although the language is arbitrary, it is nonetheless shared by a group of people and is important to them as a symbol of identity. Thus the challenge to their language and their conceptualisation of the world embodied in their language that comes from learning a foreign language, can also be a challenge to their identity.

Just how powerful and effective the challenge will be, depends on the circumstances. It is unlikely that the usual format of a few lessons a week in a foreign language will have noticeable effects. On the other hand, a full experience of living in another linguistic environment for the purpose of improving one's language competence, may well have major effects, as we saw earlier in the case of Lynn. However, the cases of Anna and John and other international pupils show that it should not be the purpose of foreign language teachers, whether in school or post-school education, to promote an alternative to the national language and the national identity it symbolises. The promotion of an international educational experience and the effects it has on self-awareness, which we can call for the moment an 'international identity', is an extension not an alternative.

Chapter 7

Chapter 7 analyses the relationship between language learning and identity. National languages are important for nation states, and the teaching of national languages is an integral part of creating national identities and in turn a crucial part of compulsory schooling developed since the rise of the nation state. The position of foreign language teaching in this context is potentially threatening to the fundamental purpose of state education, but is increasingly appropriate in a world where internationalisation and globalisation allow and encourage – and perhaps eventually will necessitate – the acquisition of additional identities. Identities are social and are acquired through socialisation, and this chapter argues that foreign language education can and should be a location for a process of tertiary socialisation that challenges the concept of national identity without trying to replace it. The chapter then illustrates these concepts through empirical data drawn from interviews with a foreign language learner who has had a complex international experience and from further interviews with young people in an international school for whom the question of identity is particularly salient. These data show the importance of national identity but the significance too of developing an international identity.

Chapter 8

Chapter 8 analyses the particular case of language learning in Europe, which is a unique situation in the contemporary world but may be an indicator of future developments elsewhere. It shows how there are signs in policies developing at European level of a desire for European identity. Education and in particular language education is expected to play an important role in this process. The chapter then examines the theoretical possibility of this notion by referring to socialisation and social identity theories as a basis for understanding data from an interview with people who had a 'European' experience and a sense of identity that does not fit neatly into the traditions of national identity. The question then arises whether a European identity will not only be an addition to national identity but also of a different kind, supported especially by education for plurilingualism.

Chapter 8
Language Learning in Europe

The Council of Europe promotes the development of plurilingual competence, a dynamic and changing repertoire of languages and language varieties one might acquire over a lifetime of interaction in a multilingual area such as Europe. The question that intrigues is whether this will create a sense of 'plurilingual identity', which might in turn be related to a European identity and, as a specific part of this, whether it will create an increase in respect for other people and their ways of life. This would be an attractive phenomenon if it really began to evolve. It would be a sign that people feel an allegiance to Europe as a socio-political and cultural entity, and this is one of the hopes of many pro-Europeans. Of more general significance, it would also be attractive if someone with a plurilingual identity demonstrated an increased understanding of and attraction towards 'otherness', both within Europe and beyond. Does becoming plurilingual create interest and positive attitudes towards 'otherness'? This is a question that is not only important for individual relationships but also for relationships among social groups, whether religious, ethnic, regional, national or international.

There are then various reasons for exploring plurilingualism: interest in the sustainability of a concept of European identity, interest in the moral development that identification with an international identity might promote, theory of social identity and socialisation, and the advantages for practical politics and the evolution of Europe.

In order to examine the theoretical and practical nature of the concept, I will consider first the promotion of the link of language and language learning with European identity. This is present in policy documents, perhaps without any theoretical underpinning but simply included as an aspiration. I will then consider theories of social identity and socialisation and in particular the role of language in identification of the individual and the social group.

A Political Aspiration

The continuing trend for European integration is most evident in the evolution of the European Union and the Council of Europe, which is strengthened by trends of economic globalisation and societal internationalisation that make all countries interdependent. It has long been recognised by both organisations that Europe is a potential whole that might overcome the fissiparous tendencies of ethnic, linguistic and religious diversity. The increasing number of member states of each organisation is a consequence of the appearance of new states in the former Soviet Union and Yugoslavia, and the role of the EU and the CoE in maintaining relationships and coherent policies among them is all the more important as the number grows.

In the age of the nation state, fissiparous tendencies were overcome by force, often including the imposition of one language on those who spoke varieties of what was deemed to be a standard, or indeed who spoke quite different languages, as examples from throughout Europe demonstrate. The imposition of English on the Welsh in the 19th century is a notorious case and there are many others, but these impositions by force are ultimately rejected even after hundreds of years. Similarly, even where force was absolute in the period of colonisation and a language was imposed on some sections of colonised populations by absolute force, as in the British Empire, the language itself begins to split into varieties and a number of Englishes are beginning to evolve that may become mutually unintelligible. There is therefore no likelihood and even less desirability of overcoming European multilingualism through the imposition of one language by force or persuasion, following the model of the nation state.

An alternative view is to encourage the acquisition of more than one language, for both economic and social reasons. This is clearly stated in the White Paper on the concept of a learning society published by the European Union in 1995. The economic advantages not only of linguistic ability but also of a capacity for cultural flexibility are stated in the following paragraph:

> Proficiency in several Community [i.e. EU] languages has become a precondition if citizens of the European Union are to benefit from the occupational and personal opportunities open to them in the border-free single market. This language proficiency must be backed up by the ability to adapt to working and living environments characterised by different cultures. (European Commission, 1995: 67)

This is followed by a second statement on the direct relationship between language learning and identity, a relationship that is presented as causal:

> Languages are also the key to knowing other people. Proficiency in languages helps to *build up the feeling of being European* with all its cultural wealth and diversity and of understanding between the citizens of Europe. (European Commission, 1995: 67; my emphasis)

This then led to the suggestion that all citizens of the European Union should learn their own and two other languages of the Union.

The position had changed by 2003 when 10 new countries joined the EU. There is no insistence of the notion of 'one plus two' Although the White Paper is still cited as a source, the focus here is on effective participation and social cohesion. The reference to identity no longer appears:

(1) knowledge of languages is one of the basic skills which each citizen needs to acquire in order to take part effectively in the European knowledge society and therefore facilitates both integration into society and social cohesion; a thorough knowledge of one's mother tongue(s) can facilitate the learning of other languages;
(2) knowledge of languages plays an important role in facilitating mobility, both in an educational context as well as for professional purposes and for cultural and personal reasons;
(3) knowledge of languages is also beneficial for European cohesion, in the light of European Union enlargement;
(4) all European languages are equal in value and dignity from the cultural point of view and form an integral part of European culture and civilisation. (Council Resolution, 2002)

There is still an emphasis on mobility, but here the professional/ economic purposes are linked to the personal, and the specific issue of enlargement from 15 to 25 countries is given prominence. There are two points to draw from these documents:

- an assumption of a causal relationship between language learning and 'feeling European' and/or being part of a cohesive European society;
- a conditional relationship between language learning and effective participation in a European (knowledge) society.

Knowledge of languages is at least a pre-condition and perhaps a causal factor in the successful evolution of European society where people are mobile and integrated, and where all European languages are equally valuable 'from the cultural point of view'. The nature of the relationship between language learning and respect for other cultures is not made clear, however. There is only an association of ideas present in the documents.

The Council of Europe has made similar statements but put much greater emphasis from the beginning on the question of diversity in language learning, and on ensuring that education systems are flexible in meeting the changing needs of European citizens throughout their lives. The following are part of a list of Recommendations to the Member states in 1982:

(1) To ensure, as far as possible, that all sections of their populations have access to effective means of acquiring a knowledge of the languages of other member states (or of other communities within their own country) as well as the skills in the use of those languages that will enable them to satisfy their communicative needs and in particular;

  (1.1) to deal with the business of everyday life in another country, and to help foreigners staying in their own country to do so;

  (1.2) to exchange information and ideas with young people and adults who speak a different language and to communicate their thoughts and feelings to them;

  (1.3) to *achieve a wider and deeper understanding of the way of life and forms of thought of other peoples and of their cultural heritage.*

(Recommendation R(82) 18; emphasis added. On WWW at www.coe. int/lang; accessed 30.9.07)

There is similarity here with the later EU statements: emphasis on living in other countries, on understanding others, on the value of cultural heritage. But there are also some interesting additional points: the importance of helping others to live in one's own society, the reference to communicating feelings, the inclusion of reference to other communities within one's own country. On the other hand, it is interesting to note that the European Union statement includes reference to mother tongue(s) and the supportive relationship between knowledge of these and learning other languages, but the Council of Europe refers only to other/foreign languages.

Almost two decades later, further recommendations were made to member states of the Council of Europe, including the following:

(1) Pursue education policies which:

  (1.1) enable all Europeans to communicate with speakers of other mother tongues, thereby developing open-mindedness, facilitating free movement of people and exchange of information and improving international co-operation;

  (1.2) develop learners' respect for other ways of life and equip them for an intercultural world, in particular through direct links and exchanges and through personal experience; [...]

(2) Promote widespread plurilingualism:

  (2.1) by encouraging all Europeans to achieve a degree of communicative ability in a number of languages;

(Recommendation R(98) 6. On WWW at www.coe.int/lang; accessed 30.9.07)

Here there is an implication in the first paragraph that speaking with others creates 'open-mindedness', and in the second paragraph that personal experience of otherness will develop respect for others. Again there is a hint of causality: plurilingualism is associated with, and assumed to create respect for, other 'ways of life'.

One important difference in the positions of the two organisations lies in the understanding of the notion of 'other people', implicit or explicit, and the treatment of language and identity. The Council of Europe position does not limit the aspiration of understanding to Europe alone, but neither does it make as strong a statement about the relationship between language learning and identity.

Taking the two organisations together, we can see a pre-occupation with the relationship between knowledge of languages or language learning and being a European in some sense, and secondly with the importance of respect for other ways of life/language and cultures.[40]

In the case of the Council of Europe this can be traced back to its origins in the founding Convention, which stated that one of its purposes was:

> to develop mutual understanding among the peoples of Europe and reciprocal appreciation of their cultural diversity, to safeguard European culture, to promote national contributions to Europe's common cultural heritage respecting the same fundamental values and *to encourage in particular the study of the languages*, history and civilisation of the Parties to the Convention. (http://conventions.coe.int/Treaty/EN/cadreprincipal.htm; emphasis added; accessed 30.9.07)

and is prominent in its contemporary self-presentation:

> The Council was set up to [...] promote awareness of a European identity based on shared values and cutting across different cultures (www.coe.int/T/EN/Com/EN/Com/About–COE/; accessed 30.9.07)

These principles have been the foundation for the work on language learning at the Council of Europe since the 1950s (Saville, 2005; Trim, 2006), of which the most well-known product is the *Common European Framework of Reference for Languages: Learning, Teaching and Assessment* (Council of Europe, 2001).

There can be no doubt about the desirability of understanding otherness, and, secondly, the hope of creating a sense of belonging to Europe is, for some people at least, a valuable idea. The question is whether there is any justification for holding the belief that language learning and being plurilingual support, facilitate or even cause these feelings to develop in individuals. The following sections discuss the theories that might throw some light on the phenomena involved and the relationships among them.

European Identity as a Social Identity?

The theory of social identity explains the behaviour of individuals when they act as members of a group, and how they feel about themselves as members of a group. It also explains the interaction among groups. Conflict arises when there is competition among groups for scarce resources, and this is particularly evident among ethnic groups, nations, or nation states. Moreover, rivalry, competition and perhaps conflict are produced not only by scarcity of resources, but also by the need for individuals to have self-esteem, and for that self-esteem to be based on the status of the group: 'My group is better than the others that I know and from which my group differentiates itself'. The first point suggests that conflict can be reduced if competition for resources is reduced, but more pessimistically, the second point implies that conflict is a consequence of rivalry and that perhaps conflicts are inevitable among groups because individuals always seek self-esteem. This also reinforces the significance of self-categorisation, i.e. the tendency of individuals to characterise themselves in terms of their belonging to a group, (self-ascription). We shall see, however, that cross-cultural research on social identity allows a less pessimistic interpretation.

Interest in social identity arose from attempts to understand and explain inter-group conflict, and psychologists have carried out experiments to investigate how people become members of a group and how they behave in group situations. Tajfel's work (1978, 1981) reports experiments to investigate this. He shows how even arbitrary groups become the basis for allegiances and loyalties and how groups differentiate themselves from each other. He then discusses the ways in which dominant and dominated groups interact and the effects on the individual, including whether an individual has the option of changing group, of 'passing' from one group to another, and therefore changing identification.

The theory appears to be most powerful in explaining interactions when the groups are large scale – gender, religious, national/ethnic – but it is argued that it also offers at least a partial explanation of how individuals behave in smaller groups, which may be transitory, such as friendship groups.

However, as noted above, the concept itself needs to be challenged so that it is not used as a total explanation of behaviour or beliefs. It can otherwise lead to a reductionist view of the individual, and a static view of the relationships between groups in a society. Secondly, the theory needs to be tested in other contexts than the ones in which it was developed, i.e. Britain and North America, and this has been done with young people on the Pacific Islands and New Zealand. This work shows that the mechanisms of group interactions may differ. Among young people of local origin, there is less prioritisation of 'my group' and more effort to maximise benefits for both 'my group' and others. It is people of European origin in New Zealand who continue to confirm Tajfel's findings. This suggests that individuals act not directly as a consequence of an automatic link between group identification and individual identity but as a reflection of the more comprehensive framework of attitudes to outsiders and insiders:

> Results like these suggest that what determines behaviour in the minimal group situation may not be an automatic psychological link between group identification and competition. What may be more crucial is the way in which group members interpret and give meaning to the intergroup situation in line with the collective frameworks of their culture and community. This sense-making will determine the consequences of group identification – whether it leads to in-group favouritism and out-group discrimination or to some other outcome. (Wetherell, 1996: 217–18)

The important inference for language teaching is that, if individuals' perceptions of the relationships between groups can be changed from egocentricity and ethnocentricity to a more altruistic sense of mutual benefit, then their understanding of and response to intergroup interactions and their own contribution to such interactions may also be changed. This remains a speculation, but one that is crucial to our discussion since the political aspiration for greater understanding is another way of saying the same thing, that people's nationally-oriented ways of seeing things can be changed to an international perspective, and that language learning can be an important force for change.

Language and Identity

One important aspect of social identity theory in the discussion of language learning is that language is one of the most important means by which groups identify themselves and others, i.e. it is one of the most important 'markers' of differences or 'boundaries' between groups (Barth, 1969). This means that, in encounters between people of different language groups, i.e. different (linguistic) social identities, a primary response of one to the other may well be through their categorisation of each other as 'speaker of language X'. Even if one person is speaking the language of the other, i.e. is a 'foreign speaker' conversing with a 'native speaker', the former will be categorised in terms of his/her language of origin. So a French person speaking German will be seen by a German interlocutor as 'French', and expected to respond and react in accord with the German person's beliefs (often stereotypes) about the French. If the French person speaks German without accent or error and therefore appears linguistically to be German, the German person may become confused by other indications (such as lack of knowledge of some aspect of life in Germany) that the speaker is not in fact German, and will therefore not know how to categorise him/her. If the person speaking German with a French accent is not in fact French but, say, Canadian, confusion may be even greater and the Canadian will also be confused or even offended by the implicit categorisation of him/her as French. Such examples demonstrate how significant categorisations can be in communication across linguistic boundaries, and how difficult it may be for the individual to escape other people's categorisations of them, and the use of national stereotypes in the interaction.

A second dimension of the relationship between language and identity is that individuals may categorise themselves in terms of their language or languages, or the variety of a language they speak. They do so in accordance with the processes of group identification, and in particular the process of marking boundaries. For example people in the German minority in Denmark see themselves as 'German' because they speak German, even though in many other respects they are indistinguishable from the Danish majority around them (Byram, 1986). This phenomenon has been best researched with respect to ethnic groups and, in his classic discussion of ethnicity, Barth (1969) places the emphasis on the ways in which boundaries are marked and function, rather than on the phenomena that may be markers of the boundaries or on the characteristics, behaviour and beliefs that are the 'content' of ethnicity. For in fact these may change, may be reconstructed over time, but the act of differentiating 'our' group from 'the others' is crucial and constant. Thus language can in principle be a marker of ethnic and/or national identity – 'I am X because I speak X' – but need not be so, or can change from being so. A European example of such a change is to be found in Ireland, where being Irish is no longer dependent on or marked by speaking Irish.

A third function of language in identity is in its embodiment of a group's shared beliefs, values and behaviours. Individuals who identify with a social group share the culture of that group. If they do not, they are not acceptable as members and may be ostracised. Identification with a group thus necessitates acceptance of the maintenance of the shared culture and this involves a process of constant interaction, not least through language.

In using the shared concepts in interactive communication, group members are constantly reinforcing the significance and meaning of those concepts that are themselves embodied in the group's shared language. Some concepts are particularly significant and become 'keywords' (Wierzbicka, 1997) and fundamental indicators of the values of the group.

The question that needs to be addressed next is how individuals become members of groups, especially ethnic/national groups, and what role language plays in this process.

Socialisation

Berger and Luckmann describe primary and secondary socialisation as follows:

The comprehensive and consistent induction of an individual into the objective world of a society or sector of it. Primary socialisation is the first socialisation an individual undergoes in childhood, through which he becomes a member of society. Secondary socialisation is any subsequent process that inducts an already socialised individual into new sectors of the objective world of his society. (Berger & Luckmann, 1960: 150)

They then go on to refer to other societies but do not develop the point:

We may leave aside here the special question of the acquisition of knowledge about the objective world of societies other than the one of which we first became a member, and the process of internalising such a world as reality – a process that exhibits, at least superficially, certain similarities with both primary and secondary socialisation, yet is structurally identical with neither. (Berger & Luckmann, 1960: 150-1)

Primary socialisation typically takes place in the family and the acquisition of shared beliefs, values and behaviours is mediated through the 'significant others' who are typically parents, but may be substitutes such as other members of the family or nursemaids and servants.[41] Language acquisition is part of this process and the acquisition of shared concepts embodied in language means that acquiring language and becoming a social being are integrated and inseparable. 'Language' here can of course mean a combination of languages and language varieties, and though Berger and Luckmann confine their perspective to that of the monolingual society and the acquisition of one language and culture, their description can be applied to more complex processes in plurilingual families.

The process Berger and Luckmann describe is one of externalisation, objectification and internalisation. Adult members of a social group constantly externalise their understandings of their shared culture, and language is a means of rendering these objective and available to others who in turn internalise them and perhaps modify their existing understandings in a constant mutual influence among members of the group. In contrast, during primary socialisation, children do not yet have their own internalised understandings of the culture that is around them and embodied in their family; for them the process is one of apprehending the objectified culture externalised by those around them and then internalising this so that they can share in that culture and be accepted into the social group that owns it.

The process of acquiring a culture in this sense of shared beliefs, values and behaviours is thus intimately connected to language acquisition. The child becomes a social being as it becomes a linguistic being, and this process cannot be repeated precisely the same way in later life.

Secondary socialisation is often but not always a continuation of primary socialisation, beyond the family, in the institutions, formal and informal, of the wider society in which the family and child exist. The crucial formal institution is school, where the process of internalisation of objectified culture continues, although the 'significant others' are no longer as emotionally significant for children as those they meet in the family. One of the functions of education is thus to continue the induction into the culture of a society, although this may not coincide exactly with that of primary socialisation, since education systems do not necessarily reflect the beliefs, values and behaviours of all the social groups within a society. This can cause conflict and contradiction.

One dimension of secondary socialisation is the internalisation of beliefs, values and behaviours concerning nationality, i.e. the sense of belonging to a nation state, of being a citizen of that state. Barrett (2007) has shown that this is a complex process with many influences involved: parental discourse, choice of abode, of school, of access to the media, as well as influences from peers and encounters with people from other countries. Among these, the school curriculum and textbooks are one location where children begin to grasp the geography of the state, that their home is part of and the idea that it is located within a country and a state (Wiegand, 1992). They are introduced to the symbols and emblems of the state and in some cases, to the behaviour expected of a citizen of the state. This process is particularly evident in the acquisition of a national geography and history. It is also evident in the acquisition of a national/official language, both written and spoken. It is here that there may be dissonance between the language of the home and the language of the state purveyed in the school, but most states require all their children to acquire the national/official language even if other languages are permitted a role in the education of children of a different culture and ethnicity. It is through this process that language becomes a marker of national identity and citizenship and identification with these happens though language: 'I am X because I speak X'. [42]

The acquisition of other languages and the concepts and values they embody is, as Berger and Luckmann say 'a process that exhibits, at least superficially, certain similarities with both primary and secondary sociali-sation, yet is structurally identical with neither.' The introduction of another language and concepts after primary and the early stages of secondary socialisation is a potential threat to the symbolic significance of the national language and to the individual's identification with this and to the use of it as a means of interpreting reality. Whether introduced in formal education or acquired in informal learning situations, a further language has the potential to begin a third stage of socialisation, 'tertiary socialisa-tion (Byram, 1990; Doyé, 1992 – see Chapter 2 of this volume).

In essence, the argument is that, as learners are confronted by another language and the concepts it embodies, they find some concepts that are incompatible with those acquired in primary and secondary socialisation. Even in the early stages of language learning, the conceptualisation of time, for example, may well be different from that of the first language. Some 'key words' are particularly heavily connoted and reveal shared meanings of another society (Agar, 1991; Wierzbicka, 1997). The acquisition of these words and their connotations is not simply a cognitive process but one that can threaten the affective attachment to the world one knows, and Berger and Luckmann (1966: 173 ff.) have an interesting discussion of situations when such threats are extreme. They argue that in any society – or as I would say, cultural group – there has to be a process of constant mainte-nance of shared reality. This happens through language and in the course of time there will be modification of shared meanings and shared reality. There can also be, for the individual, a transformation of subjective reality through this constant modification and, in extreme cases, the individual may undergo a process of switching worlds, of 'alternation' and therefore of re-socialisation. Berger and Luckmann give the example of religious conversion. Only in very rare cases is this likely to happen through lang-uage learning, although examples of extreme exophilia exist.

Intermediate cases of partial transformation are more common, and Berger and Luckmann exemplify their argument by referring to mobility from one social class to another. Where such mobility creates inconsisten-cies for the individual who meets a reality that contrasts with that of primary and early secondary socialisation, the individual may overcome the inconsistencies by re-interpretation of the past, and other people may make allowances for the changes they observe in him or her. Such processes of partial transformation may also take place in other kinds of mobility, when the movement takes people literally to another society and another interpretation of the world. In this case the threat to the existing subjective reality is likely to be far greater than that which takes place in the classroom if only because it is constant, with little respite. In the classroom, the new reality is experienced for short periods, and learners are immediately returned to their familiar reality. The following account of her experience of living in Portugal and then returning to her home country of France given by a primary school teacher involved in an exchange project makes the contrast between sojourn and classroom very clear:

> I came home by train and when I arrived at the station in Bordeaux, I needed some change to leave my case at the left luggage office. I went to get some change at a newspaper kiosk and I heard myself speaking as I would have done before, saying 'Good morning, I wonder if you could give me some change'. In other words I heard myself speaking in a way that I didn't in Portugal because I hadn't reached that level in language, that level of complexity, which I have in French. And when I heard myself speak with this kind, this level of language, I wasn't the same person any more, and I really felt at that moment that in speaking a language, there are important issues of personality. Hearing myself speak French, it was no longer me, the person who had lived for 11 months in Portugal, it wasn't me speaking. I had this French language which was part of [literally: inscribed in] me, but it wasn't me who was speaking. So then I lived for about two weeks re-teaching myself the French language which had left me, but the form of it was no longer the same. For two weeks I really felt strange, just because of using the language, and the values which I had to draw from it.
>
> I think you have to live through that experience to understand it. There really is no transfer possible from one language to another. In fact I had thought ... the courses I had done at school had given me the impression there is, that it's a code which you decode. But it doesn't work like that at all. (Byram, 1996: 89; translated from French)

The teacher tells us how she was re-socialised and acquired a new identity in Portugal, one that was unlike her usual identity because it was 'reduced' or 'simplified' by the fact that she was a beginner in Portuguese. Her explanation that she had to re-teach herself French is another process of socialisation but in two weeks she re-creates the identity she had before she went to Portugal. Her comparison with the classroom, where she had learnt

English as a foreign language, shows how some ways of teaching can in fact avoid even minimal exposure to a foreign reality by giving the impression that there is a simple one-to-one relationship between languages. During her sojourn in Portugal, but not in the language classroom, the teacher had experienced 'tertiary socialisation'.

Tertiary socialisation can, according to Doyé (1992), be analysed on three dimensions; the cognitive, the moral and the behavioural. He builds on the presentation of primary and secondary socialisation by Berger and Luckmann and others, to argue that as people meet new cultures and their norms of beliefs, values and behaviours, a relativisation can, and should, take place. The 'should' is the recognition that this may not happen without a pedagogic influence because their existing beliefs, values and behaviours are so well entrenched through primary and early secondary socialisation that the individual may not relinquish his or her own perspective on these issues at all. The 'should' also indicates that in some classrooms, as the teacher quoted above suggests, there is no attempt made to challenge the false assumption that a foreign language is just a code for learners' first language. Where tertiary socialisation does take place, it is not that one set of beliefs and schemata is replaced by others, but that new beliefs and schemata are held side by side with existing ones, the individual being ready to operate with whichever is relevant in a given context. The teacher had put aside her French language and schemata because she was immersed in Portuguese language and society, but if she had been travelling frequently backwards and forwards from Portugal to France, she would have learnt to switch between them as bicultural people do (see Chapter 4). The same argument applies to the values of moral socialisation, leading to an ability to recognise and accept other values, and where possible merge them in a universal system of human values. This corresponds to Kohlberg's post-conventional level of moral socialisation in which the relativity of the norms of one's own society is recognised (Kohlberg *et al.*, 1983). Similarly, in the behavioural dimension, the individual acquires new behaviours but, combined with an insight into other schemata and moral values, s/he does not simply adopt new ways of behaving, but finds 'middle ways' of intercultural behaviours with which he/she and people of another culture feel comfortable – not an easy task but one that a moral and cognitive perspective can facilitate. There is thus an 'is' and an 'ought' dimension to the theory of tertiary socialisation: it both describes the potential effects of language and culture learning but it also provides the principles for pedagogic action.

In thinking about 'European identity', can the theory of tertiary sociali-sation help us to conceptualise what the relationship might be between language learning in Europe and the evolution of new identities?

European Identity and Language Learning

Theories of socialisation, social identity and language have so far been developed to explain the processes of becoming and remaining a member of a national group and there is work by psychologists examining the evolution of European identity. So far however it does not deal with the role of language and language learning (Barrett, 1996; Chryssochoou, 2000; Cinnirella, 1996, 1997).

National group membership for the individual is acquired through socialisation, is internalised and maintained in interaction with others through language. Language thus embodies but is also one of the symbols of national identity. National identity, like other social identities, is reinforced by comparison and contrast with other identities, and the boundaries between the in-group nationality and out-group nationalities are marked, among other things, by language. To what extent and in what way might this process apply to the acquisition of a European identity?

The first point to note is that individuals have many social identities, and the strength of national identity may vary from group to group. Barrett's research has shown for example that Scottish and English children have differing degrees of attachment to being British and Andalusian and Catalan children have differing degrees of attachment to being Spanish:

> (in both Scottish and English groups) the age trend which we picked up in other studies, namely for national identity to become more important during the childhood years, has been replicated. However, notice also that being British is significantly more important for the English children than for the Scottish children. [...] In both groups of children (Andalusian and Catalan) being Spanish becomes more important during childhood years (although the increase is fairly minimal in the case of Andalusian children because of the considerable importance which these children attribute to Spanishness even at 6 years of age). And notice that Spanishness is far more important to the Andalusian children than to the Catalan children at all ages. (Barrett, 2000: 17)

It is also interesting to note that their national identity becomes more important to children as they grow older and this should be taken into account in deciding the starting age for language learning. *Ceteris paribus,* the younger the children the less resistance there would be to taking other perspectives than the national.

Secondly, social identity theory suggests that it is only when people might acquire two social identities of the same nature – for example being a supporter of two rival football clubs, or indeed having two national identities – that tension and difficulty may arise. People may have two citizen-ships, i.e. be legally considered citizens of two states, but it is difficult, although not impossible, to have a sense of belonging to two national groups, particularly when there are incompatible beliefs and values in their cultures (see Chapter 4; Paulston, 1992). On the other hand, a European identity could be of a different nature or 'level', not in contest with national identity, but comparable rather to a concept of 'Asian' identity, which seems to be developing in South and East Asia as a counter-balance to 'Wes-ternisation'. So European identity could be additional to, not instead of, national identity.

Thirdly, if the process of acquisition of European identity were to be comparable to that of national identity, then it would need to begin in early secondary socialisation and in school through the teaching of geography, history and other subjects. As indicated above, Barrett's research shows that the older children become the more important national identity becomes to them. In fact the exhortation that has from time to time come from the European Community/Union to introduce a 'European dimen-sion' into the curricula of schools in all member states would, if applied, begin this process.

However, the acquisition of a national identity is predicated on the notion that there is a shared culture, shared beliefs, values and behaviours, that all members of a nation internalise, and have 'always' done so because these are 'our traditions'. The existence of such traditions and a shared culture is perhaps more myth than reality for, as Hobsbawm and Granger (1983) argue, the traditions are often a 19th century invention. The 'imag-ined' shared culture (Anderson, 1991) becomes a reality through print media and the nation state has in many cases had a long period in which to establish the 'traditions' and the culture through obligatory education, especially the promotion of literacy and the inculcation of selected iconic texts. Where new nation states arise, as is currently happening in parts of Europe, the process of creating a national identity and shared culture through education is clearly observable. In some cases, where a distinct national language does not exist, it is also possible to see this being created, and in some cases this is done by excluding other languages from the education system. Is it possible to envisage an analogous process for Euro-pean identity?[43]

It can be argued that there is a shared European culture in the sense of a shared set of beliefs and values, and possibly behaviours. This becomes most evident as with all identities and cultures by contrast. The notion that there is a 'Western' as opposed to 'Asian' or 'oriental' culture is often invoked, even though it is very contentious. On the other hand, it is obviously not possible to find or create one language comparable to a national language to symbolise a European identity or embody the shared beliefs and values in the way that a national language does.[44] So neither shared culture nor shared language have sufficient reality as a basis for identity. Perhaps there is a shared history and geography – and there are attempts to create shared symbols such as the European flag and the European anthem – but are these enough? The possibility of creating the conditions for the acquisition of a European identity in a process analogous to that of national identity seems excluded.

Can there be a different but parallel process for European identity to meet the aspirations of those who wrote the documents cited at the beginning of this chapter, what Outhwaite (2006: 120) calls a 'weak or "thin" cultural identity based on a particular modulation of modernity'? We have met two avenues that are worth exploring: firstly, the notion that social identity need not be as egocentric as it appears in experiments with British, North Americans and New Zealanders of European origin; and secondly, the concept of tertiary socialisation. On the basis of these one can speculate that the acquisition of languages and the development of plurilingual competence might lead to changes in ways of understanding reality, to changes in what is taken for granted. That this is not necessarily the case, and that there is a role for pedagogy rather than mere experience of other languages is implicit in the concept of tertiary socialisation. This would mean that teachers of language would have to include this in their aims for their subject, and as our earlier research has shown there would be mixed views on this (Byram & Risager, 1999).

Will plurilingualism lead to respect for otherness, for other languages, for other cultures? The assertion by the EU is that all languages and cultures are of equal value, and by implication must be treated as such. Here again, we need to be circumspect. The implications in some of the documents that language learning – conceived by the EU with a rather narrow focus on acquiring linguistic competence rather than intercultural competence – will automatically lead to respect, or that personal experience of otherness will lead to better understanding (often called the 'contact hypothesis') are not supported by the albeit-small amount of empirical research. Byram, Esarte-Sarries and Taylor (1991) found no identifiable relationship between different styles of language and culture teaching and learners' perceptions and understanding of a national culture. More recent work in Australia (Ingram & O'Neill, 2002) has not found any causal relationship between teaching and positive attitudes either. This suggests there has to be a substantial change in the pedagogy if there is to be a hope of language teaching and learning being causally related to increased respect for otherness, let alone a change from negative to positive attitudes.

In his description of what plurilingual identity might be, Beacco (2005) also emphasises that there has to be more than simply being plurilingual, since this is 'ordinary'. The individual has to become aware of his or her plurilingualism as a valued phenomenon, but even this is not enough:

> Clearly, then, individual plurilingualism (or the ever-present possibility of its emerging) is a fact of everyday life. But awareness of the language diversity we carry within us does not automatically mean we view other people's language diversity in a positive light even in cases where our own is identical with theirs. (Beacco, 2005: 20)

In fact Beacco confines his hopes for positive attitudes and respect for other to the question of respect for languages. He agrees however that there is a serious task for education:

> The transition from a closed identity to a relaxed and welcoming relationship with languages that allows us the innumerable pleasures of plurilingualism requires an *educatio*, in the strict sense of the term, that develops pluricultural and plurilingual capability. (Beacco, 2005: 20)

This kind of education has to deal with values, and it is in the concept of 'critical cultural awareness' as one of the components of intercultural competence that language teachers meet the question of moral education (Byram, 1997). This means more than developing competences, plurilingual and pluricultural; it means encouraging learners to engage with values, beliefs and behaviours through the encounter with otherness that language and culture learning involves. It can also mean developing links with concepts and practices in citizenship education (see Chapters 10 to 13), and that too would introduce questions of belonging, of identification with international groups at a European level and beyond. Identities and attitudes may then change, but that too will be an empirical question.

Chapter 8

Chapter 8 discusses how language learning and experience of otherness can have an influence on one's sense of identity and on the evolution of identities that do not neatly fit into the traditions of national identity. This is done in the context of an analysis of policy documents that shows there is an aspiration at European level to create a European identity. There is theoretical evidence to suggest that this is possible, but the question of what ought to take place is a matter of values and purposes in education. This has implications for teachers who need to decide if and how they want to play a role in this process. Language teaching is no more value-free than any other kind of teaching.

Chapter 9

Chapter 9 considers the perspective of teachers and teacher trainers. Some theorists take the view that language teachers ought to become involved in teaching values, and especially values that reflect a particular political standpoint. There is evidence too from empirical investigations that some teachers accept that they should and do attempt to influence their pupils' understanding of the world and not just teach them linguistic competence. On this basis the second part of the chapter discusses what is necessary in teacher training to equip teachers of language to go beyond the focus on linguistic competence.

Chapter 9

Foreign Language ~~[~~ Political Action

Part

146

sory schooling, then it
that the aims of fore
contradicts the so
of compulsory
Guilherm
sion of a
foreig
pra

The learning/acquisition of language~~s~~
many locations and at many ages, not ~~(~~
On the one hand, it is important that th~~e~~
development of a 'European Languag~~e~~
document all aspects of their language learning/acquisition is an important symbol of this (www.coe.int/lang). On the other hand, there is a
unique dimension to language learning/acquisition during compulsory
schooling that makes it important to call it Foreign Language *Education*.
This dimension has tended to be forgotten since the introduction of 'communicative language teaching', partly as a consequence of the emphasis on
'skills' and 'competences'. It is often loosely referred to as 'broadening
learners' horizons' or making learners 'more tolerant'. More precisely, it is
the aim of developing a better cognitive understanding of 'self' and 'other'
and a more refined affective capacity for a desirable relationship to 'otherness'. Clearly, this formulation needs expansion and explanation; it needs an
explicit psychological theory to support it; and it needs an appropriate methodology that embraces but goes beyond that of the communicative approach
(e.g. Kramsch, 1993; Corbett, 2003). Most of all it needs a philosophical basis,
and this has been provided most convincingly by Guilherme (2002) in her
aptly named *Critical Citizens for an Intercultural World*.

Conceived in this way, foreign language education can and should play
a role in internationalisation of the curriculum (see Chapter 2), and from
this perspective it becomes evident that there is a political element in
foreign language education. The effect of language learning/acquisition
can for example affect learners' understanding of their national identity,
develop in them a European/international identity, and make them question the taken-for-granted values, meanings and behaviours of the culture
into which they have been socialised (see Chapter 8). But it need not do so; it
can also do the opposite and reinforce learners' ethnocentric attitudes.
Indeed this can be the deliberate policy when languages are learnt as part of
national security and a need to 'know your enemy'.[45]

When language learning/acquisition is guided and is part of compul-

is the responsibility of the teacher to try to ensure
gn language education are achieved, even when this
cialisation into a national culture and identity that the rest
schooling pursues.

e's analysis of the evolution of thinking on the political dimen-
l education, and her reflections on the implications of this for
language education provide the foundation on which to build the
ctice of foreign language education in a thoroughly systematic way. As a
oundation it is demanding but her empirical work shows that teachers in
Portugal are open to the ideas. Guilherme's analysis leads to a statement of
the fundamental principles of 'foreign culture education', which include
principles of 'the interaction between Self and Other', 'the cultural dimension', 'the educational dimension', 'ethical dimension' and 'the political
dimension'. The political dimension comprises the following:

- the political nature of education should be made explicit;
- the interaction between macro- and micro-contexts should be taken into consideration;
- the multiplicity and complexity of subject positionings that reflect particular configurations of power should be grasped;
- everyone's political rights independently of their cultural background should be asserted;
- the capability to challenge ongoing relations of power should be promoted;
- cultural realities should not only be interpreted but also transformed;
- the individualistic, ahistorical and depoliticised celebration of diversity should be avoided;
- the integration of citizens into new political configurations should be facilitated. (Guilherme, 2002: 123)

This is a demanding list, but one approach is through the notion that teachers should be developing in learners a 'critical cultural awareness' or *'savoir s'engager'* that explicitly enables learners to question, to analyse, to evaluate and, potentially, to take action, to be active citizens.

The significance of this view of foreign language teaching is not lost on teachers outside Portugal either, even if the dominant methodology makes it difficult for them to realise their aims in the classroom – as illustrated by these comments from a teacher of German:

I often say to my classes, you know, 'Were you watching the news last night?' At the beginning or at the end of a lesson maybe when we're rounding off. 'Did you think of me last night, when you were watching the news?' Because it was something that happened, you know, the problems they're having in Germany at the moment, or whatever. Because I want them to think that it's not just something they do in my classroom two or three times a week and that's it. There are people who speak that language and there are problems that those people have and they should be aware of that. (Byram & Risager, 1999: 103)

In a globalised and internationalised world where young people and future citizens will have a quite different experience of belonging, a different sense of national and international identities, language teaching will be 'useful' not only for the economic development of a country but, as this teacher implies, for a better understanding of other people. 'Usefulness' in this new situation will not be the preparation for the study of high culture that justified language teaching in the first part of the 20th century, nor the ability to converse with native speakers, which justified it in the second half. Though neither of these should be abandoned, in the new situation the usefulness of learning a particular language will be in the opportunities it offers for political education. Furthermore, political education will be infused with moral education, bringing new demands of 'language' teachers in their responsibilities as educators.

Teachers like Mrs H, the German teacher quoted above, are already engaged in this. Mrs H works in a small school in a remote part of England and thinks her teaching all the more important because of the remoteness. Such teachers introduce young people to other ways of living, other assumptions about what is 'normal', and thereby challenge and criticise learners' own sense of what is 'normal'. This ranges from the organisation of the school day – quite different in Germany and England – to beliefs, values and behaviours of a fundamental kind, such as family relationships, political institutions, perceptions of social problems. For if 'the other' way of living and being is compared with 'ours', then we as learners, whatever our age, begin to question what we have hitherto taken for granted. This means that our teacher, who has placed us in this questioning position by careful planning of her lessons, is pushing us into new stages of moral judgement, and thereby takes upon herself an ethical responsibility to ensure that whatever conclusions we draw are not biased by her way of presenting alternatives.

For, if Mrs H were to say that everything in German schools is better than in England, that there are no problems for young people, that the education system is obviously more successful, then she would begin to indoctrinate rather than educate. I am sure that she does not; her purpose is not to say one is better than the other, but rather to encourage her learners to see their own education from a different perspective. Furthermore Mrs H does not make this the central part of her teaching and probably does not plan her lessons on the basis of political and moral educational objectives.

Other teachers are, however, beginning to do this, even if they would not use the same terminology, and we have collected their accounts of their work (Byram *et al.*, 2001). With relatively young learners at an early stage in language acquisition, Carol Morgan, teaching French in England and English in France, experiments with ideas of 'law and order' and finds her pupils beginning to question institutions in their own country as a consequence of having to describe them to pupils in another country. With older learners, Krassimira Tupozova, teaching English in Bulgaria, takes the simple idea of an investigation of the function and types of Christmas cards in Bulgaria and England, and ends in a discussion with her learners about concepts of charity, poverty and state responsibilities in pre- and post-communist Bulgaria. In the course of this she draws upon everyday artefacts (old Christmas cards from Britain) and high culture (Dickens' *Christmas Carol*). In her lessons the political and moral issues are very clear, and made all the more evident in the bilateral comparison of Britain and Bulgaria. Yet this is more than a comparison of two countries; it ends as a discussion of morality in capitalism and communism, and as a preparation for the new European macro-situation in which these young people are living.[46]

Like Mrs H, both Carol Morgan and Krassimira Tupozova have to be aware of their responsibilities, of the risk of education becoming indoctrination. Although this is a new consideration for language teachers, it is familiar ground for teachers of other subjects, particularly citizenship education in its various forms, and if we compare with other education systems – practising an intercultural approach for ourselves – the potential relationship of political education to foreign language education becomes clearer (Alred *et al.*, 2006).

The potential of political action can be illustrated from the teaching of English in Latvia (Kalbernzina, 2000). In this case, students from all the different ethnic and language groups in Latvia found themselves in an English class where the teacher had decided to make them think about their own identities, their perceptions of others' identities, and the concept of stereotype. She did so in part by exercises that encouraged self-discovery, in part by a comparative study of the cultures and identities of young people in Ireland, where there are tensions about identity just as there are in Latvia. The use of English as the only language they all shared and the 'neutrality' of the language classroom allowed them to handle issues that were highly sensitive in Latvia at the time:

NB! In a situation where the national identity question has been a taboo for many years this lesson has to be conducted very carefully [...] and their reactions can sometimes get quite aggressive [...]. However, in my opinion, it is better that they discuss these issues openly with the teacher's participation than leave them to their own resources, leaving the issues to smoulder.

On the other hand this class was very positively charged. I had a feeling that the students really enjoyed sharing their traditions and customs on neutral ground. Since they were speaking English, it was as if they lost their partiality and became genuinely interested in each other and at the same time more confident of themselves. It also influenced my relationship with the group, as I saw later. (Kalbernzina, 2000: 115)

One year later, in October 1998, the teacher had a slightly different perspective on the risks:

Re-reading the paper a year later, I cannot help noticing that so many changes have taken place in our society during this time and the issues that seemed so painful and new have become everyday topics in the newspapers. Nevertheless I am grateful to this project that I and my students had the chance to address these topics when they seemed so painful, but in fact were actually most necessary to us all. I hope our experience would encourage teachers in other countries not to avoid topics that might seem dangerous at the time but use them as a possibility to be made use of. (Kalbernzina, 2000: 125)

Of course, not all foreign language education has a political dimension as explicitly as this. Nor should every lesson be of this kind. Yet, whether it is an explicit theme, as here, or an implicit challenge to the taken-for-granted activities of everyday life as in the work of Morgan, language teaching as foreign language education cannot and should not avoid educational and political duties and responsibilities. Yet, in her analysis of Portuguese teachers' views and their account of their practice, Guilherme points out that:

Most participants do not include critical agency in their understanding of a critical pedagogy. In other words, they do not engage into a committed transformation of their social realities, nor do they expect their students to do so in the present. (Guilherme, 2002: 204)

This is a step further than is represented in the work described above, and a step to which we shall return in later chapters.

Education for Teachers of Languages

What would be an appropriate education for teachers who would follow in the footsteps of the ones described here? It would include preparation for educating learners about values in societies – those familiar to them and those that are quite different. In the European context, this is closely related to education for democratic citizenship, and this is the most innovatory and radical element of what is needed in teacher education. For language teachers, especially in recent decades, have become focused on skills that seem to be 'value-free'. This is particularly the case where language learning has become separated from the teaching of literature, because the teaching of literature has the potential to challenge learners not only aesthetically but also morally.

The notion of 'criticality' characteristic of university education in the European tradition (Barnett, 1997) is a crucial feature of language teacher education. The inclusion of values education and education for democratic citizenship as part of the responsibility of language teachers in addition to the development of language skills in their learners requires teachers to think critically. Teachers need to question and problematise their own and others' assumptions and pre-suppositions about 'proper' values, beliefs and behaviours, as all 'intercultural speakers' should do. 'Critical cultural awareness'/*savoir s'engager* is part of intercultural competence and is defined as 'an ability to evaluate, critically and on the basis of explicit criteria, perspectives, practices and products in one's own and other cultures and countries' (Byram, 1997: 53).

Criticality in university education is defined by Brumfit *et al.* (2004: 17) as:

- the motivation to persuade, engage and act on the world ...
- through the operation of critical understanding of a body of relevant knowledge ...
- mediated by assimilated experience of how the social and physical environment is structured ...
- combined with a willingness to question and problematise our shared perceptions of relevance and experience.

What is particularly important here is that the critical person will 'engage and act on the world'. This statement is neutral about the direction such action might take but, for some writers, such as Guilherme (2002), the teacher should act for change and reform in society, the teacher should be a transformative intellectual. As Williams (1961) puts it, there is a 'long revolution' in which schools and other educational institutions have a significant role to play. This would then be the basis for the extra step that the teachers described earlier had not yet taken, a step of 'critical agency'. What should this mean in language teacher education? On the basis of their empirical research, Brumfit *et al.* produce a descriptive model of what underpins criticality in two university courses they observed, a course in modern languages and a course in social work studies. They identify two dimensions:

- work with an explicit focus on criticality, 'an attempt to shift students from being holders of opinions to users of appropriate, theoretically interpreted and structured data to inform considered views of cultural, social and linguistic phenomena';
- skill-oriented work, in which students 'were guided towards increasingly sophisticated autonomy and independence, while being provided with the information and activities necessary for the development of transferable skills (such as communicative competence in target languages or the core competences for social work), or of skills specific to the discipline, such as those of descriptive linguistics or use of social work theory'. (Brumfit *et al.*, 2004: 11–12)

Brumfit *et al.* go on to observe that there is an expectation that students will engage with the world after completion of their studies, after graduation, that they will gain 'the motivation or desire to be merged with processes of grounded interpretation and commitment to contributing to a critique and sometimes (particularly for social work students) to partial solutions to outside-world problems'.

The choice of the two courses under investigation is particularly felicitous in a discussion of education for language teachers because the researchers are interested in the disciplines of modern languages and social work, and secondly the potential commitment of the disciplines to outside-world problems. Brumfit *et al.* also point out that in the two courses in question, through one-year placement for social workers or a one year period abroad for language students, the courses in fact already bring in experience of and opportunity to critique and contribute to the solution of outside-world issues. Students do not have to await graduation to become engaged. This applies too to student teachers in most education systems who through the practice of placement in schools have a similar opportunity.

It would take us too far to produce a full specification for a course for language teachers that includes the necessary criticality, skills and outside-world engagement.[47] It is in any case likely that many courses include these to some extent, and what would be most useful in practice would be an analysis of what exists and a development of it. In other cases, such as teacher training in England, an analysis would probably show little criticality, much emphasis on skill-oriented work and no engagement with outside-world issues. It is crucial that teacher education involves all three elements, but also that it should include reflection on the ethical questions that arise when 'engagement' with the outside world involves responsibility for children and young people rather than adults.

Education for Teacher Educators?

The demands on teacher educators that are implied in these suggestions and priorities are clearly very high. We should not underestimate the needs of teacher educators themselves.

University education emphasises intellectual, affective and behavioural demands and the commitment and engagement of all teaching, including language teaching. Educating language teachers is equally demanding for those who teach them at university. Gradually an expectation is developing that university teachers should also be properly prepared for teaching, whatever their discipline. In the discipline of education, as in others, it is assumed that they should be good researchers who investigate and improve the processes of teaching and learning and the social structures and institutions within which this usually takes place. They should also be as committed and engaged as they hope their students will be. They should be advocates as well as researchers. This means teacher educators themselves need to consider and experience that same education in values and democratic citizenship that they want their student teachers to pursue. They need to be able to deal with the many dilemmas that education in values and democratic citizenship raises for all teachers.

Teacher educators and teachers need to consider, for example:

- when there are discussions of moral and political issues, what role does the teacher take – neutral chair or involved individual?
- how do teachers cope with the affective demands of mediating between conflicting views, and not just transmitting and training language skills?
- what criteria does the teacher use for deciding on topics, as some may be too sensitive or even taboo in some circumstances and societies?
- if and how should teachers encourage their own pupils to be committed and engaged in the way they are themselves?
- how do teacher educators prepare teachers for this kind of teaching?
- should we try to assess this aspect of learners' intercultural competence?

and so on.

The disciplines that can underpin an education in such matters are not only those usually associated with language teaching: linguistics and applied linguistics, second language acquisition, psychology of motivation. There is a need to draw upon social psychology to consider social identity theory because of the implications for intercultural competence, anthropology to develop an understanding of cultural values, beliefs and behaviours, and philosophy to help teachers consider matters of values, relativism and morality. No single teacher educator can specialise in all of these, and no teacher can become an anthropologist, social psychologist and applied linguist etc. It is not possible or desirable to have teachers – especially those in pre-service training – studying a range of disciplines (Byram, 1999) unless they are working at Master's level.

An alternative is to design courses which present problems or which require teachers to bring problems from their classroom experience. These problems can then be addressed from disciplinary perspectives, and teachers can pursue their study of the disciplines from their own position and identity as a language people.[48] Approaches and lessons can be drawn from medical education in this respect (Spencer & Jordan, 1999) and from a tradition of problem-based learning at Roskilde University in Denmark (Risager, 1994), but again it is beyond the scope of this chapter to pursue this in detail.

Whatever the details – and much debate on details still remains – it is clear that we need new approaches to language teacher education. Above all we need to conceptualise language learning as a significant educational experience, whenever and wherever it takes place. It implies a major educational role for teachers, who should ensure that language learning is not reduced to investing in language skills, but is a rich and deep process taking learners into new experiences and critical reflection on them.

Chapter 9

Chapter 9 makes the argument that language teachers can become involved in political education and shows that some teachers already do so, although perhaps not in a systematic way. It is therefore necessary to consider how teachers should be trained so that they can include political education in their teaching. This includes consideration of the source disciplines and to what extent teachers can access these disciplines as well as the traditional recourse to applied linguistics. The chapter concludes with some suggestions as to how this might be done and which source disciplines are important.

Chapters 10 to 14

Chapters 10–14, unlike earlier chapters, which can be read in any order, are intended to be read together and in order. They present an argument for Intercultural Citizenship Education and suggest ways in which this might be planned, taught and assessed. These chapters are theoretical, with a few illustrative descriptions of practice. They are prospective and prescriptive, a suggestion about how foreign language education should develop into the future. They are, as quoted from Hobsbawm at the beginning of this book, 'partisan' and I hope they live up to his requirement that partisanship advances science.

Chapter 10

Language Education, Political Education and Intercultural Citizenship

Although there is an attractive symmetry in the argument that the educational response to globalisation/internationalisation is to educate and socialise people into an international identity, this can be misleading because it might imply an alternative to national identity. A similar argument might be made about another frequently-used phrase, 'international/world citizenship', because it too might be seen as in competition with being a citizen of a nation state. A more nuanced view is presented in the concept of 'cosmopolitan citizenship'. Osler and Starkey (2005a) argue that, in the contemporary world, the singularity of identity is or should be no longer the norm, that people have multiple identities related to different layers of political entities. People may have more than one citizenship in the sense of holding more than one passport, and more importantly may feel allegiance to more than one political entity, whether at national, subnational or supranational level. In the view of Osler and Starkey, therefore, education should address the question of identity:

> Education for cosmopolitan citizenship must necessarily be about enabling learners to make connections between their immediate contexts and the global context; it encompasses citizenship learning as a whole. It implies a broader understanding of national identity; it requires recognition that British identity, for example, may be experienced differently by different people. (Osler & Starkey, 2005a: 23)

The approach to be taken here is different. Irrespective of identities and the role of education in developing allegiances and identification with various entities, the point to be made here is that people need certain competences in order to be able to act sensibly in and across political entities, at whatever level. I will use the phrase 'intercultural citizenship', but this is not simply a matter of labelling and convenience. It focuses on competences rather than identities (Byram, 2003). It adds a new dimension by combining language education with political education as a response to internationalisation.

Politische Bildung

The phrase 'political education' probably needs 'scare' quotation marks for many readers, anglophone readers in particular. It may have negative connotations of indoctrination, and there has been little or no tradition of political education in the anglophone world. In England 'education for citizenship' is a recent innovation, from September 2003, which has its roots in rather undefined notions of 'personal and social education', and 'civic education', the latter having disappeared from curricula many years ago. In the USA, there has been a focus on developing *National Standards for Civics and Government* in the 1990s, which is again a recent development, with a publication in 2003 of a second edition (Himmelmann, 2006)

On the other hand, attention to political education (*politische Bildung*) has been evident in Germany for several decades, since the end of the Second World War, and I shall draw on two writers from that tradition in particular as a starting point.[49]

Gagel says there are two dimensions to *politischer Unterricht* (political teaching and learning): first, social science education, with the focus on epistemology and a cognitive orientation leading to the acquisition of knowledge which has practical significance for daily life; and second, political education (in a narrower sense) (*politische Bildung*) with the focus on behaviour and an evaluative orientation in which it is intended to raise awareness of, or transmit, the characteristics of 'correct' behaviour in public political life. Gagel identifies three aims for political education in this sense:

- learning to consider personal involvement in political action as desirable;
- learning to recognise democratic forms of action (and only democratic forms) as values; these can be called democratic 'virtues';
- acquiring interest in public affairs, being prepared to be interested in political resolutions of social problems. (Gagel, 2000, 24)

He summarises this by drawing attention to the combined emphasis on cognitive, evaluative and behavioural dimensions: 'political education helps the individual towards an evaluative orientation in their environment and makes them capable of democratic behaviour' (Gagel, 2000: 24; my translation here and throughout).

These three elements of *politische Bildung* are, as Himmelmann says (2003), also to be found in documents written for the Council of Europe as part of the response to the call by all Heads of State and Governments of the member States to prioritise 'education for democratic citizenship'. This call came at the end of a meeting in 1997, another indication that it was in the 1990s that attention to political education became evident. It may be as a consequence of the end of the opposition from communism in Europe (and in the USA) that politicians became concerned to promote interest in democratic purposes and processes for fear of a growing apathy among their electorates. It may be that, in Europe, there appeared to be a need to educate in democracy whole populations that had grown up without access to democratic processes. Whatever the origins, it is evident from German writers such as Gagel, Himmelmann, and writers such as Audigier (1998), Duer *et al.* (2000) and Birzea (2000) at the Council of Europe, that democracy is the unquestioned value. The only questions are how to ensure that people understand and use their opportunities to behave democratically in public life.

This unquestioned assumption may be appropriate for North American and European societies, the societies for which these scholars are writing. American and European politicians also assume that democracy is the only form of politics that is valuable, to the extent that they are prepared to impose it on other countries. One of the issues that will arise from taking an intercultural perspective on citizenship is that even these assumptions should be questioned.

Before considering the intercultural dimension, however, it will be useful to look in more detail at the three elements of *politische Bildung*: cognitive, evaluative and behavioural, which can be also formulated as epistemological, affective/moral and active orientations. Himmelmann (2003), who prefers the term *Demokratie lernen* (learning democracy) rather than *politische Bildung*, places 'affective/moral attitudes' in first position because, without a will or disposition to achieve common purposes, there can be no acquisition of knowledge or active engagement in democratic processes. This is also the case in intercultural competence as I shall show below.

Himmelmann is concerned in his paper to define 'standards' or agreed outcomes for political education, and derives from Audigier's (1998) paper for the Council of Europe the following list of affective/moral attitudes:

- recognition of the principles of universality, interdependence and indivisibility of basic rights and freedoms;
- respect for the value, the dignity and the freedom of every individual person;
- acceptance of the rule of law, search for justice, recognition of equality and equal treatment in a world full of differences;
- recognition of the importance of peace, absence of violence, and the

participatory and constructive resolution of social conflicts and problems;
- trust in democratic principles, institutions and modes of action and
  valorisation of participatory citizenship;
- recognition of pluralism in life and in society, respect for foreign
  cultures and their contribution to human development;
- valorisation of mutuality, co-operation, trust and solidarity and the
  struggle against racism, prejudices and discrimination;
- taking action in favour of the principles of sustainable development
  as a balance between societal and economic growth and the protection of the environment. (Himmelmann, 2003)

It is evident from this list that attitudes or 'commitments', as he also
calls them, have to be directed towards a set of principles and values, which
Himmelmann and others consider to be fundamental. Some of the key
words here are: rights and freedoms, justice and equality, peace and conflict
resolution, democratic principles and participation, pluralism and co-
operation, and sustainable development.

These same principles and values are implicit in Himmelmann's second
list, which defines aspects of general cognitive capacity – the ability to:

- recognise (repeating and describing) facts, a statement, a problem, a
  situation, a conflict;
- differentiate (distinguishing and comparing) statements, assertions,
  or facts according to different interests, needs or perspectives;
- discuss (and explain) different statements in a context, and develop
  further points of view;
- investigate (and explain) origins, background or history;
- critically test (judge and evaluate) a position or perspective with
  respect to its consequences, its significance for the future, and its
  capacity for resolving problems;
- argue (and take a viewpoint) for or against a position; according to
  one's own explicit criteria;
- justify one's own position from a legal and moral perspective and
  evaluate possibilities of action;
- reflect on (and discuss) normative issues according to criteria of
  human rights, democracy, a state ruled by law, or moral beliefs; judge
  conflicts in decisions and values. (Himmelmann, 2003)

In this case Himmelmann derives the list from the *National Standards for
Civics and Government*, published in the USA. He labels this list 'knowledge'
and he also has a second list of the suggested contents of political education

curricula that learners would be expected to kno
contents is of propositional knowledge ('knowing that
will return to this later. The list of eight points presented a
dural knowledge ('knowing how') and describes the intellec
that underpin any decision to take action and to participate in t
life of a society. We shall see later that the 'society' in question n
school community, a local community, a national community or a tra
tional community.

Himmelmann's third element of political education, the behavioural, is
again derived from Council of Europe work. This final list is labelled practical-instrumental capacities or skills and strategies, the capacity to:

- grasp and take seriously the opinions and arguments of others, recognise those who have other opinions as people, be able to put oneself in
  the position of others, accept criticism and listen;
- make one's own opinions (needs, interests, feelings, values) clear,
  speak coherently, explain clearly;
- abandon every kind of violence, humiliation, insult (expressions of
  power), etc;
- take account of those who are weaker, reduce discrimination, integrate outsiders;
- organise group work, cooperate in the distribution of work, take on
  tasks, trustworthiness, perseverance, care and conscientiousness;
- tolerate plurality, divergences, differences, recognise conflicts, as far
  as possible create balance, and resolve problems in socially acceptable
  ways, accept mistakes and differences;
- find compromises, seek consensus, accept majority decisions, tolerate
  minorities, promote encouragement, balance rights and responsibilities, and show trust and courage;
- emphasise group responsibility, develop fair norms and common
  interests and needs, pursue common approaches to tasks.
  (Himmelmann, 2003)

These are the operational skills of practical activity and a realisation in
practice of the general cognitive capacities of the second list. Put together,
these three lists describe the desirable outcomes from political education in
terms of attitudes and general capacities and operational skills. They
embody what Gagel calls the narrower sense of political education, which
can be complemented by the knowledge content derived from social
sciences. Himmelmann's suggestion for content is under four headings:

- life-world and creation of social relationships (democracy as a form of *ung sozialer Beziehungen (Demokratie als*

emocracy as a form of society); [*Gesell-*
Demokratie als Gesellschaftsform)];
r (democracy as form of governance);
ung (Demokratie als Herrschaftsform)];
elations and organisations (democracy
isierung, internationale Beziehungen und
globales Projekt)]. (Himmelmann, 2003)

natically, he says, from a wide range of
curricula guidelines and textbooks. It
therefore seems to represent a common ground of consensus among those
who focus on democracy, democratic principles and institutions. Another
emphasis and a different list would be proposed by those who stress the
importance of Peace Education or World Studies. In this case the content
might be more specific, including particular emblematic events or people,
or specific skills such as conflict resolution. The question of content thus
remains open and will depend on where in the curriculum political education takes place.

In Germany, as Himmelmann points out, *politische Bildung* takes place in
many parts of the curriculum and under many labels and guises. He gives
23 labels, from *politische Bildung* (political education) or *Politikunterricht*
(study of politics) to *Weltkunde* (world studies) and *Gemeinschaftskunde*
(community studies). Not surprisingly, there is no mention of language
education, neither national nor foreign language education, even though
national language education has an implicit political purpose and foreign
language education has a potential for political educational aims. In the
following section I shall therefore explain this potential in more detail
before looking at the possible relationship between political education
and/or education for democratic citizenship and language education.

Critical Cultural Awareness

'Critical cultural awareness'/*savoir s'engager* is the central concept in a
definition of intercultural communicative competence (ICC) I proposed in
1997, when I already suggested that there is a link with political education.
Critical cultural awareness is defined as 'an ability to evaluate, critically
and on the basis of explicit criteria, perspectives, practices and products in
one's own and other cultures and countries' (Byram, 1997: 53).[50] It consists
of the ability to:

(1) identify and interpret explicit or implicit values in documents and events in one's own and other cultures;

(2) make an evaluative analysis of the documents and events which refers to an explicit perspective and criteria;

(3) interact and mediate in intercultural exchanges in accordance with explicit criteria, negotiating where necessary a degree of acceptance of those exchanges by drawing upon one's knowledge, skills and attitudes.

The other elements of intercultural competence are presented in brief here and in full in Appendix 1. Like Himmelmann, I too start with attitudes, then list knowledge objectives and thirdly behavioural objectives, as skills:

- attitudes: curiosity and openness, readiness to suspend disbelief about other cultures and belief about one's own;
- knowledge: of social groups and their products and practices in one's own and in one's interlocutor's country, and of the general processes of societal and individual interaction;
- skills of interpreting and relating: ability to interpret a document or event from another culture, to explain it and relate it to documents or events from one's own;
- skills of discovery and interaction: ability to acquire new knowledge of a culture and cultural practices and the ability to operate knowledge, attitudes and skills under the constraints of real-time communication and interaction.

These elements have also been given labels in French:

- attitudes = *savoir être*;
- knowledge = *savoirs*;
- skills of interpreting and relating = *savoir comprendre*;
- skills of discovery and interaction = *savoir apprendre* and *savoir faire*.

Together with 'critical cultural awareness' (*savoir s'engager*), these are the elements of intercultural competence defined as an aim for foreign language teaching. The purpose is to clarify how learners can acquire the ability to understand and maintain social relationships with people of another country. With some minor changes – in particular, by substituting 'social group' for 'country' – the definition could provide the objectives for an education system that had an explicit purpose of ensuring social cohesion among disparate groups within one nation state, where everyone can communicate through the national language. These could therefore be some of the objectives for national language teachers and/or other teachers in a state/public school, including teachers of political education/*politische Bildung* in any of its guises. It would cloud the issues, however, to pursue all the potential applications simultaneously, and here I will concentrate on the foreign language learning and teaching context.

My emphasis on the centrality of critical cultural awareness in foreign language teaching is similar to Gagel's suggestion that the central, unifying purpose of *politische Bildung* (political education in the narrower sense) and *sozialwissenschaftliche Bildung* (social science education more generally) is the concept of *politisches Bewusstsein* (political awareness) defined as:

> Critical awareness, independent judgement and political *engagement*. The pre-condition for democratic *engagement* is that the citizen becomes aware of the relationship between individual destiny and social processes and structures. Political awareness is formed through the recognition of one's own interests and the experience of social conflicts and relationships of governance. The politically aware and informed person should not be a passive object of politics, but as a subject should participate in politics. (Gagel 2000: 27)

Gagel draws attention to the concept of *engagement* (a loan word in German, from French) and this corresponds to my use of the French phrase '*savoir s'engager*' for the concept of critical cultural awareness.

It would be possible but laborious to make a close comparative analysis of the nature of political education and of education for intercultural competence. There are strong parallels above all in this central idea of an awareness that leads to *engagement*, but there is also the significant difference that the model of intercultural competence becomes a model of intercultural *communicative* competence when it is part of foreign language teaching and learning and when the objectives include the acquisition of linguistic, sociolinguistic and discourse competence. It is through linguistic ability that people can be intercultural speakers mediating between cultures of different countries (nation states) embodied in the (national) languages of those countries.[51] Political/democratic education as presented by Gagel and Himmelmann seems to assume a common language among all those 'learning democracy'. They do not address the practical linguistic skills necessary in international political *engagement*, even though Himmelmann's list of contents for *Demokratie lernen* (learning democracy) refers to globalisation and foreign cultures:

> Globalisation, international relationships and organisations (Democracy as a global project)
>
> • international conflicts and their causes, war and peace, peace-keeping;

- terrorism, new wars, humanitarian interventions;
- European Union, NATO, United Nations;
- variety of globalisation, international law, development politics, North–South conflict;
- global environmental problems;
- foreign cultures, foreign systems;
- system change, system development.

A foreign language education perspective can complement and enrich this element of political education/'democracy learning', not only by providing the linguistic competence necessary to engage with people of other countries and languages in democratic processes but also, in the capacity for critical cultural awareness, by introducing a perspective of mediation and negotiation that does not presuppose democracy as the only source of values and governance.

Even where 'democracy' offers apparent common ground, it is understood differently in different societies. Davies (1999) argues that a comparative analysis of definitions of democracy quickly reveals differing ideologies underlying the concept. She proposes a framework for comparison of democracy within schools that includes 'basic values', 'rights', 'system structures', 'structures within schools', 'learning content', 'balance of constraint and freedom', 'training in democracy (for teachers and pupils)' and 'outcomes', and uses this framework to compare a number of cases in different countries. Such comparisons make us aware of the differences in how democracy is understood and works in practice in different countries and therefore of the taken-for-granted ideology in any one conceptualisation of democracy and democratic action. This awareness is crucial to intercultural communication about democracy, to avoid the assumption that everyone understands democracy in the same way. It enables young people of different school systems who might want to co-operate in a common action to understand each other's assumptions about the elements of school democracy Davies identifies.

In fine, because of the emphasis on engagement with other countries and ideologies, the definition of critical cultural awareness emphasises the importance of individuals being aware of their own ideology – political and/or religious[52] – and the need to be explicit in one's criteria of evaluating other people's actions, or the documents and events of other cultures. It also promotes the engagement of the individual with people of other ideologies, to look for common ground where possible, but also to accept difference. This includes, in principle, the acceptance of other concepts of democracy and other systems of governance than democracy, and this perspective raises inevitable questions and the spectre of ethical relativism to which I shall return later. First, I shall illustrate the significance of paying attention to the demands of communication with people of other cultures and languages.

Conceptual and Linguistic Relativism

It is not difficult to demonstrate that all discourse among people of different languages, including the political, creates linguistic and conceptual complexities that cannot be overlooked. Let me do this by considering the word 'citizen' itself, and focus on European languages.

Using a French/English bilingual dictionary, 'citizen' is easily equated with '*citoyen*'. Nonetheless there are variants:

town: *habitant*; state: *citoyen*; admin.: *ressortissant*; hist.: *bourgeois*; (townsman) *citadin* (Robert Collins, 1987)

If we turn to German, the case appears to be similar:

Bürger; (of a state*) (Staats)bürger* (Collins, 1980)

However, when in 1999, a Council of Europe conference entitled 'Linguistic diversity for democratic citizenship in Europe' and '*La diversité linguistique en faveur de la citoyenneté démocratique en Europe*' took place in Austria, the collocation of '*demokratisch*' and '*Bürger*' in German was not felt to work by Austrian native speakers and the title became '*sprachliche Vielfalt für ein Europa der Bürger*' (Linguistic diversity for a Europe of citizens). Collocations and connotations are indications of semantic representations that are different in German from English or French.

As a further example, take Norwegian:

At the conceptual level, the English words 'citizen' and 'civic' lack good synonyms in the Norwegian language. The most common translation *borger*, denotes meanings like 'city dweller', bourgeois (as opposed to 'peasant' or 'worker') and 'politically conservative'. To overcome these problems the word *medborger* (co-citizen) seems to be gaining ground. To the extent that *medborger* colours the understanding of the concept, it probably gives more attention to the relational or collective elements. (Skeie, 2003: 55)

The author goes on to say that 'to an international readership it may seem somewhat narrow-minded to go into linguistic details', but that it is nonetheless revealing of historical developments and cultural values. On the contrary, I think it is important to look at linguistic details because it is reveals potential problems in public debate. Even if, as seems to be the case here, a speaker of Norwegian does not expect his/her interlocutors to understand the Norwegian connotations and collocations – a position often taken by speakers of less-widely-taught languages – the unspoken assumption that if everyone speaks English as a lingua franca, mutual comprehension will ensue, is extremely unlikely to be true. Scholars such as Skeie, who cites Marshall and knows the anglophone literature, and the British collocations and connotations of 'citizen', are not representative of other Norwegians and other users of English as a lingua franca. Less knowledgeable speakers of lingua franca English will not be able to adopt those connotations and collocations. Moreover, some would not wish to do so because of the hegemonic implications of adopting the language of the powerful, and in fact what seems to happen in lingua franca communication is that interlocutors introduce their own understandings into the language they are using (Meierkord, 2002; Taylor, 2006).

It is at this point that the concept of mediation is important. Given the problems of translation, there is a need for interpretation and mediation that pre-supposes an intercultural communicative competence and a social position for the language learner/mediator that permits them to interact with speakers of other languages on equal terms.[53]

The preliminary conclusion from these examples is that there can be considerable difficulty in understanding the word 'citizen' if one speaks Norwegian, that the concept of 'democratic citizenship' cannot be fully understood by a speaker of German, and that even a speaker of French has a number of options, which present difficulties of translation.[54]

This quickly leads to the position of linguistic relativism, attributed in the German-speaking world to Humboldt and in the anglophone world to Whorf and Sapir. This view, that language determines and limits thought, has been much debated and often ridiculed. There is however empirical work that supports it. Levinson (1997) argues that semantic representations in language are not homomorphic with conceptual representations. They are nonetheless in some proximity to each other and conceptual representations are influenced by semantic representations. If this were not the case 'memories will be unretrievable or uncodable in language, and the speaker will have nothing to talk about' (Levinson, 1997: 39). Levinson draws on empirical work with speakers of a language that does not conceptualise space egocentrically (i.e. in relation to the person, using 'left', 'right', 'in front', 'behind' etc.), but absolutely in relation to the topography of their environment ('north of', 'south of', etc). His argument is that, if people had conceptual representations in terms of absolute positions and a language that used egocentric representations, then there would be no inter-translatability between the conceptual and linguistic systems for the individual, who would then have 'nothing to talk about'.

Levinson does not address the question of inter-translatability between individuals of different languages, i.e. the ability of a 'left/right' language speaker to understand a speaker of a 'north/south' language. His article is, however, comprehensible only for a speaker of English (and other 'left/right' languages) for whom inter-translatability is possible. The translation is not at word level but at the level of explanation or mediation. Levinson explains how 'north/south' language speakers visualise and conceptualise spatial relationships, and gives examples to aid comprehension. By doing so he implicitly refutes the strong relativist view, which argues that comprehension of another language and thought is impossible because we cannot escape our own language and thought, but supports the weaker version which argues that language and thought are mutually influential. It is evident from the way in which the account is written that it is not easy to explain and understand the other system of spatial description, but that it is nonetheless possible.

It is remarkable that Levinson does not give the actual words of the language he describes, which is a dialect of Tzeltal spoken in Chiapas, Mexico. Learners of the language would, however, have to deal with the words themselves and use them to represent their own experience. They would have to acquire new conceptual representations with the new semantic representations.[55]

The implications of this version of the Whorfian/Humboldtian hypothesis for language learners have been discussed by Bredella (2001: 80–124) who argues that, with sufficient explanation and effort, learners can indeed acquire an understanding of the language and representations of other people, and he illustrates this from his classes on the American Civil Rights Movement. He shows that his university students, despite their own scepticism, could to some extent 'get inside' the concepts and beliefs of Civil Rights activists. A similar position is taken by Winch in his discussion of the ability of someone from a European–North American society, with a conceptual world based on the rationality of the natural sciences, to understand the rationality of witchcraft among the Azande in Africa.[56] He argues that in order to understand that rationality and its intelligibility 'we have to create a new unity for the concept of intelligibility, having a certain relation to our old one and perhaps requiring a considerable realignment of our categories' (Winch, 1964: 317). This requires great effort, says Berlin, citing Vico; it requires the faculty of imagination – *fantasia* – 'with which it is possible to 'enter' other minds than our own' (Berlin, 1998: 346).

What is required then is the imaginative effort to engage with, to 'enter', another conceptualisation than our own, but also to transcend both and, ultimately, establish a mode of speaking that is not weighed down by either. As Gellner (1983: 187) says, 'The possibility of transcendence of cultural limits is a fact; it is the single most important fact about human life'.

In fine, linguistic and conceptual relativism does not prevent communication, or political action, among people of different languages and cultures, as van Gunsteren 1996) also argues, but it does require the ability to decentre, to realign, to empathise, to transcend, which are some of the aims of language education and political education. In order to contextualise this further, I turn now to the question of what kinds of discourse communities intercultural speakers might participate in.

Communication in Transnational Communities

Anderson (1991) in his well-known discussion of the nation as an imagined community, points to the significance of language and argues that the close relationship between language and nation was promoted from a European, Herderian and Humboldtian perspective, and was part of the 'model' of the nation state that was borrowed – or as he says, 'pirated' – in many parts of the world. By referring not simply to language but to 'print-language' and the power of newspapers and books to create a sense of community, Anderson also emphasises the significance of literacy. A nation state is thus _inter alia_ a community of communication that needs a shared language, and usually this shared language is designated the national or sometimes the official language. Thus, linguistic identity and national identity are closely connected, at least where there is a formal, institutionalised community of communication, reinforced by schools as national institutions.

There are, however, other levels of community within a nation state that are not necessarily formalised. The organisations and institutions of civil society have differing degrees of formality and, where there is freedom of speech, these communities of communication can challenge the official discourses of the state (Kennedy & Fairbrother, 2004: 296). It is these challenges that ensure that a nation state does not become a homogeneous and static community with one set of values, beliefs and behaviours embraced by all. They are constantly if imperceptibly changing and the changes become apparent over time as what were 'extreme' values and beliefs become 'mainstream', as for example views on homosexuality have changed in Europe and North America in less than a lifetime. The discourse has changed as has the specific vocabulary. Nonetheless, discourses of challenge are likely to be conducted through the same national, officially recognised language, and again we see the significance of the national language and the reinforcement of the relationship between the national language and national identity.[57]

The significance of communication and interaction becomes all the more evident as the nature of polities changes. For Habermas, the model that should replace outdated concepts of 'the classic republican idea of the self-conscious political integration of a community of free and equal persons', is a model dependent on communication flows:

> a model of deliberative democracy, that no longer hinges on the assumption of macro-subjects like the 'people' or 'the' community but on anonymously interlinked discourses or flows of information. (Habermas, 1994: 32)

This applies to the evolution of the nation state, but all the more to the evolution of democratic processes in transnational contexts. Communication flows and the 'informal networks of public communication' at a transnational level presuppose favourable conditions for mutual understanding, and Risager has demonstrated how such communication flows need to be taken into consideration in foreign language pedagogy (Risager, 2006).

The importance of this issue is evident from the evolution of transnational civil society in response to the trend towards global governance through such organisations as the World Trade Organisation and the International Monetary Fund. Some people hope that transnational civil society will be a force for democracy limiting the power of organisations such as the WTO and the IMF. The exact nature of transnational civil society and of a democratisation of global governance is not yet clear, but it can be argued that the present legitimisation of global institutions based on the notion that experts can deliberate and come to a representative consensus is inadequate. It should be replaced by debate in a public sphere, where a public is understood as 'a collectivity of persons connected by processes of communication over particular aspects of social and political life' (Nanz & Steffek, 2004: 8). Nanz and Steffek argue that 'organised civil society has a high potential to act as a 'transmission belt' between deliberative processes within international organisations and emerging transnational public spheres' (Nanz & Steffek, 2004: 10).

Perhaps the most likely place for this to happen first is in the political space created by the European Union. Only in the case of the European Union can we see nation states gradually giving up some of their power and adopting a more international, or at least European, perspective. In such circumstances, there is encouragement for other languages to be given a status as part of the creation of identification with a community.

What makes the European example different is that it is not expected that people should be native speakers of all the languages they might acquire as part of becoming European citizens, even though there are powerful forces encouraging people to acquire as high a level of competence as possible.[58] The success of a European imagined community of communication pre-supposes plurilingual competence so that discourses at formal level and in civil society can take place, can be extended beyond the national frontiers, to European level. Thus, association of native speaker competence with identification with a polity is challenged, and replaced by plurilingual competence.

At the same time, the tensions between nations and a supra-national polity such as the European Union are strong, and it is unclear if people will feel the same loyalty to Europe as they have done to their countries. As Schnapper puts it:

> If they want to build a political Europe, European citizens have to share a minimum of common awareness, and a common desire and ability to resolve their rivalries and conflicts according to the rule of law. (Schnapper, 2002: 10)

Schnapper emphasises the process of the creation of a new public sphere, perhaps of a federal nature, which would be able to take into account the historic existence of nation states that still command a certain loyalty and sense of belonging.

A public sphere means public discourse, and communication is a fundamental factor in theories and predictions about transnational civil society, which often draw on Habermas as a philosophical basis. This is recognised by those who see the day-to-day effects of globalisation and the emergence of 'transterritorial networks' (Koehn & Rosenau, 2002: 106), and Koehn and Rosenau propose a model of 'transnational competence' as it seems to be emerging from theoretical and empirical analyses of the capacities of people engaged in international NGOs, international business and transnational civil society:

Analytic competence:
- understanding of the central beliefs, values, practices, and paradoxes of counterpart culture(s) and society(ies) – including political and ethnic awareness;
- ability to link counterpart-country conditions to one's own circumstances and vice versa;

- number and complexity of alternative cultural paths assessed;
- ability to discern effective transnational transaction strategies and to learn from past successes and failures.

Emotional competence:

- motivation and ability to open oneself up continuously to divergent cultural influences and experiences;
- ability to assume genuine interest in, and to maintain respect for different (especially counterpart) values, traditions, experiences, and challenges (i.e. intercultural/transnational empathy);
- ability to manage multiple identities;
- sense of transnational efficacy.

Creative/imaginative competence:

- ability to foresee the synergistic potential of diverse perspectives in problem-solving;
- collaborative ability to articulate novel and shared transnational synthesis;
- ability to envision viable mutually acceptable alternatives;
- ability to tap into diverse cultural sources for inspiration.

Behavioural competence – Communicative fluency:

- proficiency in and use of counterpart's spoken/written language;
- skill in interpretation and in using an interpreter;
- proficiency in and relaxed use of interculturally appropriate non-verbal cues and codes;
- ability to listen to and discern different cultural messages;
- ability to engage in meaningful dialogue; to facilitate mutual self-disclosure;
- ability to avoid and resolve communication misunderstandings across diverse communication styles.

Behavioural competence – Functional (project/task) adroitness:

- ability to relate to counterpart(s) and to develop and maintain positive interpersonal relationships;
- ability to apply /adapt understanding, sensitivity and imagination in transnational interactions;
- flexible ability to employ extensive and nuanced range of trans-nationally accommodative organisational strategies and interaction paths;
- ability to overcome problems/conflicts and accomplish goals when

dealing with transnational challenges and globalisation/localisation, pressures. (Koehn & Rosenau, 2002: 106)

It is important to note that a model with origins in empirical studies of transnational communication resembles the models presented earlier, but there are also important differences. This model includes specific skills, such as the use of an interpreter, and an attention to non-verbal communication, which are not included in educational models. On the other hand there are many rather generalised terms which would be very difficult to operationalise for teaching purposes. There is also a certain naivety that, for example, 'ability to listen to and discern different cultural messages' is just one of a whole range of matters, whereas in fact it presupposes many others and is itself extremely complex.

Furthermore, educational models are produced with pedagogical operationalisation in mind and with educational aims, not least criticality or critical cultural awareness, and these are not included in this kind of communications model. Secondly, models such as this one from Koehn and Rosenau do not problematise communication as I have done through my discussion of conceptual and linguistic relativism. It is precisely in the experience of transnational civil society that the difficulties of mutual understanding of concepts such as 'citizen' and 'citizenship' are likely to arise, and need to be overcome with imaginative effort and the specific intercultural skills of mediation.

Ethical Dimensions of Education for Intercultural Citizenship

If, despite the problems of conceptual and linguistic relativism, mutual understanding can be achieved in principle, it is possible to have a community of communication that is international. A community of practice in a transnational civil society could evolve: a community of citizenship and political practice. The question then arises as to whether a common set of values can be established as the basis for political practice. The most striking and demanding test of this possibility is currently found in the contrast between Western (i.e. European and American) and Asian (especially East Asian) philosophers of education for citizenship with their respective concepts of democracy and of the relationship of the individual to the groups to which they belong, in particular the national group (Leung & Lee, 2006). As transnational civil society emerges, these questions will no doubt be the subject of debate and pragmatic resolution; but in an education system there is a responsibility to consider what shall be done in the classroom. We have seen, for example, that Himmelmann and Gagel argue that democratic values are axiomatic, and do not recognise the complexity of the concept of democracy from a worldwide perspective.

One approach is to attempt to establish a common core of citizenship education as Kennedy proposes (2004). In this argument, citizenship education is still modelled on that of the nation state and the purpose of a common basis is to ensure that different nation states can support each other in maintaining their position in the world. The problem here is that Kennedy does not think beyond the nation state and assumes that international co-operation and comity in civil society has to be based on common values – and a common core for citizenship education. This is not the only possible conclusion. Indeed if it were, then the possibility of an international civil society would be in doubt since in practice a common core is unlikely to emerge. This is what might be called a content-orientated concept of citizenship education, a search for consensus.

In contrast, van Gunsteren (1996: 83) argues that in the contemporary world of blurred contours, where people can be citizens of different communities, the primary concern for a notion of citizenship is 'no longer to make people more equal, but to organise plurality, that is bothersome or surprising differences between people, who cannot avoid having to deal with each other'. Van Gunsteren emphasises in his conception of 'neo-republican citizenship' that education should focus on the organisation of difference, on learning how to interact with people who are different.

From this alternative perspective, the emphasis changes from content and propositional knowledge to procedural knowledge and facilitating co-operation at the level of civil society through intercultural political competence. Successful communication and co-operation need not be based on the shared meanings of a shared language as is the assumption about discourse in the nation state. Rather than seeking for common meanings, a common core in civil society communication (for example, through a uniform concept of the citizen or of democracy) we should be looking for a means of making communication across national linguistic and cultural boundaries possible whilst acknowledging linguistic and conceptual relativism. This is, however, only the first step. Communication and 'organising plurality' are not enough. The question of values has to be faced and this is where the question of ethical relativism is important.

The history of debates on relativism is a long one, as Berlin (1990) has shown, but Berlin makes an important distinction between relativism and pluralism and between judgement about facts and judgement about values, which is useful for the issues raised here.

Winch (1964) in his discussion of Evans-Pritchard's analysis of the rationality of the Azande referred to earlier points out that Evans-Pritchard appears to present witchcraft rationality and scientific rationality as of equal, relative value, and yet in the final analysis suggests that the rationality of witchcraft is mistaken, and makes errors in its analysis of the world that can be detected with the aid of the superior rationality of science. This is Berlin's 'judgement of facts'. Putting aside the question of whether Evans Pritchard is right – Winch says he is not – we can now turn to Berlin to distinguish this kind of judgement from judgement about values.

Berlin's emphasis on imaginative insight (*fantasia*) and the ability to enter (*entrare*) is the foundation for understanding, and this is what language teachers try to facilitate for their learners. But then the individual must make a judgement, which is also the aim of pedagogy as suggested here, the development of 'critical cultural awareness/*savoir s'engager*. Berlin's point is that one can enter into the other's judgement about facts – and accept the judgement to be correct – without accepting the other's judgement about values:

> Members of one culture can, by the force of imaginative insight, understand (what Vico called *entrare*) the values, the ideals, the form of life of another culture or society, even those remote in time or space. They may find these values unacceptable, but if they open their minds sufficiently they can grasp how one might be a full human being, with whom one could communicate, and at the same time live in the light of values widely different from one's own, but which nevertheless one can see to be values, ends of life, by the realisation of which men could be fulfilled. (Berlin, 1990: 10)

Berlin thus makes a distinction between understanding and accepting. This, he says, is pluralism not relativism, for relativism is trivial:

> 'I prefer coffee, you prefer champagne. We have different tastes. There is no more to be said'. That's relativism. (Berlin, 1990: 11)

A relativist view of values would preclude any further discussion and any further communication, but Berlin's description of pluralism keeps the possibility of communication open. He then makes a further distinction between those values where one can see and accept that other people might live by them, and those that are beyond the pale of human reason and value, beyond what it is to be human. In such a case, one does not accept but condemns. Of course, the definition of what is beyond the pale is a difficult one, but an important starting point for a discussion would be the Universal Declaration of Human Rights which, as Midgley points out, may have its origins in one of the central concepts of the European Enlightenment, but is now widely recognised as fundamental:

This kind of belief is not, I think, confined to the West. Oppressed people in all kinds of countries now appeal to it. And in general they don't seem to be using it merely as a foreign language, but as a kind of intercultural dialect that everybody understands. It helps us to pick out the distant matters that really do call for our intervention, despite the gulfs between our societies. (Midgley, 2003: 8–9)

Though Midgley's intention is metaphorical, her use of 'foreign language' and 'intercultural dialect' show that what she is saying is related to our concern with intercultural communication, language and citizenship.

In the next chapter I shall examine in more detail what the developments sketched here imply for language and citizenship educators, by considering the purposes and objectives they have in their own fields and the ways in which these might be combined to better face the emerging transnational communities and networks, and the possibility of a transnational civil society.

Chapter 11
Education for Intercultural Citizenship

This chapter will present an integrated Framework of Education for Intercultural Citizenship that combines appropriate parts of Himmelmann's approach to setting objectives for citizenship education/democracy learning with my approach to setting objectives for language teaching for intercultural communicative competence. It will then also discuss the principles and characteristics of the process of Education for Intercultural Citizenship through which the objectives might be attained.

The purpose of the framework developed from language and political education is not to present a comprehensive design for either, but to show the conceptual relationships between them and provide a basis for curriculum planning. There are also relationships among the different kinds of language teaching, and intercultural competence can be taught in and through the national language curriculum but this does not exhaust the aims of that curriculum. It simply shows how one of the functions of national language[59] teaching is to contribute to the creation of social cohesion through mutual understanding of different social groups – ethnic, social class, religious, gender, age – in a society. On the other hand, the pursuit of intercultural competence in foreign language education involves engagement with other languages and cultures and the search for cohesion of a different sort, and here the use of the phrase intercultural *communicative* competence (ICC) reflects the emphasis on language as well as culture learning. However just as with national language teaching, there are other dimensions to the foreign language curriculum too, and its purposes are not exhausted by the pursuit of international cohesion. Furthermore, if there were co-ordination of both national and foreign language education, the different emphases within the aims of each could require compromise and consensus from each in the practicalities of creating an interdisciplinary approach to intercultural competence.

A Framework for Political and Language Education

With respect to relationships between national and foreign language education on the one hand and political education on the other, there is a potential for enrichment of the international dimension of political education and the political dimension of language education, resulting in intercultural political competence.[60] This coherence does not exhaust the content and purposes of either, nor does it imply that all the competences of political/citizenship education are promoted only through the language education curriculum. On the other hand, as we shall see below, the general dimensions of attitudes, knowledge and behaviour common to political and language education provide a framework that makes the relationship between intercultural (communicative) competence and political competence visible, and is a tool for curriculum design and the planning of teaching and assessment.

The framework I propose has three levels:

- At the highest level, there are 'orientations' which reflect the notion of *Orientierung* in *politische Bildung* – cognitive, evaluative and action – and the comparative and linguistic orientation in language education.
- At the second level, the specific competences in each type of education – political, foreign and national language – are presented in relation to the over-arching orientations.
- At the third level, the specific objectives for each type of education are formulated; it is at this level that the interaction and mutual influence of the types of education is realisable in curriculum design.

In order to deal with the potential complexity in an accessible form, I propose to place the elements of language education within the framework and then those of political education. I will also assume that the arguments that political education should be oriented to education for democratic citizenship and 'learning democracy' are accepted, although influenced as we shall see by a comparative orientation.

Since appropriate dispositions are a necessary condition for cognitive development and taking action, I will begin with the evaluative orientation and the definition of objectives in terms of attitudes and values. If we consider the definition of attitudes/*savoir être* for Intercultural Communicative Competence (see Appendix 1), there is an emphasis on willingness/readiness to suspend belief about one's own culture and disbelief about others, i.e. a willingness to question what one usually takes for granted and to accept that others have their own taken-for-granted world that one needs to engage with. In comparison, Himmelmann's eight elements of affective/moral attitudes also refer to the need to respect pluralism, co-operation, equality, the contribution of other cultures to human development and the valuing of the fight against racism, prejudice and discrimination. The language education objectives place more emphasis on willingness to take up opportunities of living with people of other cultures, whereas political/

democratic education emphasises recognition of universal rights, trust in democratic principles and peaceful resolution of conflict. These different but complementary elements are the pre-conditions for interaction with others, whether they are from the same nation state and society or a foreign one.

From an intercultural competence perspective, there is an additional element to the evaluative orientation, the concept of critical cultural awareness/*savoir s'engager*. The emphasis here is on awareness that one's own values and ideological perspectives are culturally determined and that they may not be compatible with those of other people. This also applies to democracy, which is largely taken for granted in *politische Bildung*, or at least assumed to be the appropriate ideology for Europe and the West. In acquiring critical cultural awareness, learners become aware of the culturally-determined origins and nature of democracy and the way it can unconsciously shape their evaluative response to other ideologies and forms of government or other kinds of democracy. Secondly, they become aware that agreement is not always possible, or perhaps only partial agreement is possible, among disparate ideologies. It is therefore wrong for one group to impose its ideology on another – by any means, whether violent or not – and the learner who has critical cultural awareness can reflect critically on their own ideology as seen from the perspective of others. It is right to be pluralistic in approach whilst setting limits to that pluralism as I argued from Berlin's writings in the previous chapter.

The combination of objectives for the evaluative orientation is shown in Table 11.1 – see Appendix 1 for details of language education objectives (Byram) and the previous chapter for political education objectives (Himmelmann). It can be seen from the table that only those objectives (or 'standards', as Himmelmann calls them) that are in a more or less direct relationship are included in the model. Some are excluded because they are specific to the type of education (such as those focused on communication in language education), and some are excluded because they diverge from the common ground (such as the emphasis on 'trust in democratic principles ...' in political education).

The second orientation is the cognitive. Here, in language education there are two types of objective: those focused on propositional knowledge about one's own and one's interlocutor's culture and social identities, and those focused on procedural knowledge of the processes of intercultural interaction. The former may include knowledge of the political processes, ideologies and institutions of the culture and country of one's interlocutor, but these are not specified in the definition of intercultural competence. Where language educators wish to develop links with the cognitive orien-

Table 11.1 Intercultural citizenship: Evaluative orientation

Language education: Attitudes	Political education: Affective/moral attitude
(a) willingness to seek out or take up opportunities to engage with otherness in a relation of equality ... (b) interest in discovering other perspectives on interpretation of familiar and unfamiliar phenomena both in one's own and in other cultures and cultural practices; (c) willingness to question the values and presuppositions in cultural practices and products in one's own environment.	2. respect for the value, the dignity and the freedom of every individual person; 3. acceptance of the rule of law, search for justice, recognition of equality and equal treatment in a world full of differences; 6. recognition of pluralism in life and in society, respect for foreign cultures and their contribution to human development; 7. valorisation of mutuality, co-operation, trust and solidarity and the struggle against racism, prejudices and discrimination.
Language education: **Critical cultural awareness**	
(b) make an evaluative analysis of the documents and events which refers to an explicit perspective and criteria; (c) interact and mediate in intercultural exchanges in accordance with explicit criteria, negotiating where necessary a degree of acceptance of those exchanges by drawing upon one's knowledge, skills and attitudes.	

tation of political education, specific realisations of these general knowledge objectives will need to be introduced.

In Himmelmann's model, as pointed out in the previous chapter, the Standards listed under general cognitive capacity (*allegemeine kognitive Fähigkeit*) are focused on procedural knowledge, and 'knowledge about' is included in the specification of contents for political education/democracy-learning (Differentiated contents of political education /democracy learning [*Differenzierte Inhalte der politischen Bildung/des Demokratie-Lernens*]). As the title suggests, the propositional knowledge is focused on democratic polities, in particular Germany, in three sections, and a fourth section, listing topics under 'Globalisation, international relations and organisations'. In the Table 11.2 of combined objectives, the references to other countries and cultures imply also other ideologies and systems than democracy.

The list of topics from political education is more detailed, but is also

Table 11.2 Intercultural citizenship: Cognitive orientation

Language education: Knowledge	*Political education: Contents*
(a) historical and contemporary relationships between one's own and one's interlocutor's cultures;[61]	(1) Lifeworld • lifeworld ... • responsibility ... • family; • tasks [...] of schooling; • living in the community; • other cultures.
(d) the national memory of one's own country and how its events are related to and seen from the perspective of other cultures;	
(e) the national memory of one's interlocutor's culture and the perspective on them from one's own culture;	(2) Society • pluralism; • civil society; • public life; • social inequality.
(j) institutions, and perceptions of them, which impinge on daily life within one's own and one's interlocutor's culture and conduct and influence relationships between them;	
For foreign language education, add: other forms of governance corresponding to these in countries of the language being learnt	(3) Democracy • basic values ... • creation of representative political will; • the law in everyday life.
For foreign language education, add: other corresponding organisations and reflection on own culture and system as 'foreign' from the other's perspective	(4) Globalisation • all topics.

only a selection from Himmelmann's 'pragmatic' list. The selection is an attempt to identify those topics which would be particularly relevant to an intercultural analysis under a 'comparative orientation' to be discussed below. In addition to propositional knowledge, Himmelmann's list of knowledge standards/objectives focuses on knowing how to recognise/ summarise material, argue, reflect, critically analyse, and so on, which are competences of reasoning and argument not present in the intercultural competence model. They are, however, an important complement to references in intercultural competence to mediation, a central idea in the concept of the intercultural speaker/mediator. They may be particularly important in the mediation of conflicting ideologies as mentioned under the definition of critical cultural awareness, and are certainly present in the practice of intercultural competence.

The third orientation is developed from foreign language education. Comparison is both a means of understanding and an approach to critical analysis, provided there exists a willingness to engage with otherness in a relation of equality, as defined above under evaluative orientation. Comparison with otherness is fundamental to foreign language education and possible but not inevitable in national language or political education.

Comparison is used to make difference accessible and to identify similarity. Linguistic and cultural phenomena are presented as both similar and different and allow learners to extend their conceptions – their schemata – in ways not available within one culture since difference and contrast also force on learners a re-appraisal of their assumptions.[62] Comparison can also be used by teachers to challenge learners' assumptions. They can present a view of the familiar from the perspective of the other, 'making the familiar strange'. They can also present the unfamiliar from within the perspective of the other, 'making the strange familiar'.

The ability to interpret and see relationships between phenomena from different cultures is thus closely related to critical cultural awareness in language education and affective/moral attitude in political education, but there is no emphasis on a comparative orientation in political education (Table 11.3)

Given the lack of correspondence between language education and political education at this point, it could be argued that there is no logical interaction. One might suggest that a comparative element be introduced into political education without reference to language education. Yet, the complementarity from language education is in the emphasis on taking the other's perspective, and also on the potential to mediate between different concepts of democracy, for example, or between democratic and other systems.

That complementarity can be enhanced by the fourth orientation – the communicative orientation – even though again there is no corresponding element in political education. The focus in foreign language education on communicative competence is not only the necessary means for interacting with people who speak other languages. It also raises learners' awareness of linguistic identity and of the questions of linguistic and cultural relativity discussed in the previous chapter, which can be applied in particular to political concepts and assumptions.

Table 11.3 Intercultural citizenship: Comparative orientation

Language education: Skills of interpreting and relating	*Political education*
(a) identify ethnocentric perspectives in a document or event and explain their origins;	
(b) identify areas of misunderstanding and dysfunction in an interaction and explain them in terms of each of the cultural systems present;	
(c) mediate between conflicting interpretations of phenomena.	

Table 11.4 Intercultural citizenship: Communicative orientation

(Foreign) language education:	*Political education*
(a) linguistic competence;	
(b) sociolinguistic competence;	
(c) discourse competence.	

The communicative orientation is represented without a political education element (Table 11.4). Whereas other elements of intercultural competence can be introduced into the planning of all language education, three elements of Intercultural *Communicative* Competence were defined originally in the context of foreign language learning:[63]

- *linguistic competence*: the ability to apply knowledge of the rules of a standard version of the language to produce and interpret spoken and written language;
- *sociolinguistic competence*: the ability to give to the language produced by an interlocutor – whether native speaker or not – meanings that are taken for granted by the interlocutor or which are negotiated and made explicit with the interlocutor;
- *discourse competence*: the ability to use, discover and negotiate strategies for the production and interpretation of monologue or dialogue texts that follow the conventions of an interlocutor or are negotiated as intercultural texts for particular purposes.

The importance placed here on negotiation, on making meanings (both denotative and connotative) explicit and on co-operative creation of texts, implies the acquisition by learners of meta-linguistic awareness. Meta-linguistic awareness – or 'awareness of language' (Hawkins, 1987) – includes an analysis of linguistic relativity, and of the relationships between language and thought. It is this in particular that provides a basis for complementarity between national and foreign language teaching, since language awareness can be developed in both. Furthermore, as national language teachers place increasing emphasis on communicative competence, comparison and contrast between languages and linguistic abilities – and the development of a plurilingual repertoire (Council of Europe, 2001, 2003, 2007) – provide a potential for bridging the gap between foreign language and national language teaching.

Finally, we come to the action orientation. In an early version of the discussion of 'basic concepts and core competences of education for demo-

Table 11.5 Intercultural citizenship: Action orientation

Language education: Skills of discovery and interaction	Political education: Practical – instrumental competences
(a) elicit from an interlocutor the concepts and values of documents or events and develop an explanatory system susceptible of application to other phenomena;	(1) grasp and take seriously the opinions and arguments of others, accord personal recognition to people of other opinions, put oneself in the situation of others, accept criticism, listen;
(b) identify significant references within and across cultures and elicit their significance and connotations;	(2) make one's own opinions (needs, interests, feelings, values) clear, speak coherently, give clear and transparent reasons;
(c) identify similar and dissimilar processes of interaction, verbal and non-verbal, and negotiate an appropriate use of them in specific circumstances;	(5) organise group work, co-operate in the distribution of work, accept tasks, demonstrate trustworthiness, tenacity, care and conscientiousness;
(d) use in real-time an appropriate combination of knowledge, skills and attitudes to interact with interlocutors from a different culture taking into consideration the degree of one's existing familiarity with the culture (and where appropriate language) and the extent of difference between one's own and the other;	(6) tolerate variety, divergence, difference, recognise conflicts, find harmony where possible, regulate issues in socially acceptable fashion, accept mistakes and differences;
	(7) find compromises, seek consensus, accept majority decisions, tolerate minorities, promote encouragement, weigh rights and responsibilities, and show trust and courage;
(g) use in real-time knowledge, skills and attitudes for mediation between interlocutors of one's own and a different culture.	(8) emphasise group responsibility, develop fair norms and common interests and needs, promote common approaches to tasks.

cratic citizenship' at the Council of Europe, Audigier defined some of the capacities for action as follows:

- the capacity to live with others, to co-operate, to construct and implement joint projects, to take on responsibilities;
- the capacity to resolve conflicts in accordance with the principles of democratic law, in particular the two fundamental principles of calling upon a third person not involved in the conflict, and of open debate to hear the parties in dispute and try to arrive at the truth;
- the capacity to take part in public debate, to argue and choose in a real-life situation (Audigier, 1998).

The assumption that democratic procedures are unquestioned is evident, and appropriate in this document. However, a comparative orientation and an evaluative orientation, as defined earlier, would, in intercultural contexts, lead to a questioning of the assumptions and an attempt to discover and understand possible alternatives to democratic procedures.

In Himmelmann's model, based on further documents from the Council of Europe, the 'skills' and 'strategies' defined under 'practical-instrumental competences' (*praktisch-instrumentelle Fähigkeiten*) are generic, and do not refer directly to assumptions about democratic procedures. The element of intercultural competence that emphasises the need to take action to understand and live with others is the 'skills of discovery and interaction'. This competence is also defined in generic terms but would be applied to political co-operation, conflict resolution and public discussion as suggested by Audigier.

The integrated representation of an action orientation is shown in Table 11.5. The elements included from each list of objectives/standards are those that involve communicative competence, in particular where success depends upon mutual understanding despite linguistic and cultural differences.

* * *

The integrated framework[64] presented here in the form of objectives/ standards is the basis for introducing into language education a curriculum that responds to the demands of globalisation/internationalisation. It does so by drawing on political education theory and on proposals for education for democracy. The realisation of the framework in the curriculum could be carried out by language educators, both foreign and national language educators, working in co-operation. The framework could however also be realised by language educators working in co-operation with those who are usually seen as responsible for political education. This second option is more desirable but also more innovative and demanding.

Whatever the approach chosen, the principal aim is to ensure that those who leave an education system, at the end of compulsory schooling perhaps, have a sense of belonging to an international community, a capacity to interact on socio-political matters with people of other languages and cultures, with a critical awareness of the particular nature of socio-political action and interaction in international and intercultural contexts.

In fine, the purpose is to characterise intercultural political competence and to implement an 'education for intercultural citizenship', a phrase that emphasises the significance both of intercultural communicative competence and of education for citizenship. It is to the characterisation of this that I turn next.

Education for Intercultural Citizenship

Principles

The principles of education for intercultural citizenship (EIC) can be presented as four related axioms.[65]

(a) *Intercultural experience* takes place when people from different social groups with different values, beliefs and behaviours (cultures) meet.

It is the social nature of human beings that causes them to form groups that give them a sense of security and, if the group has a sufficiently high status, self-esteem (Tajfel, 1981). Status is relative and is measured by comparison with other, parallel groups. It is only when one's own group is perceived to be of high status that high self-esteem follows. Individuals acquire their values, beliefs and behaviours by socialisation into the shared languages and realities of the social groups around them – including national groups but also professional, social class, regional, religious and so on.

Intercultural experience takes place when people of different groups meet, and is particularly striking and even unnerving, when there is a clash of values, or beliefs, or behaviours. Intercultural experience can take place within a society or across societal boundaries. The outcomes are unpredictable.

(b) *Being 'intercultural'* involves analysis and reflection about intercultural experience and acting on that reflection.

The individual becomes an 'intercultural person' only when intercultural experience becomes the focus of his/her attention, analysis and reflection. Individuals who either do not apprehend or refuse to acknowledge the particular nature of an encounter with another from a group with different values, beliefs and behaviours, are not intercultural. Such individuals assimilate what they take to be common values, beliefs or behaviours to their own, and reject, criticise or condemn what appears to be different. The intercultural person on the other hand reflects on the commonalities and differences and acts according to principles of human comity.[66]

(c) *Intercultural citizenship experience* takes place when people of different social groups and cultures engage in social and political activity [intercultural *democratic* citizenship experience takes place when people of different social groups and cultures engage in social and political activity founded on democratic values and practices].

Intercultural citizenship experience is a particular kind of intercultural experience. It includes action that, following initial experience and becoming a continuation of that experience, is focused on social and political engagement. This may include the promotion of change or improvement in the social or personal lives of the intercultural individuals or their fellows. Whenever the political context of intercultural citizenship experience is democratic, it has a specific nature that includes the obligation to judge values, beliefs and behaviours according to agreed definitions of democracy and democratic principles. The criteria for judgement and the values from which they are derived, are developed as part of the experience and activity.

(d)   *Intercultural citizenship education* involves:
   causing/facilitating intercultural citizenship experience, and analysis and reflection on it and on the possibility of further social and/or political activity – i.e. activity which involves working with others to achieve an agreed end;
   creating learning/change in the individual: cognitive, attitudinal, behavioural change; change in self-perception; change in relationships with Others (i.e. people of a different social group); change that is based in the particular but is related to the universal.

Experience of intercultural (democratic) citizenship can take place in many locations and on many occasions, and individuals may reflect and act together with people of other groups accordingly. The role of education is to anticipate and prepare people for such experience and to promote reflection, analysis and appropriate action. Given the tendency of individuals to remain within the security of their own group and to protect their own self-esteem, there is a significant role for education in preparing them to resist this tendency and meet the challenges involved.

Education for intercultural citizenship therefore deliberately facilitates or creates experiences where the qualities of being intercultural are developed. It focuses on experiences that are political, in the sense of working together with people of other groups to achieve an agreed purpose. Because of this focus, education for intercultural citizenship expects to create change in the individual, to promote their learning. Becoming an intercultural citizen involves psychological and behavioural change, including change in self-perception and understanding of one's relationships to others in other social groups. Where a particular emphasis is placed on learning to be a democratic citizen, the educational purpose is to enable individuals to recognise the particularity of all groups and their cultures, whilst seeing them in the context of universal human values and aspirations.

Education for intercultural (democratic) citizenship is thus a response to ubiquitous intercultural experience within and beyond societal boundaries, and to the political opportunities, for co-operation and the pursuit of agreed goals, which are plentiful in the contemporary world, for example in the emergence of transnational civil society. The specific characteristics of this kind of education can be itemised as follows, although this is simply a way of clarifying aspects of education for intercultural citizenship which overlap and are interdependent:

Characteristics

(1) *A comparative (juxtaposition) orientation in activities of teaching and learning,* such as juxtaposition of political processes (in the classroom, school ... country ...) and *a critical perspective* that questions assumptions through the process of juxtaposition.

Perhaps the most important difference between citizenship education and education for intercultural citizenship is the focus on comparison, understood as juxtaposition, since this serves as an epistemological tool for 'making the familiar strange and the strange familiar'. Juxtaposition, in other words, raises to consciousness that which is too familiar and taken for granted, whilst making the unfamiliar apprehensible. This process leads to a questioning of that which is otherwise taken for granted because it has been internalised as the 'natural' reality, even though it is in fact no more than an agreed and shared interpretation within social groups.

(2) *Emphasis on becoming conscious of working with Others* (of a different group and culture) through (a) processes of comparison/juxtaposition, (b) becoming aware of the influence of language on perceptions, whether L1 or L2/3/... and (c) becoming conscious of their multiple identities.

Intercultural citizenship involves working with people of different social groups to shared ends and, in order to pursue this through comparative juxtaposition, individuals need to make conscious efforts to make explicit the processes of communication. Whether a different language or a variety of the same language, each group maintains and adjusts its interpretation of the world through its language. Co-operation and comparison therefore inevitably involve a raising to consciousness of the need to clarify differing concepts and where necessary invent new ones. However because each individual has multiple social identities, belonging even in his or her own society to multiple social groups each with their own language or language variety, growing awareness of the relations between language and reality also makes individuals more conscious of their multiple social identities and is a phenomenon both internal to the individual and also inter-individual.

(3) *Creating a community of action and communication* that is supra-national and/or composed of people of different beliefs, values and behaviours which are potentially in conflict – without expecting conformity and easy, harmonious solutions.

Intercultural citizenship involves co-operation with others to actively pursue agreed purposes, and this presupposes the creation of a new community of action and communication, which may be temporary or permanent. It is through this process of re-alignment with Others that distinctions of insider and outsider – and the stereotyping and prejudice involved – are overcome. Intercultural citizenship education promotes in particular the formation of communities that go beyond the boundaries of the nation state, and this requires a new composition of individuals with values, beliefs and behaviours that frequently conflict. Such communities challenge the effects of socialisation, and can therefore expect resistance and conflict. It is not the aim of intercultural citizenship education to seek conformity and harmony where conflicting perspectives exist, but rather to seek a mode of political action that is acceptable to all involved.

(4) *Having a focus and range of action* different from that which is available when not working with Others, i.e. all those of whatever social group who are initially perceived as different, as members of an out-group.

It is a peculiarity of intercultural citizenship education that it creates a new focus and a range of activity hitherto unfamiliar to the individuals involved. It challenges the assumption that political action is limited by the boundaries of the individuals' familiar social groups and identities. Education thus helps individuals to consider these new options, to suspend their usual categorisations of others as members of their in-groups or as outsiders, in order to find common aims and modes of co-operation.

(5) *Emphasis on becoming aware of one's existing identities*, and opening options for social identities additional to the national and regional, etc. – paying equal attention to cognition/knowledge, affect/attitude, behaviours/skill.

Education for intercultural citizenship provides the means by which individuals re-consider their existing social identities, and become aware of the multiplicity of their identities and the groups to which they belong. Education for intercultural citizenship facilitates the acquisition of new identities and a sense of belonging to new communities of action. In doing this, the educator is aware that the sense of belonging involves cognition, i.e. shared knowledge and interpretations of reality; attitudes and feelings; a sense of affinity with others and a willingness and curiosity to apprehend their realities; and behavioural change – i.e. the ability to adapt to new contexts in ways acceptable to all concerned.

(6) *All of the above with a conscious commitment to values:* rejecting relativism, whilst being aware that values sometimes conflict and are differently interpreted; but being committed, as citizens in a community, to finding a mode of co-operation on the basis of shared aims and values.

Education for intercultural citizenship must take place within a framework of values and reject a relativist perspective, since co-operation and comity would otherwise be impossible. A relativist perspective is a betrayal of the common humanity of individuals from different social groups with different social identities. The values are themselves part of the creation of the shared reality of a community of action, and are subject to maintenance and adjustment through communication. Intercultural educators need to make their learners aware of the potential conflicts in interpretations and the difficulties in communication. Whilst basing their teaching on the pursuit of common purposes, actions and a community of citizens, intercultural educators must also provide learners with the means of recognising that 'Forms of life differ. Ends, moral principles, are many. But not infinitely many: they must be within the human horizon. If not, then they are outside the human sphere' (Berlin, 1990: 11).

Chapter 12

Policies for Intercultural Citizenship Education

My argument so far has focused on language education and its potential contribution to political education, or education for citizenship. In presenting a comparison of objectives for intercultural competence and for political education or 'learning democracy', I have shown the parallels, the possibilities of complementarity and the ways in which language teachers could modify their purposes. In the characterisation of intercultural citizenship education, I have suggested a framework of objectives and the principles and characteristics that should be present in curriculum development.

The purpose of this chapter is it to further contextualise the approach taken in the previous one, to consider in more depth the opportunities for exercising intercultural citizenship, and to analyse the ways in which education systems as a whole are responding to these. The focus will include educational policies and curricular programmes, after an initial consideration of the communities in which intercultural citizenship will be the crucial factor. In particular I will introduce the European situation since this is so far unique, but could well be an indication of future events elsewhere in the world.

Citizens and Their Communities

As contrasting yet comparable starting points, let us consider citizenship education in England, one of the oldest nations, and in Singapore, one of the youngest. In both countries, governments are concerned to engage young people with the country and its communities, a preoccupation in many other countries fearful of the disaffection of young people from public life and political interest.[67] The social and geographical mobility required by industrial societies, the crucial characteristic that divides them irreversibly from agrarian societies (Gellner, 1983), has made of them anomic societies where 'the threads which in the past had woven human beings into social textures' are broken (Hobsbawm, 1994: 334). The creation of different forms of citizenship education is an attempt to recover those threads and to weave them back together, so that 'communities' – a hint at the distinction between *Gemeinschaft* and *Gesellschaft* – will re-appear.

In England, where politicians can be heard frequently referring to the need for 'communities',[68] a process of consultation and recommendation was published as the 'Crick Report' (Qualifications and Curriculum Authority, 1998), and this became the basis for the national curriculum for citizenship education. This is described on the ministry website as having three elements:

- *Social and moral responsibility*: Pupils learning – from the very beginning – self-confidence and socially and morally responsible behaviour both in and beyond the classroom, towards those in authority and towards each other.
- *Community involvement*: Pupils learning about becoming helpfully involved in the life and concerns of their neighbourhood and communities, including learning through community involvement and service to the community.
- *Political literacy*: Pupils learning about the institutions, problems and practices of our democracy and how to make themselves effective in the life of the nation, locally, regionally and nationally through skills and values as well as knowledge – a concept wider than political knowledge alone.

The outcomes of citizenship education are then summarised in the following terms:

> Pupils develop skills of enquiry, communication, participation and responsible action [...] through creating links between pupils' learning in the classroom and activities that take place across the school, in the community and the wider world. (Online at http://www.dfes.gov. uk/ citizenhip/section.cfm?sectionId=3&hierachy=1.3; accessed 12.06)

It is important to note here the definition of communities and the nature of the individual's relationship to those communities. There are three kinds and levels of community: 'local', 'regional' and 'national'. The individual is expected to have both propositional and procedural knowledge in order to participate in communities and be effective in the life of the nation. (It is also stated that activities should take place not only in school and the community but also in the 'wider world', a vague phrase that could be interpreted to refer to communities beyond the nation.) This knowledge has to be supported by appropriate attitudes, but there is no explicit reference to emotional attachment to a community, at whatever level, no explicit reference to nationalism or patriotism.[69]

In Singapore, the situation is different. As a country with only half a century of history and a population of various ethnic origins, there is a need to deliberately create nationalist attachment, even if the word patriotism is not used. At the launch of 'National Education', which is expected to permeate the curriculum and complement the subject 'Civics and Moral Education', the minister in charge declared:

> National Education aims to develop national cohesion, the instinct for survival and confidence in our future. [...] we must equip (students) with the basic attitudes, values and instincts which make them Singaporeans. This is the common culture that will give them a shared perception of life, and draw them closer together as one people when confronted with serious problems. This will give them a well-founded faith in the country's future. This is the DNA to be passed from one generation to the next. (DPM Lee Hsien Loong. Launch of National Education, 17 May 1997. Online at http://www.moe.gov.sg/ne/keyspeeches/may17-97.htm; accessed 12.06)

The metaphorical passing of DNA from one generation to the next suggests that adherence to the country should be biological, and hints at the notion of a country and its people being bound together by blood, which has been one of the defining characteristics of nationality in some older nation states, most notoriously in the extremes of Nazi Germany. The purpose of National Education is stated quite explicitly to be not only knowledge, skills and attitudes, as in England, but also emotional attachment and commitment for Singapore and against some unnamed enemy:

- First, to develop an *awareness of facts, circumstances and opportunities* facing Singapore so that they [students] will be able to make decisions for their future with conviction and realism.
- Second, to develop a *sense of emotional belonging and commitment* to the community and nation so that they will stay and fight when the odds are against us. (Online at http://www.moe.gov.sg/ne/aboutne/approach.htm; accessed 12.06. Emphasis in original)

This is, moreover, seen as a matter of psychological development, since 'at the primary level, the students are encouraged to Love Singapore; secondary students are taught to Know Singapore; and Junior College/Pre-University students are urged to Lead Singapore'.

There are similarities and differences between England and Singapore. In Singapore what is beyond the nation is threatening and must be repulsed: 'stay and fight when the odds are against us'. This is part of the image of Singapore as an island state surrounded by other, hostile states that might at any time invade. In the English national curriculum, the relationship with other countries is less fraught. There is a reference to students' knowledge and understanding of 'the United Kingdom's relations in Europe, including the European Union, and relations with the Commonwealth and the United Nations', all of which are political relations with governmental organisations. There is no hint that students should see themselves as part of and participate in communities of people beyond the national.

Each of these two countries has its own history, which affects the national perspective, but each is representative of many others. It is easy to see why national curricula are likely to emphasise preparing young people for life in their own country. Nonetheless, a limited national perspective on citizenship education is ultimately a denial of the changes that are taking place through globalisation, and is a failure to prepare young people for them. As Hobsbawm argues, 'nation' and 'nationalism' are no longer satisfactory analytical concepts, and contemporary history:

> will inevitably have to be written as the history of a world which can no longer be contained within the limits of nations and nation states as these used to be defined, either politically, or economically, or culturally, or even linguistically. It will be largely supranational and infranational, but even infranationality, whether or not it dresses itself up in the costume of some mini-nationalism, will reflect the decline of the old nation state as an operational entity. (Hobsbawm, 1992: 191–2)

Hobsbawm points out that national history and culture will continue to be present in education systems, especially of small countries, and he is vindicated by the two cases presented here. But he also says that national identity will become just one of many as nationalism declines. In fine, the communities within which young people will live and participate will include not only the local and the national but also the transnational.[70]

In his *Language and Solitude* (1998), Gellner argues that there is a long-existing tension between two modes of envisaging the social world. On the one hand, there is Tönnies' *Gemeinschaft*, a mode of living and thinking based on an organic theory of knowledge, on tradition and conservatism. Then, there is *Gesellschaft*, where individuals live as individuals with a knowledge of the world which analyses and dissolves the organic linkages among people and groups assumed to be natural. The organic vision becomes self-aware as a consequence of the analytical, individualistic attempt to build up our knowledge from a Cartesian reliance on the self. The organic *Gemeinschaft* is promoted as a reaction and has led to the extremes of fascism. The extremes of individualism ignore the needs of human beings for comity and a sense of place. What is needed instead is a 'cultural pluralist nationalism and [...] political internationalism' (Gellner, 1998: 187).

The concept of intercultural citizenship discussed in the previous chapter should lead to people having a sense of belonging to a *Gemeinschaft*, and a plurality of such communities, whilst allowing them to act in international (or transnational) networks that have the political characteristics of *Gesellschaft*, may also develop, albeit in tempered and temporary form, the attributes of *Gemeinschaft*.

The existence of transnational communities is not new, but is becoming increasingly present and relevant to everyone in society. Transnational communities in the past were better known as diasporas, for example the Jewish diaspora (Castles 2004: 28). In the post-1945 era, the diasporas of workers ('guest workers' and others) have become a visible part of many societies of the industrially developed world.[71] Singapore (and countries in the Gulf) experiences this as much as Britain and the rest of Western Europe. Nonetheless, these new diaspora communities with ties to their country of origin and often to family members in third countries, have until now been seen as a peripheral phenomenon by mainstream society. In some countries, there has been acknowledgement of their presence in the education system through the introduction of various forms of multicultural education, but this too is usually a response that is centred on the nation state, on integration into the existing polity.

What is increasingly evident to teachers is that their learners of all ages are already members of transnational networks as a consequence of globalisation and communications technology. They notice that children are absent from school because they are visiting their grandparents in the country of origin and they see how computer technology and the Internet allow constant interaction across large distances. The question is whether these networks are the forerunner of transnational communities which will have a political purpose and status. They certainly have the potential to be so, as Castles points out:

> Transnational communities are groups whose identity is not primarily based on attachment to a specific territory. They therefore present a powerful challenge to traditional ideas of nation state belonging [...]. The notion of a transnational community puts the emphasis on human agency; such groups are the result of cross-border activities which link individuals, families, and local groups. (Castles, 2004: 27)

The realisation of this potential for action is so far to be seen in the work of Non-Governmental Organisations (NGOs). These are the existing bodies that have joined together to influence global politics, and which are seen as the basis for more complex developments. The evidence for their success is mixed. In a study of NGOs concerned with environmental issues,

Rohrschneider and Dalton (2002) conclude that NGOs generally, and public interest groups such as women's groups or ethnic movements, will not necessarily become globalised and truly internationalised, but may rather continue as national groups that seek allies among other national groups. On the other hand, Mundy and Murphy see in the emergence of transnational groupings of NGOs new levels of 'civility', i.e. 'the development of a dense pattern of sustained interaction and collaboration' (Mundy & Mundy, 2001: 92).

Writers on transnational civil society thus discern the growing political significance of transnational communities, with the possibility that new concepts of citizenship can be developed. Wagner distinguishes between those writers who hope to see the emergence of a cosmopolitan citizenship[72] and others who favour transnational citizenship. The former would like to break away from the constraints of nation states, and establish a new dimension that is 'dialogic and built on communicative communities that have the power to contest unjust social structures'. The latter recognise that the nation state is a reality, but wish to see the increasing numbers of people with affiliations to more than one nation state being recognised in 'an institution of citizenship that will give them rights in all the countries with which they identify: where they work, where their roots lie or where they have their cultural ties' (Wagner, 2004: 284).

Whether the outcome is cosmopolitan citizenship or transnational citizenship, there will be a need for interaction and communication, for propositional knowledge about communities beyond the nation, and for procedural knowledge of how to act and interact. It is here that intercultural citizenship is crucial.

As Wagner points out, the European Union is the only case so far of a supranational body that functions as a polity with citizens to which it accords rights. It does not, however, extend these to everyone living within it, only to nationals of the member states, and not to immigrants from other states who then become illegal, '*sans papiers*', but who form a substantial minority of at least 5 million people in Europe. Their presence cannot be ignored as the occasional declaration of amnesty by a government demonstrates. Outhwaite too analyses in some detail differing views on whether a European society is emerging, accepting that some consider this naïve, others believe that the forces against it are too strong. He concludes that there are sufficient signs, despite the doubters, to be able to say 'in a slightly pale Galilean way, something of a societal kind *is* moving at the level of the EU, the European Economic Area or Europe as a whole' (Outhwaite, 2006: 117; emphasis in original). Despite the caveats, the European Union offers the first framework within which a transnational civil society engaging in political activity might flourish, and it is therefore important to consider the educational response.

Education for Citizenship beyond the Nation State: Europe

The European situation is, thus far, unique. For people living in the 47 states that are members of the Council of Europe (CoE), there is a consensus among governments to pursue education for democratic citizenship in their education systems, and there are numerous modes of implementation of agreements about language education and education for citizenship, although as yet few explicit links between the two. For people living within the European Union (EU) of 27 states, there already exists an international citizenship in the sense of being a member of a democratic polity. Citizens of EU countries elect their representatives both at national level – for the parliament of their nation state – and at supranational level – for the European parliament. The EU has many political characteristics of a nation state and the historical trend is to ever more such characteristics, despite resistance in some areas.

One area where resistance has been strong is in the organisation of compulsory education. Nation states have resisted the imposition of a European education system, although resistance has been lower in higher education than in compulsory education. Nation states use their education systems to cultivate a national identity, not least through the teaching of the national language(s). The emphasis on a distinction between national languages and foreign languages serves the purposes of national education, but creates a problem for the EU and the CoE because it is in tension with the need to communicate at European level in a range of languages for economic, political, social and cultural purposes. Furthermore, it is in tension with any hope of creating a sense of European identity in parallel with the introduction of European citizenship.

The logical development would be to have a 'European' language for European identity, but this does not exist. The alternative, of developing an existing shared lingua franca – which at this point in history could only be English – is not politically acceptable since there would be accusations of linguistic imperialism and/or of allowing unfair and unequal dominance to native speakers of English. Whether these are justified or not – and the case is far from proven – a lingua franca would not be efficient. Transnational discourse cannot rely on a single, taken for granted, shared language and its meanings. The discourse that is necessary is not simply a matter of establishing an agreement on and/or an exchange of information such as might be achieved through a lingua franca. The topics that arise in social discourse are shot through with contemporary and historical nuances, and the likelihood of misunderstanding in a lingua franca is strong (Meierkord, 2002; Taylor, 2006). Perhaps more important still, the relationship between language and thought, between language and worldview is crucial, and when people engage in co-operation in civil society, they do so as social beings whose social identities are embodied in the language they speak. To use a lingua franca is reductive of their social identities, and diminishes them as human beings.[73]

The real-world option is to change the relationship between national languages and foreign (European) languages. This logic is evident in the EU 'White Paper' on education published in the mid-1990s (see Chapter 8):

> Multilingualism is part and parcel of both European identity/citizenship and the learning society. (European Commission, 1995: 67)

So it is the notion of proficiency in languages which is linked to and implicitly seen as in a causal relationship with a sense of being European, with European identity, which in turn seems to be synonymous with citizenship. The subsequent recommendation for practice is that European citizens should speak their mother tongue(s) plus two other languages, and this implies that a knowledge of three or more languages – perhaps to different degrees and in different ways – will create a sense of European identity and citizenship, and a potential for participation and integration into an international/European society and polity. A similar statement was made in 2003:

> (5) knowledge of language is one of the basic skills which each citizen needs to acquire in order to take part effectively in the European knowledge society and therefore facilitates both integration into society and social cohesion; a thorough knowledge of one's mother tongue(s) can facilitate the learning of other languages. (Council Resolution, 2002)

The EU policy on language education thus has three features:

- a relationship between national language/mother tongue learning and foreign language learning;
- an assumption of a causal relationship between language learning and identity/citizenship;
- and a conditional relationship between language learning and participation in European society.

Learning several languages is at least a pre-condition and perhaps a causal factor in the evolution of citizenship in the sense of being an elector, in an affective bond with an international society, and in an action orientation involving participation in the economic, political and cultural life of the society.

In fine, the EU offers an example of language education policy that reaches beyond the national level of education even though the realisation of the policy in curricula is yet to evolve. On the other hand, there are no signs of change in the objectives of language education to take into account transnational community and the need for political education. There is no vision of an 'intercultural citizen' but rather an unchanged vision of a person who learns languages, is economically mobile, has a feeling of being included in a cohesive society. There is an acknowledgement of the need for intercultural competence, crucial in all heterogeneous societies, but there is no mention of the critical cultural awareness that is crucial to intercultural citizenship.

The policy for citizenship education in the EU vision is similarly under-developed. In 1997, Davies surveyed the 15 countries of the EU and the Commission itself, by approaching in person the ministries and other education authorities. His intention was above all to find out what policies existed, recognising that the implementation of these might be quite another matter. Quoting a previous survey of EU documentation, Davies points out that there already existed an expectation that European citizens should have knowledge about the EU, its functions and history, that they should be willing to believe in co-operation, have a sense of European identity and share values of democracy, pluralism, tolerance, friendship between peoples, social justice and respect for human rights. Davies found that, though there were various initiatives (including the White Paper mentioned above), there was at EU level 'a lack of consistency in the way that the word "citizenship" is used[74] and at times it is ignored altogether in favour of terms which seem to imply that a somehow neutral collection of data or movement of people for vocational purposes is all that is required' (Davies, 1997: 105).

At country level, the picture was even less encouraging, with a very wide range of interests and practices being found, from a stress on a new intercultural approach (which in this case meant racial and ethnic harmony within a country), to a complacency that nothing needs to be added to current practice. Davies's summary suggests that three kinds of activity can be identified: language learning (which seems to be considered in itself to be a preparation for European citizenship), investigations into a common cultural heritage, and partnerships among schools. This is, as he points out, inadequate in that there is no attention to political aspects of Europe, and he argues *inter alia* that 'Concerns over the democratic deficit will not be addressed in classes which focus on language learning' (Davies, 1997: 113).

Davies is no doubt right about this, and that is why the argument is made in these pages that language teaching should be conceived differently so that it is able to contribute to political education.

Another location for the evolution of European citizenship is in the work of the Council of Europe. At the moment of its founding in the first years after the Second World War, language learning was seen as important for European culture and heritage. This would be one way of creating a sense of unity after 1945 and the emphasis was on a shared cultural heritage, as stated in the summary of the Cultural Convention, the foundation for co-operation among member states:

> to develop mutual understanding among the peoples of Europe and reciprocal appreciation of their cultural diversity, to safeguard European culture, to promote national contributions to Europe's common cultural heritage respecting the same fundamental values and to encourage in particular the study of the languages, history and civilisation of the Parties to the Convention. (Online at http://conventions.coe.int/Treaty/EN/cadreprincipal.htm; accessed 10.04)

In today's documents, the Council of Europe statement of purposes is presented as a question of identity:

> The Council was set up to [...] promote awareness of a European identity based on shared values and cutting across different cultures. (Online at (www.coe.int/T/EN/Com/About_COE/; accessed 10.04)

The importance of language was evident from the beginning, and the link with identity is implicit in the ways in which language, culture, heritage and history are presented as related concepts. There is a clear parallel here with the ways in which national and ethnic groups are defined.

The importance of language has been formulated with increasing precision, and in the last few decades a language education policy position has evolved, which was stated in a document to celebrate the 50th anniversary of the signing of the Cultural Convention:

Council of Europe language education policies aim to promote:

- *plurilingualism*: all are entitled to develop a degree of communicative ability in a number of languages over their lifetime in accordance with their needs;
- *linguistic diversity*: Europe is multilingual and all its languages are equally valuable modes of communication and expressions of identity; the right to use and to learn one's language(s) is protected in Council of Europe Conventions;

- *mutual understanding*: the opportunity to learn other languages is an essential condition for intercultural communication and acceptance of cultural differences;
- *democratic citizenship*: participation in democratic and social processes in multilingual societies is facilitated by the plurilingual competence of individuals;
- *social cohesion*: equality of opportunity for personal development, education, employment, access to information and cultural enrichment depends on access to language learning throughout life. (Council of Europe, 2006)[75]

What is apparent here is that language learning is considered to be a condition *sine qua non* for the success of particular aspects of social policy. The terminology has changed and become more precise, with phrases such as 'social inclusion' complementing the older concept of 'mutual understanding' and the emphasis on diversity that was already present in the Cultural Convention. Most importantly, an explicit link is established between language learning and democratic citizenship.

The policy is articulated in more detail in other documents. The essential notion is that individuals ought to be encouraged and enabled to become 'plurilingual', which means having 'proficiency of varying degrees, in several languages, and experience of several cultures [...] not seen as the superposition or juxtaposition of distinct competences, but rather as the existence of a complex or even composite competence on which the user may draw' (Council of Europe, 2001: 168). The reasons for postulating this aim for language teaching are expressed in clearly political formulations:

- *language rights are part of human rights*: education policies should facilitate the use of all varieties of languages spoken by the citizens of Europe, and the recognition of other people's language rights by all; the resolution of social conflicts is in part dependent on recognition of language rights;
- *the exercise of democracy and social inclusion depends on language education policy*: the capacity and opportunity to use one's full linguistic repertoire is crucial to participation in democratic and social processes and therefore to policies of social inclusion;
- *economic or employment opportunities for the individual and the development of human capital in a society depend in part on language education policy*: individual mobility for economic purposes is facilitated by plurilingualism; the plurilingualism of a workforce is a crucial part of human capital in a multilingual marketplace, and a condition for the free circulation of goods, information and knowledge;

- *individual plurilingualism is a significant influence on the evolution of a European identity*: since Europe is a multilingual area in its entirety and in any given part, the sense of belonging to Europe and the acceptance of a European identity is dependent on the ability to interact and communicate with other Europeans using the full range of one's linguistic repertoire. (Beacco & Byram, 2007: 9)

The Council of Europe thus articulates a view that language learning and a sense of being a member of a democratic society with a European identity are in a causal relationship, as can be found in the documents of the EU. But here too there is no reference to a critical cultural awareness or a community of action that is crucial to the realisation of 'the exercise of democracy and social inclusion'.

The Council of Europe also works in the field of citizenship education, and in particular in education for democratic citizenship (EDC). EDC is defined as 'a set of practices and principles aimed at making young people and adults better equipped to participate actively in a democratic life by assuming and exercising their rights and responsibilities in society' (Council of Europe, 2004: 12). The term 'society' here is open enough to include all levels of activity both national and supranational. In practice, the focus is on encouraging activity at national level or below. The Council of Europe's own analyses of policies and of their implementation do not reveal any concern with supranational activity or transnational civil society.

In one document, it is interesting to note, the different interpretations of the phrase 'civil society' are commented on. It is argued that there is a gap between the Anglo-Saxon world and the 'continental approach':

> The Anglo-Saxon world considers this notion (civil society) to include the whole body social, namely the private sector, the market and non-governmental organisations (NGOs). It is only the State that is not part of this definition. For its part, the continental approach makes a strict distinction between the three domains which are the state, the market and civil society. According to this approach, civil society is clearly separate from the market, whereas this is not the case with the Anglo-Saxon approach. (B. Wicht in a report 'Civil society or "everyone for themselves"? Culture as an agent for democracy in Europe.' Online at www.coe.int /e/cultural-co-operation/education/E.D.C./; accessed 10.04)

This remark raises again the importance of mutual understanding in the discourse of citizenship that I illustrated with the example of the word 'citizen' in Chapter 10. If a transnational civil society emerges, two interpretations of the concept have the potential to create misunderstanding about the activity and purpose. So far, however, the Council of Europe has not articulated the concept of transnational civil society, nor has it seen the relationship between the key concept of plurilingualism and the promotion of education for democratic citizenship.

****

In summary, what seems to be happening in Europe, whether in the European Union or the Council of Europe, is a process of creating a supranational polity and an identity modelled in some respects on the nation state. There is a flag, an anthem, a parliament and a proposed constitution (for the EU). Unlike the evolution of nation states from below, from a 'protonationalism' (Hobsbawm, 1992), European 'nationalism' does not have a base but is being created 'from above'. Furthermore, it does not have a single language, as a nation state might, but a concept of 'plurilingualism'. This is difficult to grasp for many people, but is actively promulgated by the Council of Europe, and by the European Union under the label 'multilingualism'. Neither does Europe have a transnational civil society comparable with civil society at national or infranational levels.

The role of education systems in the process of creating a European polity and identity, and an interest in and capacity for European citizenship, is restricted by the pre-occupation of nation states with their own identity and citizenship. Member states of the European Union and Council of Europe have not allowed access to their schools for 'European' education. Only in foreign language learning do member states accept a full European commitment, many of them using the *Common European Framework of Reference* (Council of Europe, 2001) and European Language Portfolio in curriculum development, or taking advantage of EU funds to create links between schools that are seen as beneficial to language learning even if this is not the main purpose for the EU. However, neither the European Union nor the Council of Europe yet has a policy for what I have defined as 'intercultural citizenship'.[76]

Chapter 13
Curricula for Intercultural Citizenship Education

The 'native speaker' of a language is a much-debated concept (Kramsch, 1998; Davies, 2003) but is nonetheless frequently used as a goal by many – probably the majority of – language teachers. They hope their learners will move ever nearer to being native speakers and therefore assess their learners against this goal. Because it is extremely difficult, though not impossible, to achieve this goal, learners have a constant sense of failure.[77] Davies points out that a distinction needs to be made between the goal as inspiration and the definition and measurement of attainment of the goal:

> The native speaker is a fine myth: we need it as a model, a goal, almost an inspiration. But it is useless as a measure; it will not help us define our goals. So in spite of [...] my conviction that there is a continuum between native speakers and non-native speakers, nevertheless, I recognise that for language teaching purposes what is crucial is the description of adequate partial competences. (Davies, 2003: 197)

The definition of partial competences, says Davies, is a matter for tests, but this approach can also be complemented by describing levels of attainment, as is done in the *Common European Framework of Reference for Languages* (Council of Europe, 2001) and by determining which skills a learners needs in a given set of circumstances.

Although this is a very important issue in language teaching, I have introduced it only briefly here in order to make the point that, even if the native speaker is a model or inspiration for linguistic competence, it should not be a model for (inter)cultural competence. In this respect, language learners need a different goal, one that is no less complex but more appropriate than the native speaker. The 'intercultural speaker', discussed in Chapter 4, has linguistic and cultural competences that enable them to take up a 'privileged' position (Kramsch, 1998) with a new perspective on their own and other people's cultural assumptions, values, beliefs and behaviours. The precise description of what an intercultural speaker should set themselves as a goal depends on circumstances, on the analysis of their learning opportunities and of their foreseeable needs, as well as the potential they might wish to acquire for further learning at a later point in their lives (Byram, 1997).

If the analysis of actual needs and future potential includes their activity as intercultural citizens, as I have argued it should, then the divergence from some notion of a 'native speaker' or a 'national citizen' is all the more evident. The intercultural citizen is a citizen of his/her own state, not someone attempting to imitate or identify with citizens in another state. The intercultural citizen is someone who acquires the competence to act in transnational communities. Just as I argued in Chapter 4 that intercultural competence to act differs from bicultural identity, which is a state of being, the intercultural citizen is someone who has competence to act transnationally, which is not the same as being a citizen of two states, having dual citizenship.

In this chapter my purpose is to discuss and illustrate how the learning goals of education for intercultural citizenship can be realised in varying circumstances and according to varying needs and opportunities.

Transnational Political Activity in Education

Since the essence of intercultural citizenship is taking action, we can conceive the planning of curricula in terms of tasks.[78] The specific characteristics of such a task will be that it takes learners beyond the assumptions of their own cultures and involves them in an activity that is transnational. Their task will be undertaken in a transnational community, perhaps as a member of a transnational civil society. As a consequence, it urges them to critical reflection on their own society and what it expects of its citizens. However, as I pointed out in an Chapter 10, transnational civil society is only just emerging, and its characteristics are much debated. Similarly what counts as a transnational community and political activity in such a community is far from clear. It needs to be clarified by experiment and experience as much as by definition and analysis. In the following pages, I will use some specific examples from experiments in teaching to identify different kinds of transnational political activity and the intercultural citizenship competences involved.

Let us recall the principles and characteristics of intercultural citizenship education from Chapter 11:

Principles

(a) *Intercultural experience* takes place when people from different social groups with different values, beliefs and behaviours (cultures) meet.

(b) *Being 'intercultural'* involves analysis and reflection about intercultural experience and acting on that reflection.

(c) *Intercultural citizenship experience* takes place when people of different social groups and cultures engage in social and political activity [intercultural *democratic* experience take place when people of different social groups and cultures engage in social and political activity founded on democratic values and practices].

(d) *Intercultural citizenship education* involves:
       causing/facilitating intercultural citizenship experience, and analysis and reflection on it (and on the possibility of further social and/or political activity – i.e. activity which involves working with others to achieve an agreed end;
       creating learning/change in the individual: cognitive, attitudinal, behavioural change; change in self-perception; change in relationships with Others (i.e. people of a different social group); change that is based in the particular but is related to the universal.

Characteristics

(1) *A comparative (juxtaposition) orientation in activities of teaching and learning,* such as juxtaposition of political processes (in the classroom, school ... country ...) and *a critical perspective* that questions assumptions through the process of juxtaposition.

(2) *Emphasis on becoming conscious of working with Others* (of a different group and culture) through (a) processes of comparison/juxtaposition, (b) becoming aware of the influence of language on perceptions, whether L1 or L2/3/... and (c) becoming conscious of their multiple identities.

(3) *Creating a community of action and communication* that is supra-national and/or composed of people of different beliefs, values and behaviours which are potentially in conflict – without expecting conformity and easy, harmonious solutions.

(4) *Having a focus and range of action* different from that which is available when not working with Others, i.e. all those of whatever social group who are initially perceived as different, as members of an out-group.

(5) *Emphasis on becoming aware of one's existing identities,* and opening options for social identities additional to the national and regional, etc. – paying equal attention to cognition/knowledge, affect/attitude, behaviours/skill.

(6) *All of the above with a conscious commitment to values:* rejecting relativism, whilst being aware that values sometimes conflict and are differently

interpreted; but being committed, as citizens in a community, to finding a mode of co-operation on the basis of shared aims and values.

The demands of this list are high. They provide an ideal towards which to aim in policy and practice, but such ideals are a necessary formulation of the position I have explained in this book. Analysis of contemporary education systems reveal that this ideal is present in at least embryonic form in some countries.

In Alred, Byram and Fleming (2006) the ideal was used as a basis for analysing education in four countries, Japan, Poland, Portugal and Spain. In Japan, the potential for promoting intercultural citizenship is present in conceptualisations of curriculum as revealed in policy documents, but it is limited to the national:

> The characteristics of working with others through comparison and communication, creating a community of action and a community composed of people of different values and behaviours, awareness of identities and commitment to values and to finding co-operation are encouraged in various spheres of Japanese education. These characteristics tend to be promoted at various levels up to the national level but not beyond. (Parmenter, 2006: 162)

Parmenter argues that some of the characteristics could easily be transferred to a transnational level although others – a comparative orientation and critical questioning of assumptions – are not yet accepted in most Japanese classrooms.

In Portugal, too, there is potential for education for intercultural citizenship expressed in the current educational philosophy of the curriculum and other documents and 'It is noticeable that interculturality and citizenship have been gradually strengthened throughout the last two decades and, with great evidence, in basic education' (Guilherme et al., 2006: 231). The authors of this study emphasise that Portugal is a country that escaped a dictatorship only three decades ago, that democracy and education for democratic citizenship are new phenomena there.

This is all the more the case for Poland, where the encouragement of critical skills and criticality as an attitude is yet to appear:

> The analysis of the core curriculum reveals that Citizenship Education with the core curriculum, rather than developing critical, active citizens, transmits knowledge and basic skills that enable pupils to act as Polish nationals and in this way strengthen their national identity. (Walat, 2006: 183)

Walat suggests that the acquisition of a European identity, which might be expected after Poland joined the European Union, is not yet pursued in the education system. National identity is the main focus, as in Japan.

As I have shown in earlier chapters, the question of identities is always related to education for (intercultural) citizenship, and in Spain, there is a definite focus on how education can help young people to acquire several identities:

> From the foregoing considerations, one can deduce that in Spain [...] citizenship education is beginning to be approached from a multilayered perspective and the different identities are balanced, respected and fostered. Both in the National Curriculum and in the textbooks, regional, national, European and global identities turn out to be conjugated and presented as complementary, that is to say, 'multiple citizenships' constitute a priority in Spanish education. (Méndez García, 2006: 183)

This notion of multiple identities underpins curricula already. As Parmenter says of Japan (2006:163), membership of family, school, community and nation is accepted and promoted. However there is no identity beyond the nation; the only identity the education system permits is that of 'the Japanese person'. It is not impossible for 'Japanese persons' to communicate with, say, 'Portuguese persons', if both have intercultural competence and linguistic competence. They would not, however, interact as intercultural citizens in a transnational community of purpose unless they were also encouraged to identify with a group beyond the nation.

The cases analysed by these authors were an opportunity sample and may not be representative of other education systems. Nonetheless they pinpoint the importance of clarification of concepts within national education systems as represented in their curriculum documents. They also show that change is taking place in some countries, that the ideal of the model of intercultural citizenship is being pursued at national level.

Change does not only come from the top, however, and bottom-up, grassroots change can have its own effect on curriculum development. In the criteria set out above, teachers are asked to work with learners to create new communities that will be politically active i.e. seek to create change in their own and others' environments and in their opportunities for living in society. What evidence is there that this can be done?

In an earlier book, we collected examples of teachers planning their curricula with intercultural competence objectives in mind (Byram *et al.*, 2001). These teachers introduce into their methodology a strong comparative element, which leads to the reassessment of assumptions and knowledge about learners' own selves and society. For example, learners can reassess their understanding of 'law-and-order' (Morgan), of welfare and charity (Tupozova), of their stereotypes of the landscapes of other countries (Vigneron). This involves empathy and understanding of other perspectives and leads learners, under the guidance of teachers, to challenge existing assumptions in their own culture from the perspective of the other. Learners thus take a supranational perspective, being in neither their own nor the other culture, but suspended above both. They do so temporarily before 'returning' with a new, critical understanding of the previously all-too-familiar world in which they live. Analysing these examples against the characteristics of intercultural citizenship education cited above, we see that teachers have created an opportunity for 'intercultural experience' for their learners in which the 'meeting with others' takes place in the documents and artefacts of another culture. Through their pedagogical approach, they have then taught their learners to 'be intercultural' through causing them to reflect on their intercultural experience. If and how learners 'act' on their reflections is not always noted by these teachers, probably because the action is expected to take place in learners' lives outside the classroom, and perhaps in the future rather than immediately.

The challenge is to go a stage further in the classroom, to create opportunities to meet others not only in texts and artefacts. The challenge is to form a transnational community – even if only temporary – and to take some immediate political action to benefit themselves and others.

Examples already exist of transnational communities being formed for intercultural experience and communication. It is not surprising that the European Union encourages through its Comenius programme the creation of networks of schools working together on projects. The main characteristics are clear from the statement of overall objectives:

> The overall objectives of COMENIUS are to enhance the *quality* and reinforce the *European dimension* of school education, in particular by *encouraging transnational co-operation* between schools, contributing to the improved professional *development of staff* directly involved in the school education sector, and promoting *intercultural awareness.*

> COMENIUS seeks to help those learning and teaching in schools to develop a sense of belonging to a broader and outward-looking European community – a community characterised by diverse traditions, cultures and regional identities, but rooted nevertheless in a common history of European development. (Online at http://europa.eu.int/comm/education/programmes/socrates/comenius/; accessed 11.04. Emphasis in original)

What is important to note here is the emphasis on 'community' and on 'transnational co-operation'. The concept of community is, as we have noted in Chapter 12, used loosely in the contemporary world, and the notion of a community characterised by various identities does not correspond well with the notion that a community tends by its nature to homogeneity. It is also clear from this statement that language learning and intercultural awareness are related to the basic concepts of a 'European dimension' in the curriculum. What is lacking in this list of overall objectives, and in the detailed definitions of the key concepts, is the notion of political activity, in the sense of making some change in the social environment.

The actual practice of projects tends not to venture into political action either. A project on 'European citizenship' aims to set up meetings and other mechanisms for the development of curricula. Another with the same title has as its main objectives support for the 'values debate in schools and outside of schools, demonstrating a common canon of values', with a focus on interreligious and intercultural dialogue. The outcome is intended to be 'material about' these issues where the emphasis is to be on finding a 'common culture' (Compendium of Projects, Comenius Action 3, 2003 – see http://europa. eu.int/comm/education/programmes/socrates/comenius/). Though perhaps laudable, this nonetheless ignores the importance of maintaining and accepting difference. Another network aims to enhance 'Euro-Arab dialogue' with exchanges of video materials among schools, with the following:

Résultats escomptés:
- *une meilleure connaissance de sa propre culture et de la culture de l'autre;*
- *l'aptitude au dialogue interculturel, avec moins de préjugés et plus d'esprit de découverte;*
- *le désir de participer à des projets communs avec des partenaires venus de différents horizons.* (Compendium of Projects, Comenius Action 3, 2003, 2.1: 2. See http://europa.eu.int/comm/education/programmes / socrates/comenius/)

[Expected results:
- a better knowledge of one's own culture and of the culture of the other;
- aptitude for intercultural dialogue, with fewer prejudices and more spirit of discovery;
- desire to participate in common projects with partners from different horizons.]

Although the creation of a potential, of an interest in common projects, is present in this report, what is lacking in this and other projects is the final stage of intercultural citizenship education: the engagement in political action.

We might also look at the traditions of school exchanges but here too we would find that though temporary transnational communities are created, the focus is on the potential they afford for communication practice – and enjoyment of a new environment (Tarp, 2006). That such practice is best fostered when there is a common project is well recognised by teachers, and the opportunities (and limitations) of the Comenius programme in Europe is one approach to making exchanges work. The Comenius programme has the advantage that it encourages projects which are not just bilateral, as is the tradition in school exchanges.

These European examples arise from the particular political circumstances of the European Union, with its agenda of creating 'European citizens'. The examples cannot be imitated in other parts of the world where political circumstances are different. On the other hand, networks can be created with a common purpose among schools anywhere. In East Asia, virtual networks could be founded to bring schools from Japan, Korea and China together, with English being the lingua franca, with all the caveats this involves and complemented by pupils' (receptive) knowledge of other Asian languages. What is important in all of this is to define clearly the nature of the network, and to ensure that it includes the potential for political action, if not in the first instance – since we must acknowledge this may be politically unacceptable in some education systems – then certainly in the longer term.

Levels of 'Acting Interculturally'

If transnational communities are to become the basis of political action, five levels of engagement need to be pursued:

(Pre-political)
(1)   learners engage with others (through documents and artefacts or 'in person', which might be face-to-face or virtual) and reflect critically on their own assumptions, and those of the other;
(2)   learners engage with others, reflect critically and propose/imagine possible alternatives and changes;

(Political)
(3)   learners engage with others seeking their perspective/advice, reflect critically, propose change and take action to instigate change in their own society;

(4) learners create with others a transnational community, reflect together, propose and instigate change in their respective societies;
(5) in a transnational community, learners from two or more societies identify an issue that they act upon as a transnational group.

To illustrate the first level, I will refer to a number of articles in the book mentioned above, *Developing Intercultural Competence in Practice*, a collection of accounts of their lessons by teachers attempting to put into operation the theory of intercultural communicative competence (Byram *et al.*, 2001). In one project, English students in upper secondary education with intermediate language skills studied family life in France (Duffy and Mayes). They watched video-recorded scenes from family life, they prepared interview schedules for their peers in France, they analysed interviews with people of their own age, they compared national statistics in France and England on family structure, and so on. The constant comparison made them aware of their own assumptions about norms of family life in England, and to what extent these can be generalised. The study of some families in France and some statistical data gave them insight into the country whose language they were learning, but above all challenged their own experience of family life.

In another project with upper-secondary students, this time in Bulgaria, the focus was on student–teacher relationships (Madjarova, Botsmanova and Stamatova). The students started with a letter to a magazine from an English girl in which she told about falling in love with her teacher and how he had reported the love letter she sent him to the head of the school, her parents and the school counsellor. The Bulgarian students discussed how they thought their own teachers would and should react, interviewed or listened to interviews with Bulgarian teachers and English native-speaker teachers in their own school, and found quite different responses. Bulgarian teachers would deal with the problem on a personal level, not involving the school as an institution. As a consequence, they began to understand better the nature of the relationships in 'the same' institutions in different countries and the assumptions behind them, particularly in their own country. They thought about the traditions and values of schooling in Bulgaria and the ways in which these are changing.

The third example, from Denmark (Parsons and Junge), shows how lower language competence need not be a problem. In this case, adult immigrants from countries such as Afghanistan, Iraq, Somalia, Lebanon, Romania and others, were learning the host language, Danish, as beginners – some of them not being literate in their own language. The teachers believed in taking their learners out into the community as 'ethnographers' discovering the community and country in which they intended to live. In one case, the learners had asked worried questions about the way older people in Denmark are treated by their families and by society. They were worried because these people seemed to be abandoned by their families to live in old people's homes, whereas in the learners' own societies they would be looked after by their families. Instead of reading texts that would be too difficult anyway, they went to observe in old people's homes and similar institutions, having prepared simple questions for the people they met, and recorded the answers in order to listen to and understand them better in class. The experiences and findings were complex, but broadly speaking the immigrants found that their assumptions that old people would be unhappy and feel abandoned were not confirmed. They began to see alternative conceptions of living actively and independently as older people, conceptions that do not exist in their own societies. And perhaps they worried less about their own future as old people in Denmark.

All of these examples show people with considerable experience of their own society, with various degrees of intellectual and emotional maturity and capacity to decentre. The question arises whether the principles can be applied with younger learners, without that maturity and also with limited linguistic skills, although the latter factor as we have seen is not crucial. As I pointed out in Chapter 5, it can be shown both in principle – drawing on Bruner's theories – and in practice in several different countries that there is no reason to assume that primary school children cannot be engaged in cultural learning.

In an account (Parmenter and Tomita) in the same book of a television programme teaching English in Japanese primary schools, the material and methodology makes young learners take the perspective of the Other on their own society and language. As Japan becomes a multicultural and immigrant country, this is important. With a very limited linguistic competence – the words of greeting and saying one's name – young learners see Japanese children and children from countries such as former Yugoslavia, Chile, Italy and so on, introducing themselves in their own languages and in Japanese. The Japanese children learn to speak slowly and clearly to help others understand them and, in discussion with some young learners, it was evident that the programme had helped to make them aware of how immigrants living in their neighbourhood experienced Japan. In this shift of perspective lies the key to self-analysis and a challenge to one's own assumptions.

Where the concept of criticality is linked to imagining alternatives to the assumptions revealed by these comparisons, then there is a further refinement of the pre-political types of engagement. The distinction between the first two levels may not always be easy to make, but in one example, the changing political situation encouraged learners actively to imagine alternatives to existing institutions in their society. In this case, starting from a simple lesson comparing Christmas cards in England and Bulgaria (Topuzova), teacher and students in an upper secondary school found themselves considering changing concepts and institutions of charity and the welfare state in Bulgaria. The students were asked to collect and analyse Christmas cards in Bulgarian shops and then compared their findings with a parallel analysis of Christmas cards from Britain. One difference was the concept of contributing to a charity by buying a Christmas card sold by the charity. This led to an explanation of charities in British society and their role alongside the provisions of the welfare state, and then to a discussion of the appearance of charities to relieve poverty in post-Socialist Bulgaria. Students began to ask themselves why charity organisations were appearing, how they differ from but nonetheless imitate some features of charities in Capitalist societies, and what might happen in the future. It is not recorded if these students began to act differently, or to engage politically in their own lives outside school as a consequence of these insights.

The third level of engagement takes us explicitly into political action. It suggests learners need to seek out other people's perspectives as part of their own planning to take action, and it is at this level that teachers need to plan their teaching with the objectives of intercultural citizenship in mind.

In Chapter 11, I presented an analysis of the common ground in language teaching and education for citizenship under different 'orientations': evaluative, cognitive, comparative, communicative and action. We can now draw on this framework as a means of ensuring that the planning of teaching addresses all the objectives. The use of the framework can be exemplified from a project in Slovenia, where the option available was to work within the foreign language curriculum and to introduce into it some of the insights from *politische Bildung*.[79] In order to make the framework easy to use in planning, the lists for each orientation are abbreviated.

For each unit in a course of English for students from a range of disciplines, the framework was used to classify objectives that the teacher had already in mind as a language teacher. It then became evident where there were orientations and objectives that were not being given sufficient emphasis, and this led to modification of the plans for the units. It is not expected that every unit shall deal with every aspect of the framework, but rather that the framework shall be used to ensure that a whole syllabus includes the intercultural experience and education which is characterised above. As an example of how the framework relates to the specific plans for a unit of work, consider Table 13.1.

Table 13.1   A framework for Intercultural Citizenship with examples from the unit on media: 'Reading between the lines'

Cognitive orientation	Knowledge Contents	of social groups and their products and practices in one's own and in one's interlocutor's country; of the processes of societal and individual interaction.	students read about the role of language for human beings (article). view video spots on languages; read Whorf's and Sapir's claims on language and thought.
		knowledge of the present world; knowledge of the principles and values of human rights and democratic citizenship.	consider the importance of linguistic presentation in news.
Evaluative orientation	Attitudes Affective/moral attitude	curiosity and openness, readiness to suspend disbelief about other cultures and belief about one's own; respect for persons, acceptance of law and recognition of pluralism.	compare alternative presentations of events to official views and compare these with their own views; recognise and reflect on a biased presentation of a topic – in Slovene and English.
	Critical cultural awareness	ability to evaluate critically and on the basis of explicit criteria; adherence to values of freedom, equality and solidarity; valorisation of mutuality and trust.	make evaluative analysis of news articles and detect biased language.
Action orientation	Skills of discovery and interaction	elicit concepts and values; identify significant references and processes of interaction; use knowledge and skills in real time.	students search for information on the language rights of minorities (legislation in EU and Slovenia); students search for websites with alternative views.
	Practical-instrumental competences	take others' opinions seriously; co-operate and tolerate divergence; find compromise and group responsibility.	reflect on use of English as an international language and the implications.

Table 13.1 – *continued*

Comparative orientation	Skills of interpreting and relating	Identify ethnocentric perspectives, areas of misunderstanding; mediate between conflicting interpretations.	
Linguistic orientation	Linguistic competences	ability to apply knowledge of rules.	
	Sociolinguistic competences	ability to give meaning – taken for granted or negotiated.	
	Discourse competences	ability to discover and negotiate strategies for production and understanding of texts.	compare the linguistic tools used in both languages to present news, to give biased views.

In the example in Table 13.1, the teacher has used the 'political' topic of the language rights of minorities and linked it with a common theme in language teaching: the analysis of the media and linguistic bias. The knowledge orientation includes knowledge about the significance of language *per se*, and the importance of analysing the language of the media. The action orientation requires students to search for more information and a range of views on the question of minority language rights. The evaluative orientation then includes the process of comparing different views with their own.

This is a beginning, but the action orientation does not require students to actually engage with the issues outside the classroom, to become active in the pursuance of language minority rights for example, since some of them are members of linguistic minorities. In another project, however, students majoring in tourism studies focused on the topic of sustainable tourism and became engaged in developing an approach to the advertising of sustainable tourism in Slovenia, including writing advertising materials which could be used by their local tourist board.

The fourth level would be reached if Slovenian students were linked to students in other universities in other countries to deal with the question of sustainable tourism, such as students of tourism studies in Germany, from where many tourists to Slovenia come. Together the students would produce campaign materials that would promote sustainable tourism among German tour operators and not just in the materials produced within Slovenia.

The fifth level would mean students from two or more countries forming a group to lobby politicians or otherwise act on a problem of transnational significance.

For example, Slovenian students can act with Italian and Austrian students on language rights for minorities in the region by organising and holding a conference of young people from the minorities.

As yet these ideas have not been realised, but in the last two decades there has been much change in foreign language education towards ensuring that language teaching is for intercultural communicative competence. Perhaps in the next two decades, language teachers will begin to contribute to education for intercultural citizenship

Chapter 14

Assessment and/or Evaluation of Intercultural Competence and Intercultural Citizenship

It was the intention of the authors of the *Common European Framework of Reference* (Council of Europe, 2001) to include in its contents indicators of intercultural competence on one or more scales similar to the scales produced for linguistic competence. The wish to do this, and the failure to achieve it, are symptomatic of a process that is still taking place. The attempt is unlikely to be abandoned because of the demand for scaled quantified levels of competence in all aspects of education, as Hu has pointed out (Hu, in press). This demand from education authorities is integral to their most recent attempts to 'raise standards' by making standards more explicit. It is acknowledged by teachers or theorists, who have long recognised that 'what is not tested, is not taught', but the question remains both crucial and intractable.

'Assessment' and 'Evaluation'

The discussion of the issues at an international level makes some of the difficulties more apparent. At the Council of Europe where English and French are the official languages, the terminology presents some complications because of the 'false friends' of English/French translation familiar to generations of learners.

'Assessment' (Eng) is usually equated with '*évaluation*' (Fr) and this has had the effect in some quarters of 'evaluation' (Eng) being used where 'assessment' (Eng) might be expected. In French there is a further distinction, between '*évaluation*' and '*reconnaissance*', which puts emphasis on measurement and quantification (*évaluation*) in opposition to recognition (*reconnaissance*) of capacities, characteristics or competences that are not measured or quantified (or maybe not measurable or quantifiable). Instead, there is recognition and acknowledgement of competences through description and discussion in qualitative terms – through language, which uses words such as 'good', 'excellent', 'poor' (Zarate & Gohard-Radenkovic, 2004).

All of this may be treated merely as a linguistic curiosity arising from problems of translation, but it is not without importance when assessment is a matter of international concern, with international comparisons having an effect on national policies. The best case of this in recent times has been Germany, which found itself unexpectedly low in the international league table of results from a test of reading competence in adolescents – the so-called PISA-shock. Hu (in press) compares this to the Sputnik-shock in the USA in the 1950s and 1960s.

In order to maintain simplicity and clarity, from this point I will use only English terms, but give them some connotations and meanings thar draw on the international terminology.

In the *Shorter Oxford English Dictionary*, 'assessment' is associated only with taxation, 'the determination of the amount of taxation etc. to be paid' (Shorter Oxford, 1944), but in educational discourse it connotes any means of placing an individual's achievement on a scale. Scales are usually quantified: in percentage terms (England), on a scale of 1–20 (France), or of 1–6 (Germany) and so on in different ways in different countries. *The Shorter Oxford English Dictionary* defines the verb 'to evaluate' first, with mathematics in mind, as 'to work out the value of' and 'to find a numerical expression for' and second, in general use, as 'to reckon up, ascertain the amount of; to express in terms of the known'. Thus the notion of quantification is not absent from 'evaluation' any more than it is from 'assessment'. In educational discourse, however, it has often been given the particular meaning of a process of analysing whether a course of study is working successfully, meeting its own intentions, rather than the description of the success of individuals within the course of study. For my purposes here, I propose to use both 'assessment' and 'evaluation' to refer to individuals and in doing so I will discuss 'scaling'– i.e. placement of an individual's behaviour on a numerical scale and attaching value to that behaviour.

Attributing Value

My main point can be made in a preliminary way by referring to the five meanings of 'good' we find in the *Shorter Oxford English Dictionary*. The five are: 'a term of general or indefinite commendation'; 'morally excellent – of persons, of conduct'; 'agreeable, amusing, salutary, wholesome'; 'useful, reliable for a purpose, or efficient in a function, pursuit, creed etc.'; 'adequate, effectual, thorough'. There is here a distinction between effectiveness and efficiency and, on the other hand, morality. An effective and efficient intercultural competence may be based on a morality which would gain our 'commendation'; it may also be 'useful and reliable for a purpose' without winning our moral approbation. So, if we were to say that someone is assessed as having 'good' intercultural competence, gaining a high score on a universal scale, the statement is ambiguous. It is this ambiguity that must be addressed before time is spent on dealing with the technical matters of testing and other forms of assessment, which unfortunately often dominate the debate.

One approach to resolving this ambiguity is to establish, with Berlin, the limits of pluralism, as discussed in Chapter 10. Approbation is restricted to that behaviour which is 'within the pale' of humanity, of being and acting as a human being. This can then be linked with an explicit pluralism which, as defined under 'critical cultural awareness' and _'savoir s'engager'_, acknowledges the criteria and values underpinning any commendation, but especially any refusal to commend. If an intercultural action is assessed as not commendable because it flaunts the moral standards of the one who makes a judgement, then that person must make the criteria explicit and be willing to reflect critically upon them. Action in the world, as expected of the intercultural citizen, must be judged and commended or not, but only if the criteria are explicit and defensible. This is one position.

A pragmatic alternative that nonetheless derives from the same source is to consider the purposes of assessment. In this case, the particular forms of assessment are important, and this in turn means that technical feasibility has to be taken into account. From the general starting point of the 'purposes' of assessment, we can discuss first the 'desirability' of a particular process and focus of assessment and, as a second stage, the 'practicality' of what is deemed desirable.

Taking the model of the five _savoirs_ (see Appendix 1), it is intuitively desirable to assess an individual's knowledge (_savoirs_) whereas it might appear undesirable to assess his or her willingness to decentre and suspend (dis)belief (_savoir être_). The former is akin to the knowledge assessment that is well established and characteristic of most teaching and learning. It may be associated with approval for and commendation of the effort needed to acquire knowledge, but approval of this kind is unlikely to disturb. On the other hand, a 'poor' achievement which is attributed to 'lack of intelligence' rather than lack of effort will, in some education systems, be unacceptable as a mode of assessment because it reveals belief in an innate (lack of) competence, a belief which is considered ideological and hegemonic. Thus, even the assessment of _savoirs_ raises ethical questions.

Assessment of _savoir être_ is even more problematic. To assess a disposition, a willingness to act in an approved way, to be 'open', to be 'curious', can be interpreted as ideological, reflecting a particular set of values that is not necessarily shared by all social groups. In some countries it is not acceptable for people to be open to other cultures and beliefs. The imposition of openness as 'good' through a system of assessment that may allow or prevent access to a career or further education, would be hegemonic.

There is an alternative position. When assessment takes place within an education system – particularly during the years of compulsory education – it is simply part of the process of passing the values which are fundamental to the society from one generation to the next. This has always been one of the purposes of education – and of schooling in particular – as we have seen in earlier chapters. To deny this function of schooling is to court anarchy. The values of openness to others, of critical self-awareness and self-analysis, of action in the world which realises such values, are in this view crucial to the longevity of the group and to its harmonious and peaceful relationships with other comparable groups. Assessment of the acquisition of these values would in this scenario be acceptable, verifying whether an education system is being successful in its task.

The decision to use assessment in this way may not be a conscious one, but it is certainly political, in the sense that it pre-supposes a tacit consensus, a consensus that is constantly reinforced by political decisions and actions. In some education systems however, the decision-making is highly conscious, and carried out in the name of social cohesion. In circumstances where social cohesion is problematic due to the increasing heterogeneity of a society – a widespread phenomenon in the 21st century due not least to migration – the explicitness of the values is strong and the use of assessment to promote them is more acceptable. Assessment of both *savoirs* and *savoir être* can thus be deemed desirable.

Assessment of *savoir s'engager* raises similar questions, since the notion of critique of the values and assumptions of one's own social group – be they secular or religious – is not acceptable in every society or religion. And yet, assessment may be deemed desirable if the values of critical cultural awareness are in harmony with the values of the society being served by its education system.

Assessment of the skills of *savoir comprendre* and *savoir apprendre/faire* is likely to be less controversial, because they serve and are in a sense subordinate to *savoirs* and *savoir être*. They cannot, logically, operate if *savoir être* does not exist, although pragmatically it is possible that exercise of the skills will promote *savoir être* in a process of reciprocal influence.

In fact, there is no reason in principle to avoid assessment of all the *savoirs*, if there is political will and ethical honesty. In practice, I know of no education system which assesses *savoir être* or *savoir s'engager*, or which considers the practicalities of doing so. Reluctance might spring from fear of the responsibility of blocking access to opportunities through an examination system based on values of openness and critical self-awareness, which are not universally acknowledged as desirable by all social groups within a society and its education system. This may well be the case among religious sects which require obedience to specific beliefs and condemn self-analysis, self-critique and openness to alternative views from other religions or secular groups.

On the other hand, traditional examinations in the humanities and social sciences – including examinations in university studies of foreign literature – are implicitly founded on values of openness and critical analysis of values. This does not cause a problem in practice; first because the issues remain largely implicit, and second because people from religious or other groups with strict restrictions, are not drawn to such studies, and are not obliged to study at university level.

To illustrate, consider the following incident in the final examinations in English in a German university. The student was being examined by his professor in an oral discussion of events in Northern Ireland at a period when 'the Troubles' were severe and emotions were running high. The discussion became an argument in which, in the eyes of the professor, the student displayed deeply prejudiced attitudes towards Catholicism and the professor, in the eyes of the student, tried to impose an historical reading of the situation as an example of English colonialism.

The purpose of the discussion was to allow the professor to assess the student's competence. Linguistic competence was high, comparable to C2 on the *Common European Framework of Reference* scales. Intercultural competence, in the view of the professor, was very 'poor', because there was no evidence of openness or self-awareness (*savoir être* or *savoir s'engager*, to use my terms, although the incident took place before these were invented). If the professor had been required to assess both linguistic and intercultural competence, he would have given high and low marks, but the student might have objected that the professor demonstrated a lack of openness and was using his position and power to impose a particular view and block the student's access to a career by giving him a low mark. In other words, assessment involves both assessor and assessee in ways that would make such an examination invalid and unreliable. In the event, the student was given a high mark for the examination reflecting his linguistic competence.

If this kind of problem can arise in university studies where people choose to study, it would be all the more difficult to handle if assessment were introduced into compulsory schooling. The safeguards which would be needed can be envisaged: careful selection of topics, use of more than one examiner, examination of different aspects of intercultural competence in separate as well as holistic procedures, production of a profile of marks rather than a single summative assessment. This would be very costly but necessary in high-stakes examinations, and this is probably why little progress has been made in practice despite the demand from education authorities.

An example of such demand is described by Hu (in press) in her account of the PISA-shock in Germany. She too points out the major difficulties of using existing approaches to assessment of intercultural competence for the purposes of national assessment and international comparisons. Her focus is more on the technical than the moral problems but she comes to the conclusion that assessment for pedagogical purposes rather than setting standards is much more likely to be successful. In pedagogical assessment, whether a profile of feedback to a learner or a self-evaluation in the form of a portfolio, the focus is on diagnosis and planning of further learning.

A similar dilemma is described by the American Association of Teachers of German (Schulz et al., 2005) in their attempt to bring a more systematic and rigorous approach to the 'pursuit of cultural competence in the German Language classroom'. Schulz (2007) proposes a portfolio approach as does Hu (forthcoming) who refers to Byram's (1997) conclusion that self-assessment through a portfolio is the only feasible solution at the moment.

Portfolios and Profiles

In fact, portfolios have been developed and tested. The INCA portfolio is available online (INCAproject, 2004) and Catteuw (2007) and Kennedy and others (2007) have produced similar schemes, each with three levels of competence defined for several dimensions of intercultural competence. Each level has one or more descriptors and learners may use these to place themselves on the three-point scale. Alternatively, as Catteuw argues (2007) learners may engage in peer-assessment – asking their peers to access them – or in co-assessment, where learner and teacher discuss the assessment and agree on the scale point. The descriptors have, in all cases, been invented although the dimensions or sub-competences are derived from theory. The fact that there has been no empirical collection of data as a basis for descriptors means that they would not be sufficiently valid or reliable for high-stakes testing, but can well serve in assessment for pedagogical purposes.

A further development of the portfolio notion that links foreign language education more explicitly and systematically with education for citizenship is the documentation of 'Intercultural Encounters' developed at the Council of Europe. This too is based on theoretical definitions of several dimensions of intercultural competence, but there is no attempt or intention to define levels. The *'Autobiography of Intercultural Encounters'* is instead focused entirely on helping learners to analyse an encounter with otherness, which may be within their own society – perhaps through friendship with someone of another religion – or in experience of another society, perhaps through a family holiday. Users are invited to describe and analyse the encounter reflecting on their own experience and how they imagine the 'others' involved understood the experience (see Appendix 4). Such reflection requires some degree of maturity if the document is to be used without help and a version for younger children requires an adult to act as facilitator and interlocutor.

The autobiography refers to just one encounter but could be used as often as a user wishes and would thus build up a portfolio of accounts of encounters. Again, the pedagogical function is pre-eminent here, with potential for discussion and reflection with peers or teachers, whether the user is a child or an adult.

The *'Autobiography of Intercultural Encounters'* offers a number of questions to stimulate reflection, leaving it open to the user to decide if they wish to consider every question or only some. There is a sequence in the questioning developed from the theory and the final questions are crucial in making the autobiography a basis for the action orientation that is the essential characteristic of intercultural citizenship.

In the final section, there is first a group of questions developed from the concept of *savoir s'engager*, where judgement needs to be grounded in explicit and conscious criteria and philosophical standpoint:

9. THINKING BACK AND LOOKING FORWARD

If, when you look back, you draw conclusions about the experience, what are they?

Complete as many of these as you can ...

- I *liked* the experience for the following reasons ...

- I *disliked* the experience for the following reasons ...

- There were some things that I *approve of* and these are my reasons ...

- There were some things that I *disapprove of* and these are my reasons ...

- Try to imagine that you are telling someone you know well about all this. It could be your brother or sister for example. Do you think they would have the same opinions as you? Would they approve and disapprove of the same things for the same reasons?

- Try to think about why people you know well and who belong to the same group(s) as you (same family, same religion, same country, same region etc.) might have the same reactions and write down your explanation ...

Did the experience change you? How?

Did you decide to do something as a result of this experience? What did you do?

Will you decide to do something as a result of doing this Autobiography? If so what?

The pedagogical function is very evident and there is no intention to provide data for the setting of standards or other high-stakes procedures. The moral dimension is addressed by the focus entirely on self-analysis. No-one but the individual evaluates whether their response to an encounter was 'good' in any of the senses introduced above and, in some circumstances, the document could remain entirely confidential and not open to be read by a teacher or anyone else.

This is one approach to the dilemmas of 'assessment' and 'evaluation'. It remains to be seen if solutions to the problems of high-stakes testing can be found.

Conclusion

The word 'education' appears twice in the title of this book and also appeared in my first book on this topic in 1989: *Cultural Studies in Foreign Language Education* (Byram 1989a). This choice of terms encapsulates the purpose then and now: to locate the teaching of foreign (and other) languages within general pedagogy in the forms it takes in compulsory schooling. Perhaps it would have been more precise but also more clumsy, to use the phrase 'liberal education'. This would have made more explicit my argument that the teaching of foreign languages within compulsory schooling should not focus exclusively on the usefulness of being able to communicate (especially orally) in a foreign country. The phrase would also have tied the argument too much to a British tradition of liberal education when the argument can apply to other education systems each with its own tradition.[80]

The emphasis on a cultural studies dimension as an integral part of foreign language teaching (FLT) is the means of making teachers conscious of the opportunity to pursue education as originally conceived for a few, whilst presenting language learning as useful to the many. FLT is caught up in the tensions of obligatory, and therefore mass, education which affect all school subjects, but language teachers have been less aware of this than others, not least those other 'language teachers', the ones who teach national languages. The 'obvious' value of teaching a 'useful' subject like a foreign language in an internationalised and globalised world tends to push aside the value of (liberal) education.[81]

There are, of course, critiques of liberal education and its values as 'elitist', suggesting it is a means of maintaining the status quo and existing positions of power by creating a barrier for children and young people from disadvantaged circumstances. I have heard these critiques in the discourse of teachers and in debates about comprehensive education in Britain and other parts of Europe. They exist also in the educational literature, but this is not the place to analyse such debates, nor to present a historical exposition of liberal education or its equivalent in other countries – such as *Bildung* in Germany, or *dannelse* in Scandinavia. Nor is this the place to compare different traditions of education and values in different systems. What is important is the emphasis that FLT cannot and should not avoid the questions of education and values in any education system. Traditions and values differ, but it is everywhere important that teachers and others in FLT should think about educational value and not only instrumental use for languages.

The essays in this book are founded on this view. My purpose has been to consider policies, practices and research in foreign language teaching from a position of emphasising the significance of 'cultural studies' or 'the intercultural dimension' as the means through which educational values are analysed. In former times, this role was played by teaching literature and literary criticism, and it is not my intention to replace this, but to embrace it in a broader concept of intercultural competence. The advantage of intercultural competence over literary competence is that not only does it refer to other documents than the literary, but it also has an instrumental application in a self-evident way. It is easier for learners to understand that knowledge of and skills in interaction with the daily values, beliefs and behaviours of other people is useful in communication as well as valuable in stimulating reflection. Knowledge of literature and skills of literary criticism can also do this, but it is not immediately obvious that this is the case.

Another theme throughout this book has been the interplay between language learning, acquiring intercultural competence and identification with a nation state or an international entity such as the European Union. Language acquisition in early life, whether there is just one or more than one language involved, has a crucial role in identification with different social groups and in the process of socialisation. Learning a further language can have substantial effects on one's social identities, adding more or maybe altering those that already exist. Intercultural competence needs to be distinguished from being bicultural because it is not intended that learners acquiring intercultural competence should be affected in their identities. It is a potential for taking action, for mediating and reflecting the values, beliefs and behaviours of one language group to another – and the opportunity for reflexivity, i.e. to critically analyse one's own values, beliefs and behaviours.

In addition to repetition of the word 'education' in the title, this book also refers to a movement 'from' and 'to'. When, for many people but by no means all, experience of the contemporary world is a realisation of 'internationalisation' and 'globalisation', the utility value of FLT might seem greater than ever. Certainly, for learners in compulsory primary and secondary schooling – a phenomenon and privilege that are not universal, it must be remembered – the chances are that they notice the effects of a global market in their daily lives and can participate in international networks, both at home and in school. It might seem, then, that learning a foreign language is above all useful. It might seem that English as a lingua franca is a particularly useful 'tool' for communication, and one that is not attached to any specific country or culture.

It is the notion of taking action that links the concept of intercultural communicative competence with education for citizenship. My argument in the final chapters of this book is that, whatever learners might believe, it is the purpose of FLT and the duty of teachers, not only to combine utility and educational value, but also to show learners how they can and should engage with the international globalised world in which they participate. 'Citizenship' is a term that conveniently embodies the issues that arise: the need for self-aware judgement, the willingness to become engaged, the skills and knowledge which facilitate engagement. This is a move 'from' FLT within education 'to' FLT that brings a specific additional contribution to education for (democratic) citizenship. That contribution is captured in the term 'intercultural citizenship', a focus of citizenship education on the understanding and action involved when one is a member of an international society, especially of an international civil society. Here, again, there is inevitably a question of values of FLT, but there is also an extra dimension: engagement in action.

This is a new step, in my experience of foreign language teaching, and one that has not yet been taken by more than a few teachers. As a consequence, this final part of the book has few illustrations or practice. It is a proposal for an agenda, for 'things to be done'. It is avowedly a 'partisan' agenda, to quote Hobsbawm again from the Introduction. I hope that it does in a small way, 'advance science' as Hobsbawm requires, that it advances our understanding of language teaching in the contemporary world, and our planning for the future of foreign language teaching on the basis of that understanding.

Appendix 1

Intercultural Competence[81]

SKILLS
interpret and relate
(*savoir comprendre*)

KNOWLEDGE	EDUCATION	ATTITUDES
of self and other; of interaction: individual and societal (*savoirs*)	political education critical cultural awareness (*savoir s'engager*)	relativising self valuing other (*savoir être*)

SKILLS
discover and/or
interact
(*savoir apprendre/faire*)

Figure 1 Factors in intercultural communication

Attitudes:
curiosity and openness, readiness to suspend disbelief about other cultures and belief about one's own.

Objectives

- willingness to seek out or take up opportunities to engage with otherness in a relationship of equality; this should be distinguished from attitudes of seeking out the exotic or of seeking to profit from others;
- interest in discovering other perspectives on interpretation of familiar and unfamiliar phenomena both in one's own and in other cultures and cultural practices;
- willingness to question the values and presuppositions in cultural practices and products in one's own environment;
- readiness to experience the different stages of adaptation to and interaction with another culture during a period of residence;
- readiness to engage with the conventions and rites of verbal and non-verbal communication and interaction;

What I have in mind here is the kind of learner many teachers will have noticed when they take a group to another country. It is the curiosity and wonder expressed in constant questions and wide-eyed observations, in the willingness to try anything new rather than cling to the familiar. In the classroom, these attitudes are sometimes evident in the willingness to improvise in using the language, or in the question at the end of a lesson about something noticed in a textbook, or in the learner who talks about what they have heard from relatives about another country. Among university students spending a period of residence in another country, there are those who become fully engaged with their environment rather then live almost encapsulated in the links with home. Often such learners are not the ones most successful in academic work, in the acquisition of linguistic accuracy in the classroom, for example.

I also want to distinguish this kind of engagement with otherness from the tourist approach, where the interest is in collecting experiences of the exotic, and from the commercial approach where the interest is in a business arrangement and the making of a profit. Both of these have a rightful place in international relations, but they are not conducive to developing intercultural competence.

Knowledge:
of social groups and their products and practices in one's own and in one's interlocutor's country, and of the general processes of societal and individual interaction.

Objectives (knowledge about/of)

- historical and contemporary relationships between one's own and one's interlocutor's countries;
- the means of achieving contact with interlocutors from another country (at a distance or in proximity), of travel to and from and the institutions that facilitate contact or help resolve problems;
- the types of cause and process of misunderstanding between interlocutors of different cultural origins;
- the national memory of one's own country and how its events are related to and seen from the perspective of one's interlocutor's country;
- the national memory of one's interlocutor's country and the perspective on it from one's own;
- the national definitions of geographical space in one's own country and how these are perceived from the perspective of other countries;
- the national definitions of geographical space in one's interlocutor's country and the perspective on them from one's own;
- the processes and institutions of socialisation in one's own and one's interlocutor's country;
- social distinctions and their principal markers, in one's own country and one's interlocutor's;
- institutions, and perceptions of them, which impinge on daily life within one's own and one's interlocutor's country and which conduct and influence relationships between them
- the processes of social interaction in one's interlocutor's country;

Much of the knowledge involved here is relational, e.g. how the inhabitants of one country perceive another country and what effect that has upon the interaction between individuals. It is also related to socialisation, since perceptions of others are acquired in socialisation. In learning the history of one's own country, for example, one is presented with images of another; in learning about the geography of one's own country, the boundaries with other countries are the defining characteristics. As an example, an English learner of French inevitably meets at some point the two versions of the story – rather than the history – of Joan of Arc. The French collective, national memory of this story is different from the English, and the historical relationships between the two countries encapsulated in the difference form the kind of knowledge envisaged here. There are doubtless similar examples in every country.

There is also a more theoretical kind of knowledge. Behind the example just mentioned, is the socialisation process itself, and an intercultural speaker needs to understand how this creates different perceptions, rather than having to acquire knowledge of all specific instances and examples. Awareness that one is a product of one's own socialisation is a pre-condition for understanding one's reactions to otherness. Similarly, awareness of how one's 'natural' ways of interacting with other people are the 'naturalised' product of socialisation, and how parallel but different modes of interaction can be expected in other cultures, is part of the knowledge an intercultural speaker needs.

Skills of interpreting and relating:
ability to interpret a document or event from another culture, to explain it and relate it to documents from one's own.

Objectives (ability to)

- identify ethnocentric perspectives in a document or event and explain their origins;
- identify areas of misunderstanding and dysfunction in an interaction and explain them in terms of each of the cultural systems present;
- mediate between conflicting interpretations of phenomena.

Documents depicting another culture – television reports, tourist brochures, autobiographical travellers' tales, or even language learning textbooks – may honestly claim to give an 'impartial' or 'objective' account. Knowledge about the ways in which ethnocentric perspectives are acquired in socialisation is the basis for developing the skills of 'reading' such documents, and identifying the sometimes insidious and unconscious effects of ethnocentrism. Similarly, an intercultural speaker will notice how two people are misunderstanding each other because of their ethnocentrism, however linguistically competent they might be, and is able to identify and explain the pre-suppositions in a statement in order to reduce the dysfunction they cause.

Skills of discovery and interaction:
ability to acquire new knowledge of a culture and cultural practices and the ability to operate knowledge, attitudes and skills under the constraints of real-time communication and interaction.

Objectives (ability to):

- elicit from an interlocutor the concepts and values of documents or events and to develop an explanatory system susceptible of application to other phenomena;

- identify significant references within and across cultures and elicit their significance and connotations;
- identify similar and dissimilar processes of interaction, verbal and non-verbal, and negotiate an appropriate use of them in specific circumstances;
- use in real-time an appropriate combination of knowledge, skills and attitudes to interact with interlocutors from a different country and culture, taking into consideration the degree of one's existing familiarity with the country and culture and the extent of difference between one's own and the other;
- identify contemporary and past relationships between one's own and the other culture and country;
- identify and make use of public and private institutions that facilitate contact with other countries and cultures;
- use in real-time knowledge, skills and attitudes for mediation between interlocutors of one's own and a foreign culture.

These are the skills that enable some people quickly to establish an understanding of a new cultural environment and the ability to interact in increasingly rich and complex ways with people whose culture is unfamiliar to them. They are able to draw upon whatever knowledge they have, but above all they have the skills of the ethnographer entering into a new 'field' of study, whether in a remote community, in a street corner gang or in the staff room of a school. The foreign correspondent of newspaper or television is another example of someone who develops such skills, quickly discovering the streams of thought, power, influence underlying the events that they are to report. The intercultural speaker has different purposes from the ethnographer and the correspondent, but operates similar skills under similar constraints of time and place.

Critical cultural awareness/political education:
an ability to evaluate critically and on the basis of explicit criteria perspectives, practices and products in one's own and other cultures and countries.

Objectives (ability to)

- identify and interpret explicit or implicit values in documents and events in one's own and other cultures;
- make an evaluative analysis of the documents and events that refers to an explicit perspective and criteria;
- interact and mediate in intercultural exchanges in accordance with explicit criteria, negotiating where necessary a degree of acceptance of them by drawing upon one's knowledge, skills and attitudes.

The important point here is that the intercultural speaker brings to the experiences of their own and other cultures a rational and explicit standpoint from which to evaluate. Teachers are familiar with learners of all ages who condemn some particular custom in another country as 'barbaric'. They have no rationale other than that of the original meaning of 'barbaric', i.e. that it is different and from beyond the limits of our 'civilised' society. Although the teacher may not wish to interfere in the views of their learners, for ethical reasons, they can encourage them to make the basis for their judgements explicit, and expect them to be consistent in their judgements of their own society as well as others.

Appendix 2

Sources for Teacher Training for Intercultural Competence

Consider the elements of intercultural competence, the five *'savoirs'* (Appendix 1) and the disciplines which they rely on, with some texts which might be useful in teacher training.[83] The specific chapters identified might be used in courses where teachers are to read original texts for themselves:

Savoir être:
curiosity and openness, readiness to suspend disbelief about other cultures and belief about one's own.

Attitudes to other countries and people are formed early, and the work of social psychology is important here. Fortunately, in Europe at least, there has been substantial work by Barrett and colleagues in recent years which makes theory and empirical findings available for language teachers.

Text:

- Barrett (2007) *Children's Knowledge, Beliefs and Feelings about Nations and National Groups.* Chapter 4: Children's knowledge, beliefs and feelings about nations and states construed as historical and cultural communities; Chapter 6: The development of children's subjective identifications with their own nation and state.

The formation of attitudes is part of the broader process of socialisation into a national identity, among others, and the creation and maintenance of groups and their boundaries is fundamental to socialisation.

Texts:

- Tajfel (1981) *Human Groups and Social Categories: Studies in Social Psychology.* Chapter 13: The achievement of group differentiation.
- Barth (1969) *Ethnic Groups and Boundaries.* Introduction.

Because attitudes are not only formed early but are subject to many influences in a society (not least the historical relationships of a society with other countries and peoples), the teacher needs to understand if and how attitudes can be changed 'Prejudice' and 'stereotype' are crucial concepts discussed in social psychology since Allport (1954).

Texts:

- Allport (1954) *The Nature of Prejudice.* Chapter 1: What is the problem; Chapter 2: The normality of prejudgement; Chapter 17: Conforming.

- Stangor & Scaller (1996) Stereotypes as individual and collective representations.
- Eberhardt & Fiske (1996) Motivating individuals to change: what is a target to do?

Savoir comprendre:

ability to interpret a document or event from another culture, to explain it and relate it to documents or events from one's own.

A comparative understanding of texts of all levels in other countries refers to the importance of learning how texts that may appear similar have different functions and hence different meanings. At the same time, texts differ in structure and rhetorical impact. Cultural studies form an interdisciplinary area of study that pursues the hermeneutics of texts and contexts. Discourse and conversation analysis focus on close textual analysis and are important in the relationship of language learning and learning intercultural competence.

Texts:

- Kramsch (1993) *Context and Culture in Language Teaching*. Chapter 7: Teaching language along the fault line.
- Kramsch (2003) From practice to theory and back again.

Savoirs:

knowledge of social groups and their products and practices in one's own and in one's interlocutor's country, and of the general processes of societal and individual interaction.

If learners are to acquire a body of knowledge about, say, Germany, then teacher trainers need to be familiar with the debate about the nature of knowledge about beliefs, values and behaviours, in particular the question of boundary-marking phenomena. There are many possibilities here, and teachers of German will have their own favourites, but the following text is particularly interesting.

Text:

- Sommer (2004) *Leben in Deutschland*.

A second kind of knowledge, about the nature of personal interaction, will be drawn from sociology, notably from the analysis of personal interaction and the influence of linguistic and social norms.

Texts:

- Goffman (1963) *Behavior in Public Places*. Chapter 6: Face engagements.
- Goffman (1969) *The Presentation of Self in Everyday Life*. Chapter 1: Performances.

Savoir apprendre/Savoir faire:

ability to acquire new knowledge of a culture and cultural practices and the ability to operate knowledge, attitudes and skills under the constraints of real-time communication and interaction.

The ability to investigate a new environment, whether a localised and restricted environment such as a small village or a school, or a large-scale entity such as a national group, is pre-eminently represented in the work of ethnographers. Examples of the working methods can be found in some ethnographic descriptions of communities, large and small, and there are collections of accounts of methods used.

Texts:
- Agar (1980) *The Professional Stranger An Informal Introduction to Ethnography.* Chapter 4: Ethnography.
- Spradley (1979) *The Ethnographic Interview.* Chapter 2: Language and fieldwork; Chapter 3: Informants.
- Burgess (1984) *The Research Process in Educational Settings: Ten Case Studies.* Chapter 2: The researcher exposed: A natural history (Hammersley).

The application to language learning has been investigated for advanced learners but also experimented with for young learners with less language competence.

Texts:
- Roberts *et al.* (2001) *Language Learners as Ethnographers* Part II: The Ealing ethnography project.
- Snow & Byram (1997) *Crossing Frontiers: The School Study Visit Abroad.*

When learners have the opportunity for a period of residence – whether study or work or tourism – immersion in a new environment can be very demanding. The field of study here can be encapsulated in the notion of 'culture shock', and there has been a recent focus on the experience of students and how to investigate and profit from residence.

Texts:
- Ward *et al.* (2001) *The Psychology of Culture Shock.* Chapter 2 Intercultural contact: processes and outcomes.
- Byram & Feng (2006) *Living and Studying Abroad.* Chapter 3: Recording the journey: diaries of Irish students in Japan (Pearson-Evans) and Chapter 4: The one less travelled by... The experience of Chinese students in a UK university (Burnett and Gardner).

Savoir s'engager:
ability to evaluate critically and on the basis of explicit criteria perspectives, practices and products in one's own and other cultures and countries.

This, the most educationally significant of the *savoirs*, takes us into the relationship of language teaching and learning with the general purposes of an education system. It thus opens up the questions of educational philosophy and traditions that differ from one country to the next. Within a European tradition, all education but especially higher education, encourages learners to question constantly the learning they are offered and the society in which they live. In its broadest and fullest sense this is political education / politische Bildung or 'education for democracy'.

Texts:
- Barnett (1997): *Higher Education: A Critical Business.* Chapter 1: Conditions of critical thinking; Chapter 6: Critical action.

- Himmelmann (2001): *Demokratie Lernen als Lebens-, Gesellschafts- und Herrschafts- form. Ein Lehr- und Studienbuch.* Chapter 1: Einleitung: politische Bildung – das Identitätsproblem.

Political education and education for democracy have also been discussed with particular reference to language learning:

- Guilherme (2002) *Critical Citizens for an Intercultural World. Foreign Language Education as Cultural Politics.* Chapter 3 The critical dimension in foreign culture education.
- Byram (this volume) Chapter 10: Language education, political education and intercultural citizenship.

Appendix 3

Framework for Intercultural Citizenship

Cognitive orientation		Evaluative orientation	
Language education: Knowledge	*Political education: Contents*	*Language education: Attitudes*	*Political education: Affective/moral attitude*
historical and contemporary relationships between one's own and one's interlocutor's cultures; the national memory of one's own country and how its events are related to and seen from the perspective of other cultures; the national memory of one's interlocutor's country and the perspective on it from one's own culture; Institutions, and perceptions of them that impinge on daily life within one's own and one's interlocutor's culture and conduct and influence relationships between them.	*Lifeworld* lifeworld ... responsibility ... family; tasks [...] of schooling; living in the community; other cultures. *Society* pluralism; civil society; public life; social inequality. *Democracy* basic values ... creation of representative political will; the law in everyday life. *Globalisation* all topics.	Willingness to seek out or take up opportunities to engage with otherness in a relation of equality ... Interest in discovering other perspectives on interpretation of familiar and unfamiliar phenomena both in one's own and in other cultures and cultural practices. Willingness to question the values and presuppositions in cultural practices and products in one's own environment. *Language education: Critical cultural awareness* (2) Respect for the value, the dignity and the freedom of every individual person. (3) Acceptance of the rule of law, search for justice, recognition of equality and equal treatment in a world full of differences. (6) Recognition of pluralism in life and in society, respect for foreign cultures and their contribution to human development.	(b) Make an evaluative analysis of the documents and events that refers to an explicit perspective and criteria. (c) Interact and mediate in intercultural exchanges in accordance with explicit criteria, negotiating where necessary a degree of acceptance of those exchanges by drawing upon one's knowledge, skills and attitudes. 7. Valorisation of mutuality, co-operation, trust and solidarity and the struggle against racism, prejudices and discrimination.

Comparative orientation	Action orientation		Communicative orientation
Language education: Skills of interpreting and relating	*Language education: Skills of discovery and interaction*	*Political education: Practical – instrumental competences*	*(Foreign) language education:*
a) Identify ethnocentric perspectives in a document or event and explain their origins. (b) identify areas of misunderstanding and dysfunction in an interaction and explain them in terms of each of the cultural systems present. (c) Mediate between conflicting interpretations of phenomena.	(a) Elicit from an interlocutor the concepts and values of documents or events and develop an explanatory system susceptible of application to other phenomena. (b) Identify significant references within and across cultures and elicit their significance and connotations. (c) Identify similar and dissimilar processes of interaction, verbal and non-verbal, and negotiate an appropriate use of them in specific circumstances. (d) Use in real-time an appropriate combination of knowledge, skills and attitudes to interact with interlocutors from a different culture[84] taking into consideration the degree of one's existing familiarity with the culture (and where appropriate language) and the extent of difference between one's own and the other.	(1) grasp and take seriously the opinions and arguments of others, accord personal recognition to people of other opinions, put oneself in the situation of others, accept criticism, listen. (2) make one's own opinions (needs, interests, feelings, values) clear, speak coherently, give clear and transparent reasons. (5) organise group work, co-operate in the distribution of work, accept tasks, demonstrate trustworthiness, tenacity, care and conscientiousness. (6) tolerate variety, divergence, difference, recognise conflicts, find harmony where possible, regulate issues in socially acceptable fashion, accept mistakes and differences (7) find compromises, seek consensus, accept majority decisions, tolerate minorities, promote encouragement, weigh rights and responsibilities, and show trust and courage. (8) emphasise group responsibility, develop fair norms and common interests and needs, promote common approaches to tasks.	(a) linguistic competence; (b) sociolinguistic competence; (c) discourse competence.

Autobiography of
Intercultural Encounters[85]

COUNCIL OF EUROPE   CONSEIL DE L'EUROPE

What is the Autobiography of Intercultural Encounters?

This autobiography has been designed to help you analyse a specific inter-cultural encounter that you have experienced. You do this by answering a sequence of questions about various aspects of that encounter.

An intercultural encounter can be an experience you had with someone from a different country, and it can also be an experience with someone from another cultural background in your own country. It might be, for example, someone you met from another region, someone who speaks a different language, someone from a different religion or from a different ethnic group.

This focus is on **ONE** event or experience that you have had with someone different from yourself. For example, avoid talking in general terms about a holiday that you have had, and instead choose just one specific encounter or meeting that you have had with a particular person from another country or culture.

The event could be a visit to that person's house. It could be a meeting with someone from a foreign country or another region of your own country. It could be something that happened whilst on a trip abroad, and so on. Here are some examples from other people:

- For the first time I met a foreigner in Turkey. My mother and I talked to him because we got lost in the town.

- This January I went for a holiday to Egypt. There I got acquainted with a local girl of 11. We met on the beach and first communicated with the help of gestures. I learned that her parents worked at the hotel where my family was staying.

- I went to stay at my friend's house. His parents came to this country from Japan but he was born here.

Choose an experience that was important for you (one that made you think, that surprised you, one that you enjoyed, or difficult etc.) *and give the experience a name or title*, e.g. 'A South African visitor', 'My Greek experience', 'My first conversation in a foreign language' or 'Staying with a Japanese friend'.

This autobiography helps you to think about the experience by asking you questions about it. Try to answer the questions as honestly as possible. It does not matter if the experience is positive or negative. All experiences are important.

****

Name . . . .

Date of birth . . . .

Male/Female . . . .

Country . . . .

Region of country where you live . . . .

Religion . . . .

Languages I speak . . . .

Encounter number . . . . **Today's date:** . . . .

1. THE ENCOUNTER

Title
Give the encounter a name that says something about it.

Description
What happened when you met this person/these people?

Location
Where did it happen? What were you doing there?

Was it ... (please tick one or more)

- study?
- leisure?
- on holiday?
- at work?
- at school?
- other?

Importance
Why have you chosen this experience?

- It made me think about something I had not thought about before.
- It was the first time I had had this kind of experience.
- It was the most recent experience of that kind.

Was it because ...? (please tick one or more)

- It surprised me.
- It disappointed me.
- It pleased me.
- It angered me.
- It changed me.

Add any other reactions in your own words, and say what you think caused your reaction.

2. THE OTHER PERSON OR PEOPLE

Who else was involved?

- Give the name of the person or people if you know it ...
- Write something about them ...

What was the first thing you noticed about them?
What did they look like?
What clothes were they wearing?

Were they were male/female? Older/younger than you? Did they belong to a different nationality or religion or region? Is there any other thing you think is important about them?

****

3. YOUR FEELINGS

Describe how you felt <u>at the time</u> by completing these sentences:

- My feelings or emotions at the time were ...
- My thoughts at the time were ...
- What I did at the time was ... (for example did you pretend you had not noticed something that was strange? Did you change the subject of the conversation that had become embarrassing? Did you ask questions about what you found strange?) ...

****

4. THE OTHER PERSON'S FEELINGS

Imagine yourself in the other person's position.

How do you think the other person felt in the situation at the time? This can be difficult, but try to imagine what s/he felt at the time. Happy or upset/stressed, or what? How did you know?

What do you think the other person was thinking when all this happened? Do you think they found it strange, or interesting, or what?

Choose one or more of the following, or add your own and say why you have chosen it:

- For them it was an everyday experience/an unusual experience/a surprising experience/a shocking experience/because ...

Choose one or more of the options below and complete the sentence or add your own ideas ...

- The other people involved in the experience appeared to have the following feelings – surprise/shock/delight/no special feelings/...
- I noticed this because of what they did/said and/or how they looked, for example they ... (say what you noticed) ...
- I am not sure because they seemed to hide their feelings.

5. SAME AND DIFFERENT

Are there *similarities* between the ways you saw the situation and they way they saw it?

- Looking back, if I now compare my ways of seeing it with the other people's/ person's, I can see the following *similarities* ...

- When I talk with them about it, we find there are some *things similar,* for example (please write in the space below *as many things that are similar* as you can) ...

- When I talk with them about it, we find we have the *same opinions,* for example (please write in the space below as many things you *agree about and have the same opinions on* as you can):

Are there *differences* between the ways you saw the situation and they way they saw it?

- Looking back, if I now compare my ways of seeing the situation with other people's, I can see the following *differences* ...

- When I talk with them about it, we find there are some things different, for example (please write in the space below as many *things that are different* as you can)...

- When I talk with the other people about it, this is how we disagree about it ...

- When I talk with them about it, we have some opinions that are different, for example (please write in the space below as many things you *disagree about and have different opinions on* as you can):

How do you see your own thoughts and feelings now?

Choose <u>one or more</u> of the following and complete the sentence OR <u>invent your own</u>:

- The way I acted in the experience was appropriate because what I did was ...

- I think I could have acted differently by doing the following ...

- I think the best reaction from me would have been ...

- My reaction was good because ...

- I hid my emotions by ...

****

6. TALKING TO EACH OTHER

When you think about how you spoke to or communicated with the other people, do you remember that you made adjustments in how you talked or wrote to them?

First thoughts ...

Further ideas – for example:

- I was talking to them in my own language and I noticed I needed to make adjustments to help them understand me, for example ...

- I wasn't speaking in my own language and I had to make adjustments to make myself understood – to simplify/explain using gestures, by explaining a word, by ...

- I noticed things about how they spoke – that they simplified, that they used gestures, that they spoke more slowly ...

When you think about how you communicated, do you think you already had some knowledge or previous experience that helped you to do this better?

First thoughts ...

Further ideas – for example:

- I already knew things about how people communicate and behave in other groups that helped me to understand the experience and communicate better – I knew for example that ...

- I knew that other people involved in the experience thought and acted differently because of what they had learnt as children, for example ...

****

7. FINDING OUT MORE

There may have been things in the experience that puzzled you, and you tried to find out more at the time. If you did so, how did you do it?

If you have found out an answer since, how did you do it?

For example:

- There were things I did not understand, so I tried to find out by asking questions at the time/ reading about it / looking on the Internet / asking questions ...

- I used the following sources for information ...

- When finding new information I noticed the following similarities and differences with things I know from my own society ...

- The following things still puzzle me ...

8. USING COMPARISONS TO UNDERSTAND

People often compare things in other groups or cultures with similar things in their own. Did you do this? Did it help you to understand what was happening?

For example:

- The experience involved some things that were similar to what I know in my own group and these are the things I noticed ...
- There were some things that were different from my own group ...

****

9. THINKING BACK AND LOOKING FORWARD

If, when you look back, you draw conclusions about the experience, what are they?

Complete as many of these as you can ...

- I *liked* the experience for the following reasons ...

- I *disliked* the experience for the following reasons ...

- There were some things that *I approve of* and these are my reasons ...

- There were some things that *I disapprove of* and these are my reasons ...

- Try to imagine that you are telling someone you know well about all this. It could be your brother or sister for example. Do you think they would have the same opinions as you? Would they approve and disapprove of the same things for the same reasons?

- Try to think about why people you know well and who belong to the same group(s) as you (same family, same religion, same country, same region etc.) might have the same reactions and write your explanation here:

Did the experience change you? How?

Did you decide to do something as a result of this experience? What did you do?

Will you decide to do something as a result of doing this Autobiography? If so what?

****

Notes

1. For more than 20 years I witnessed this enthusiasm at first hand as a teacher trainer, and it constantly renewed my own enthusiasm – a privilege that is not available to everyone in teaching.

2. The evolution of the South American trade block of Mercosur (comprising Argentina, Brazil, Paraguay and Uruguay) may be similar. It is significant that identity cards refer to Mercosur as well as to the country of the holder.

3. On the other hand, in times of crisis, another perspective can be taken, as in this quotation from a report on language teaching in Britain after World War I:

   The war has made this people conscious of its ignorance of foreign countries and their peoples [...] The masses and the classes alike were ignorant to the point of public danger. Ignorance of the mental attitude and aspirations of the German people may not have been the cause of the war; it certainly prevented due preparation and hampered our efforts after the war had begun; it still darkens our counsels. Similar ignorance of France, greater ignorance of Italy, abysmal ignorance of Russia, have impeded the effective prosecution of the war, and will impede friendly and co-operative action after the war is over. [...] In this field Modern Studies are not a mere source of profit, not only a means of obtaining knowledge, nor an instrument of culture; they are a national necessity. (Leathes Report, 1918: 32)

   But such sentiments and arguments do not last and in Britain, the Leathes Report had no significant impact on how language teaching was considered (for further discussion of the report see Hawkins (1981: 147ff).

   Two generations later, a similar sentiment could be found in the USA as the government sought to pursue its 'war on terror' and link language learning to national security, as we shall see below.

4. For example, in France the recent decree establishing a *'socle commun'* (common base) of essential skills and knowledge as the crucial purpose of schooling refers to the law which states that *'la nation fixe comme mission première à l'école de faire partager aux élèves les valeurs de la République'* ['the nation determines the first purpose of the school to be that it should make pupils share the values of the Republic'] and thus the new *'socle commun'* is *'le ciment de la nation: il s'agit d'un ensemble de valeurs, de savoirs, de langues et de pratiques dont l'acquisition repose sur la mobilisation de l'école et qui suppose, de la part des élèves, des efforts et de la persévérance'* [the cement of the nation: a collection of values, knowledge, languages and practices, the acquisition of which depends on the activities of the school and assumes effort and perseverance on the part of pupils] (*Décret n° 2006-830 du 11 juillet 2006 relatif au socle commun de connaissances et de compétences et modifiant le code de l'éducation* [Decree on the common base of knowledge and competences and modifting the code of education]).

5. See note 2 above.

6. A more restricted comparison is available for English in European countries (Bonnet, 2002).

7. An experiment at the University of Lleida in Catalonia, Spain, which encourages teachers to combine the teaching of English, Catalan and Castilian is an exception which, symptomatically, teachers and others in the education system find challenging.

8. Writing in the same tradition, a century later, Gadamer says the acquisition of foreign languages and conceptual words is, like the process of our earliest cultural initiation, part of the process of *Bildung* (quoted in Standish 2002: iii).

9. It is also worth noting that there have been moments when foreign language teaching was used in very nationalist ways. In 1925 a high civil servant of the Prussian Ministry of Education (*Ministerialrat*) used the curriculum documents and guidelines which determined what was required in school to insist that *'Nationalerziehung'* (national education), *'Erziehung zum Gemeinsinn'* (education towards a common way of thinking) and *'staatsbürgerliche Erziehung'* (citizenship education) should be pursued with young people in Germany. This was to be done by *'kulturkundlicher Unterricht'* (cultural knowledge lessons) which included the teaching of English (Schreiner, 2007).

10. Here it is notable that a migration background means that pupils tend to do less well in learning German which is deemed to be an L1 – even if in practice it is not – and on the other hand they do better when learning a foreign language (L2), English.

11. This is a 'convenience sample' based on my work in Norway for the Council of Europe (see *Language Education Policy Profile: Norway* http://www.coe.int / lang; accessed 30.09.07) and a period as a Visiting Professor at Tokyo Gakugei University. Since I can read Norwegian but not Japanese I have translated some Norwegian documents but have to rely on published translations for Japanese documents.

    I am grateful to Ms Jorunn Berntzen of the Norwegian Ministry of Education and Professor Lynne Parmenter of Waseda University in Japan, for their help.

    The quotations are from websites and policy documents at a given point in time and will doubtless change by the time of publication, but this does not change the argument I present here.

12. The curriculum documents in Japan do nonetheless refer to 'deepening understanding of language and culture' as one of the aims, albeit without further specification.

13. There is, however, little evidence in practice that this hope of Norwegians learning several more languages is realised.

14. More recently, in East Asia, comparisons have been made on the basis of TOEFL tests and the percentage of the population achieving success in these. However such comparisons are bedevilled by a lack of compatibility between the samples, since a higher proportion of students in Japan take the test than in Korea, for example. This means that a simple comparison of percentages of successful test-takers is not valid (Oka, 2003; Koike, 2004).

There has also been a recent comparison among European countries focused on the learning of English (Bonnet, 2002).

15. These proposals show an increase but in response to an EU report on language teaching in Europe, the Norwegian ministry points out (http://www.regjer ingen.no/en/dep/kd.html?id=586; accessed 2.05) that the amount of time spent on languages in lower secondary is among the lowest in Europe, although the time spent in primary/elementary school in Norway puts it in a middle position. They point out that in most countries, the earlier the start, the larger the total number of hours spent, whereas Norway (and Austria) differs from this trend, starting early but having a low total.

16. My anonymous reviewer suggests that the presence of the Internet means that Japan has a 'for free' input, and that the number of loanwords might be an index of Anglicisation. Loanwords have always been an index of how fashionable a language might be at a given time – the presence of loan words in German from the 17th century is an example – but I doubt if this indicates a competence in a foreign language.

17. In Norway, too, there is still dissatisfaction with the competence of students in written English, which is said to be too low when they arrive in higher education and need to read and write in English to study other subjects, but this is not given as much public attention as in Japan (Norway: Country Report www.coe.int/lang; accessed 29.2.08).

18. Himeta (2006) points out that a distinction is made in French between '*acteur social*' and '*agent social*' which is lost in the English translation of both as 'social agent'. The active agency of '*acteur social*' is distinguished from the greater emphasis on the constraints under which a 'social agent' acts. At a later date, as Himeta points out, Zarate (2003a) argues that the learner is envisaged in the CEFR as limited in agency, and yet such agency is fundamental to the notion of an intercultural speaker.

19. For a more detailed explanation of socialisation, see Chapter 8.

20. Being bicultural as described here is also only emblematic for people who, in the highly complex societies of multicultural cities, have more complex identifications with more then two ethnic groups, but the issues remain *mutatis mutandis* similar. Since my purpose is to contrast bicultural with intercultural, a focus on people with allegiance to two cultures will suffice here.

21. Personal communication: Yoko Arashi.

22. Risager (2006, 2007) (and others more informally) have challenged this assumption. There are difficulties with the concept of a national culture, and Risager suggests that the sense of belonging to a national network is probably very tenuous, although Billig's (1995) work shows how strongly national identity can be maintained in an unconscious way. Whatever the conclusion on this matter, national identities are perceived as linked to if not created by national language and traditions of teaching have made this assumption. Teachers thus feel most comfortable with the notion of national culture – even if they have to be wary of national stereotypes – and as long as it is treated as a starting point that is later problematised, knowledge about a national culture is an appropriate means to an end. All pedagogy needs simplification, followed by refinement and complexity.

23. This account is based on the assumption that there is no major disjuncture between primary and secondary socialisation, i.e. that the basic values are common to both, as is typically the case in a homogeneous society. In most societies this is a simplification since there is often a significant difference between the world of primary socialisation in the family and the world of school where much of secondary socialisation takes place. Most classes include learners who are, or are becoming, bicultural. Foreign language learning could therefore be yet another world with new values and it is an interesting question whether children who have already bridged one socio-cultural gap are more or less likely to find the second one easier to deal with. This would however complicate the argument here too much and I consider the simplification necessary for the purposes of the argument.

24. This chapter is based on an article written together with Peter Doyé, Technische Universität Braunschweig, Germany, to whom I am deeply grateful for many years of collaboration and friendship (Byram & Doyé, 1999).

25. In anglophone countries, the phenomenon is similar, but here the language is increasingly Mandarin Chinese, as shown in newspaper reports of American families employing Mandarin speaking *au pairs* or English private schools introducing Mandarin Chinese as a first foreign language.

26. The meaning of 'primary education' differs from country to country with respect to the starting and finishing ages of children and the educational philosophy, but for my purposes here, it can be used generically to refer to the education of children from about age 5–6 to about age 10–11.

27. This process might be guided by the use of the *Autobiography of Key Intercultural Encounters* (see Chapter 14), which helps children in interaction with teachers or others to identify and reflect on an experience of an encounter with otherness in some form (Council of Europe, in press).

28. This chapter is based on a survey article by Anwei Feng and myself in *Language Teaching* (Byram & Feng, 2004). I am grateful to Anwei for his co-operation in this and many other aspects of our work.

29. There is a useful distinction in German between '*ein Ist-Zustand*' and '*ein Soll-Zustand*'.

30. Examples from students I have supervised include: using video and cinema clips with students of English in a Hong Kong university (Marshall Yin); introducing moral dilemmas and discussions with students of English in a Japanese university (Stephanie Houghton); using process drama to create experience of otherness among school pupils in Taiwan and Korea (Yoon Jeong Choi, Chih-Hui Lai, Irene Chen); combining teaching English as an international language with the educational purposes of intercultural competence in Taiwan (Jessie Hsieh); using poetry with Portuguese learners of English (Ana Matos) and so on. Some of these are described at http://millennium.arts.kuleu ven.ac.be/cultnet (accessed 29.2.08).

31. In Japan, the possible generic term '*gengo kyoushi*' ('language teacher') is not used, and the term '*gaikokugo kyoushi*' ('foreign language teacher') is used only sometimes in schools since in practice the only foreign language taught in most schools is English, and '*eigo kyoushi*' ('English teacher') is much more common.

32. The reference to 'national culture' might be challenged insofar as few, if any, nation states have a single, homogeneous culture shared by all citizens. This was probably never the case but the myth of a national culture is crucial to the sense of an 'imagined community' (Anderson, 1991). It is, in most cases, the culture shared by the socially and economically dominant groups in a society and it is the culture promoted by schools, even in multicultural societies. It is in this sense that I shall use the concept of a national culture here and later.

33. The difficulty of simplification for the sake of clarity is also evident in these cases. In the last decade there have been calls for an explicit policy to make English the official language in the USA, as a consequence of the increasing and, for some people, threatening presence of Spanish. In Britain, one minister for home affairs called for an emphasis on the learning of English by the children of recently-immigrant communities. These reactions to the presence of other languages reveal the symbolic significance of the national language, even when the defenders of the national language say they are simply being practical.

34. This phenomenon returned at the time of the war between Britain and Argentina. Patriotism was the watchword of Prime Minister Thatcher, and my children's primary school teacher showed them maps of where 'our boys' were in the advance against the enemy.

35. We will come later to the special case of the European Union which may be moving towards the establishment of a single industrialised entity that would then imply, in Gellner's model, the emergence of a single education system and a 'standard idiom'. On the one hand there may be sufficient common ground and common history to overcome the difficulties of not having a single education system and idiom. On the other hand, the strength of the nation state, national identity and national idiom(s) may yet prevent the entity working as a single industrial society.

36. Consider two striking examples of this. In the United States the pledge to the flag is routine, and unquestioned, whereas in Japan, with its troubled history of nationalism and jingoism, it is a hotly debated issue. In 2004, teachers in Tokyo were obliged to force their pupils to sing the national anthem that for many Japanese is still tainted with imperialist history (Befu, 2001) In circumstances of conflict with other nations, this reinforcement often becomes explicit as schools become instruments of indoctrination.

37. This is a good decision as the National Trust has played and continues to play a significant role in the definition and preservation of what is deemed to be 'national heritage' and, as Cannadine says, 'for many of its dominant figures, the National Trust was indeed the pursuit of politics by other means' – a politics that was not partisan but 'the definition and preservation of "national heritage" are activities which inescapably carry political messages' (Cannadine, 2003: 243).

38. This, too, is a good decision since, as Billig points out (1995), the sense of belonging to a nation state is taken for granted in national news casting (and weather forecasting); the effect would be different if they watched BBC World, where the banality of nationalism is less strong, and it is not taken for granted that the audience is British.

39. This and other extracts presented here are from interviews carried out by Kim Dray for a doctoral thesis and I am grateful for permission to use them. The

interpretation is, however, mine and does not engage Dr Dray in any responsibility.

40. In February 2007, at a conference on the Common European Framework of Languages, Gouillier (2007) argued that the first signs of a 'new European educational space' are to be discerned, in which the separations of states and their jealously-guarded independence in educational matters are disappearing. This is initially a matter of administrative co-operation, but may eventually impact on the experience of being a European for all language learners.

41. When substitutes are of the same language and society, there will be no great distance between the culture of parents and substitutes, as was the case in European bourgeois families who employed someone to look after their children. When the employees are of a different language and culture, there is potential for conflicting frames of reference for children. Anecdotally this seems to have been the case among families in the British Empire in India and today among families in Hong Kong and Singapore who employ 'maids' from the Philippines.

42. I have simplified the explanation here and do not refer to multilingual states, but the principles are applicable *mutandis mutatis* in such states too.

43. My anonymous reviewer reminds me that there has been one attempt to create a European newspaper, *The European*, and that there are websites that have a similar aim. These may be the media that will over time help to create a European imagined community.

44. For arguments to the contrary, which I do not however find convincing, see Berns (1995).

45. This happened in the Soviet Union (Pavlenko, 2003) and might happen in the USA with a boost in the teaching of Arabic, Chinese, Hindi, Russian and Farsi announced by the president in 2006 (www.actfl.org; accessed 1.06). When language learning is seen as part of national security, with the use of military terminology such as the formation of a corps of 'language reservists' the implications are clear, and the choice of languages points to the countries considered a threat of some kind.

46. For further proposals for classroom practice, see Brown & Brown (2003).

47. Such a specification is attempted in a report on teacher training in Europe but in the description of 'a composite profile of the ideal 21st century (foreign) language teacher in Europe' there is no reference to intercultural competence or the training needed to develop such competence in learners (Kelly *et al.*, 2002).

48. For some suggestions of texts on which a course might be constructed, see Appendix 2.

49. I am grateful to Professor Peter Doyé who first suggested comparing *politische Bildung* and language education in his article of 1993, and who has continued to help me with these ideas (Doyé, 1993b).

50. For a detailed contextualisation of the model presented here and comparison with other models, see Guilherme (2002: Ch. 3) and Risager (2007: Ch. 8).

51. Risager (2007) has argued for a transnational paradigm in foreign language and culture pedagogy and criticised my emphasis on the national. If and when

language teaching and teachers themselves accept this perspective, my argument will need to be modified but in principle will remain the same. Whether the people with whom one interacts identify and are identified by others with a nation state in their interactions will not affect the political dimension, the *savoir s'engager*, of intercultural communicative competence.

52. The relationship between political ideologies and religious ideologies, and the fact that, in some Islamic countries, religious, political and legal systems are unified, takes the discussion on political education and intercultural competence into the field of inter-faith dialogue.

53. The concept of the mediator as social actor in the European context has been discussed on several occasions by Zarate (2003a, 2003b).

54. It is evident that, if these difficulties arise within the European context and among European languages, they are likely to be even more complex in a European/Asian interchange. Feng's (2006) discussion of the concepts in Chinese makes this clear.

55. They would not be able to 'make do' with a one-to-one translation that makes the foreign language merely a code of the learner's language (see Chapter 8).

56. The question of competing rationalities is discussed by Lloyd who points out that early scientists of the modern era often managed to subscribe to two rationalities:

> In the form of divination, prediction figures among what used to be called the pseudo-sciences. In the early days of the history of science, in the middle of the 19th century, they were always an occasion of embarrassment. [...] Astrology, alchemy, physiognomy, later phrenology, all had to be dismissed as essentially deluded. The historian of science was not to be distracted by their presence in the same periods, even in the very same authors as those he or she was interested in, except insofar as he or she had a duty to point out how mistaken the pseudo-sciences were [...] from the 1950s on, it was remarked that techniques of divination had their own internal coherence and obeyed certain rules, and on that score and by that criterion do not fail to be rational. (Lloyd, 2002: 21)

Gellner also provides an interesting historical perspective in his discussion of the development from agrarian to industrial societies, and in doing so introduces the important factor that people may become bilingual conceptually, which implies a linguistic bilingualism too, although he does not refer to this:

> I am deeply sceptical about the applicability of the incommensurability thesis even to agrarian societies. I do not believe it can legitimately be used to deny the possibility of inter-cultural communication, or of the comparative evaluation of agrarian and industrial cultures. The incommensurability thesis owes some of its plausibility to a tendency to take too seriously the self-absolutising, critic-anathematising official faiths of late agrarian societies [...] the adherents of these faiths have, in practice, known how to transcend their own advertised blinkers. They are and were conceptually bilingual, and knew how to switch from commensurate to incommensurate idioms with ease and alacrity. [...]What is relevant however, is that somehow or other we are not helplessly imprisoned within a set of cultural cocoons and their norms, and that for some very obvious reasons (shared cognitive and produc-

tive bases and greatly increased inter-social communication) we may expect fully industrial man to be even less enslaved to his local culture than was his agrarian predecessor (Gellner, 1983: 120)

57. As always this analysis has to be modified _mutatis mutandis_ for nation states where there are more than one national language or where the speakers of a minority language are accorded legal rights to use their language in public discourse.

58. The development in Brussels at the European Union of a 'Europass' including languages or in Strasbourg at the Council of Europe of a 'European Language Portfolio' is a sign of the recognition by European authorities, and the national authorities that support them, that plurilingual competence of some kind is crucial.

59. The phrase 'national language' is used here for simplicity, although as discussed in earlier chapters, there are many variants.

60. I note here Beacco's view that there is a danger of losing the relationship with _language_ teaching, that there is no specific methodology but only an attitude of raising awareness, of creating respect, part of a common educational endeavour. He argues that this means _'qu'il n'y a pas de méthodologie langagière spécifique à l'éducation interculturelle susceptible de guider techniquement les enseignants qui ne peuvent alors se fonder que sur leur personnalité civique'_ ['that there are no language teaching methods specific to intercultural education capable of technically guiding teachers and therefore teachers can only base themselves on their civic personality'] (Beacco, 2006b: 14). He warns against activities related to citizenship education if they lead to discussion in the first language or a language other than the target language as this means there is no linguistic benefit. He also points out that such discussions may be limited by language competence. He therefore argues for teaching objectives which are close to language objectives, objectives which he describes collectively as _'bienveillance et civilité linguistique'_, defined in concrete terms as:

- _ne pas se scandaliser d'entendre des sons inconnus_ [not to be scandalised by hearing unfamiliar sounds];
- _ne pas imaginer que si des locuteurs parlent en votre présence une langue inconnue de vous, c'est pour tenir des propos négatifs à votre égard_ [not to imagine that if people speak a language you do not know in your presence that it is to make negative comments about you];
- _ne pas trouver systématiquement que les locuteurs de langues étrangères parlent trop fort, de manière inarticulée ..._ [not to say automatically that people who speak foreign languages speak too loudly, or in inarticulate ways, etc];
- _ne pas associer la difficulté à utiliser la langue-cible à des difficultés cognitives ou intellectuelles_ [not to associate difficulties in using the target language with cognitive or intellectual difficulties];
- _considérer comme une preuve de disponibilité le fait que votre interlocuteur choisisse de parler dans votre langue 1_ [consider as a positive signal the fact that your interlocutors choose to speak your language 1];
- _faire l'effort d'utiliser ne seraient-ce que quelques mots de la langue 1 de votre interlocuteur, comme signe de votre disponibilité_ [make an effort to use even a few words of your interlocutor's language 1 as a sign of your flexibility];

- *faire l'effort de parler de manière articulée et avec un débit plus lent pour faciliter l'interaction avec le locuteur non natif* [make the effort to speak in a clear manner and at a slower speed to aid interaction with a non-native interlocutor];
- *proposer des remédiations ou des corrections des formulations de l'interlocuteur de manière discrète et non évaluative* [suggest remedies or corrections to the formulations of the interlocutor in a discreet and non-evaluative way];
- [...].

This is a starting point but, as will be evident here, my proposals for language education – both national language and foreign language – go further. It is important for example to envisage a co-operation among language education teachers that would allow some issues to be taken further in the national language classroom that may be too complex for the language level in the foreign language classroom. Having said that, there is no reason in principle for banning discussion in the learners' first language in a plurilingual classroom, and the issue of transnational civil society needs to be addressed by foreign language teachers too.

61. The original use of 'country' in the foreign language model of ICC has been replaced with 'culture' – an abbreviation to refer to the complexity of beliefs values and behaviours of a social group with which a person is identified in a given interaction – so that the model applies equally to national language education.

62. I do not propose to discuss the psychological dimension further here, since I have done so elsewhere (Byram, 1989a; Byram, Morgan *et al.*, 1994). It is to be noted that cognitive development as part of all learning is also discussed in Gagel (2000).

63. In national language education too, communicative competence is an essential part of the teaching aims and there is much said here about foreign language teaching that applies *mutatis mutandis* to national language education, but to deal with this simultaneously would be unnecessarily complex at this point.

64. See Appendix 3 for an overview.

65. I am grateful to all the participants at the Durham Symposium on 'Being intercultural and being an intercultural citizen' 2004 and especially to contributors to the ensuing book (Alred *et al.*, 2006), but especially to Geof Alred and Mike Fleming, with whom I have worked for many years.

66. These first two axioms are developed and illustrated in Alred *et al.* (2003).

67. In 2005, David Bell, the Chief Inspector of education in schools in England made an explicit link between a lack of political interest among young people and the need to develop citizenship education:

> interest in politics is falling among young people. There is a line of argument that young people do care about political and social issues, but not necessarily traditional party political issues. However, in a small scale opinion poll conducted by Ofsted, 45% of 14 to 16-year-old pupils said they didn't think it was important for them know more about what the major political parties stand for, and 70% were not involved in any kind of community activity outside school.

Facts and figures like these demonstrate the importance of ensuring young citizens feel connected with their society. Citizenship education is one way of trying to do this. (Bell, 17 January 2005. Online at www.educationguardian. co.uk/ofsted; accessed 17.1.05)

68. Never was the word 'community' used more indiscriminately and emptily than in the decades when communities in the sociological sense became hard to find in real life – 'the intelligence community', 'the public relations community', the 'gay community' (Hobsbawm, 1994: 428).

69. However, the danger of slipping from citizenship as activity in community and democracy to education for national identity is demonstrated by the speech of the inspector cited earlier (note 67):

> One of the most ambitious aspects of national curriculum citizenship requires pupils to understand the diversity of national, regional, religious and ethnic identities in the United Kingdom, and the need for mutual respect and understanding. At its heart, lies the thorny question of national identity. What is it that binds us together as a nation? What does national identity mean in practice? Can we possess multiple identities?

The inspector then goes on to equate citizenship education with the development of 'allegiance to British nationality' which is not a matter of ethnicity but of being subject to common laws, payers of taxes students and workers with shared interests, a description that hovers between Tönnies's (1887/1963) notion of community and society.

70. Like other writers on these issues, I shall use the term 'transnational' at this point, rather than 'international'; it carries better the idea of crossing borders.

71. When describing the evolution of Amsterdam, Buruma points out that new technologies make it possible for these diasporas to maintain close ties with their country of origin:

> Slowly, almost without anyone's noticing, old working-class Dutch neighbourhoods lost their white populations and were transformed into 'dish cities' linked to Morocco, Turkey and the Middle East by satellite television and the Internet. Gray Dutch streets filled up, not only with satellite dishes, but with Moroccan bakeries, Turkish kebab joints, travel agents offering cheap flights to Istanbul or Casablanca, and coffee houses filled with sad-eyed men in djellabas whose health had often been wrecked by years of dirty and dangerous labour. (Buruma, 2006: 21)

72. One example of this is in the work of Osler and Starkey (2005b), who have related their work in citizenship to language teaching.

73. This argument is not incompatible with the *de facto* evolution of English as a lingua franca in international bodies, such as the European Commission itself, or the use of two official languages at the Council of Europe since the meanings are created within the institutions, as are the identities that people develop in them. The difficulty arises when outsiders to the institutions do not understand the connotations created for such institutional languages.

74. See Chapter 10 for a discussion of the problems of linguistic relativism and in particular the understanding of 'citizenship'.

75. I must note here that I was one of the authors of the first drafts of this and some

other texts analysed here, but they are an approved expression of the consensus and commented on and revised in a process of consultation.

76. For a related analysis of national education systems, see Alred *et al.* (2006).

77. A modification of this view, and one that seems to have evolved pragmatically as a means of encouraging new learners, is to judge whether they would be able to communicate successfully with 'a sympathetic native speaker'. This reduces the demands, but introduces a lack of clarity in assessment.

78. There are potential links with 'task-based learning' here, but it would divert us too far from the focus to pursue these at this point. Nonetheless the case for task-based learning (which concentrates almost exclusively on the acquisition of linguistic competence), could well be integrated with the case being made here since the principles are that learners should be given appropriate tasks with a focus on meaning rather than the forms of language, and these are the principles that are essential to the discussion of curricula in this chapter (Long & Norris, 2000; Ellis, 2003)

79. It was during the development of this project that the framework was developed and I am grateful to the members of the Labicum Project, and in particular Neva Čebron, for their co-operation and help.

80. The British tradition was particularly well articulated soon after the First World War, there was a major report, the 'Leathes Report', on the teaching of languages but in its discussion of the aims of language teaching, it demonstrated that the authors had not yet seen the link between mobility, language teaching and intercultural communication. Language learning was seen as an interesting puzzle and a good source of training of the mind:

> Language teaching in schools has and should have a disciplinary and educative aim. It should train the mind, the taste and the character. Language is a means of expressing thought, and the study of a foreign language reveals the anatomy of thought. Each language has its own modes of expression, and the contrast of and comparison of different modes of expression leads to a more accurate sense of logical processes and a closer observation of the finer shades of meaning. (Leathes Report, 1918: 86)

Although 'different modes of expression' were recognised, the interest that was foremost was not in how they might be part of the experience of engagement with another culture, but in the refinement of analytical skill. The report is nonetheless a crucial moment in British language teaching even though it is insufficiently known.

81. At the Council of Europe, it is interesting to see that as the focus moves towards work on 'national' languages as they are taught in themselves and as they are used for teaching other subjects, an explicit concern with values, and the use of the German concept of '*Bildung*' has arisen (see Biesta, 2002, for a brief explanation of *Bildung*). National languages are clearly seen as related to values whereas foreign languages are not. This is not to say that previous projects concerned with foreign languages at the Council of Europe did not have an eye to values and European citizenship, but the man focus remained on how to ensure the usefulness of language teaching and learning.

82. Taken from Chapter 2 of Byram (1997).

83 Much of the proposal here is based on a module I taught at the University of Durham as part of an MA course in 'Teaching Japanese as a Second Language' and on another module at the University of Jaen (Spain) taught with Mari-Carmen Mendez Garcia in a PhD course for teachers of English as a foreign language.

84 The original use of 'country' in the foreign language model of ICC has been replaced with 'culture' – an abbreviation to refer to the complexity of beliefs values and behaviours of a social group with which a person is identified in a given interaction – so that the model applies equally to national language education.

85 *Autobiography of Intercultural Encounters* © Council of Europe. The layout has been adapted to fit the present publication.

References

Agar, M. (1980) *The Professional Stranger*. London: Academic Press.

Agar, M. (1991) The biculture in bilingual. *Language in Society* 20, 167– 81.

Agar, M. (1994a) The intercultural frame. *International Journal of Intercultural Relations* 18 (2), 221–237.

Agar, M. (1994b) *Language Shock: Understanding the Culture of Conversation*. New York: William Morrow.

Aleksandrowicz-Pedich, L. and Lazar, I. (2001) Cross-cultural communicative competence in teaching English as a foreign language: Research project in four European countries (Estonia, Hungary, Iceland and Poland). In T. Siek-Piskozub (ed.) *European Year of Languages* (pp. 139–144). Proceedings of the 3rd CER-FIPLV conference, 26–28 September 2001, Poznan, Poland. Poznan: Adam Mickiewicz University.

Allport, G. (1954) *The Nature of Prejudice*. Cambridge, MA: Addison-Wesley.

Alred, G., Byram, M. and Fleming, M. (eds) (2006) *Education for Intercultural Citizenship: Concepts and Comparisons*. Clevedon: Multilingual Matters.

Anderson, B. (1991) *Imagined Communities* (2nd edn). London: Verso.

Arbex, M. (2001) La diversité culturelle dans les méthodes de FLE uilisées au Brésil. *Dialogues et Cultures* 44, 92–98.

Armour, W.S. (2001) 'This guy is Japanese stuck in a white man's body': A discussion of meaning making, identity slippage and cross-cultural adaptation. *Journal of Multilingual and Multicultural Development* 22 (1), 1–18.

Audigier, F. (1998) *Basic Concepts and Core Competences of Education for Democratic Citizenship*. DECS/CIT (98) 35. Strasbourg: Council of Europe.

Balbi, R. (1997) Resources. In P. Doyé and A. Hurrell (eds) *Foreign Language Education in Primary Schools*. Strasbourg: Council of Europe.

Barnett, R. (1997) *Higher Education: A Critical Business*. Buckingham: Open University Press.

Barrett, M. (1996) English children's acquisition of a European identity. In G. Breakwell and E. Lyons (eds) *Changing European Identities: Social Psychological Analyses of Social Change*. Oxford: Butterworth Heinemann.

Barrett, M. (2000) The development of national identity in childhood and adolescence. Inaugural lecture, University of Surrey. Online at www.surrey. ac.uk. Accessed 29.2.08.

Barrett, M. (2007) *Children's Knowledge, Beliefs and Feelings about Nations and National Groups*. London: Psychology Press.

Barth, F. (1969) Introduction. In F. Barth (ed.) *Ethnic Groups and Boundaries*. London: Allen and Unwin.

Beacco, J-C. (2005) *Languages and Language Repertoires: Plurilingualism as a Way of Life in Europe*. Strasbourg: Council of Europe.

Beacco, J-C. (2006a) *Langues et repertoire de langues: Le plurilinguisme comme 'manière d'être' en Europe*. Strasbourg: Council of Europe.

Beacco, J-C. (2006b) Education à la citoyenneté et enseignement des langues: Valeurs et instruments. *Lingua e nuova didattica* 35 (5), 11–19.

Befu, H. (2001) *The Hegemony of Homogeneity*. Melbourne: Trans Pacific Press.

Belz, J.A. (2001) Institutional and individual dimensions of transatlantic group work in network-based language teaching. *ReCALL* 13 (2), 213–31.

Berger, P. and Luckmann, T. (1966) *The Social Construction of Reality*. Harmondsworth: Penguin.

Berlin, I. (1990) *The Cracked Timber of Humanity*. Princeton, NJ: Princeton University Press.

Berlin, I. (1998) *The Proper Study of Mankind*. London: Pimlico.

Berns, M. (1995) English in Europe: Whose language, which culture? *International Journal of Applied Linguistics* 5 (1), 21–32.

Berrier, A. (2001) Culture et enseignement de l'oral en français langue seconde: Quel cadre et quels aspects présenter en classe. *Les Langues Modernes* 1, 12–18.

Biesta, G. (2002) How general can '*Bildung*' be? Reflections on the future of a modern educational ideal. *Journal of Philosophy of Education* 36 (3), 377–90.

Billig, M. (1995) *Banal Nationalism*. London: Sage.

Birzea, C. (2000) *Education for Democratic Citizenship: A Lifelong Learning Perspective*. DG IV/ EDU/ CIT (2000) 21. Strasbourg: Council of Europe.

Boers, F. and Demecheleer, M. (2001) Measuring the impact of cross-cultural differences on learners' comprehension of imageable idioms. *ELT Journal* 55 (3), 255–62.

Bonnet, G. (ed.) (2002) *The Assessment of Pupils' Skills in English in Eight European Countries*. Online at http://cisad.adc.education.fr/revn/. Accessed 6.06.

Bourdieu, P. (1977) *Outline of a Theory of Practice*. Cambridge: Cambridge University Press.

Bourdieu, P. and Passeron, J-C. (1970) *La réproduction*. Paris: Editions de minuit.

Bredella, L. (2001) *Literarisches und interkulturelles Verstehen*. Tübingen: Gunter Narr.

Bredella, L. and Richter, A. (2000) Sapir-Whorf hypothesis. In M. Byram (ed.) *Routledge Encyclopedia of Language Teaching and Learning* (pp. 522–24). London: Routledge.

Breugnot, J. (2001) L'institution scolaire en France et en Allemagne: Différences et proximités. *Les Langues Modernes* 3, 13–20.

Brown, K. and Brown, M. (eds) (2003) *Reflections on Citizenship in a Multilingual World*. London: CILT.

Brumfit, C., Johnston, B., Mitchell, R., Ford, P. and Myles, F. (2004) Description of the 'Criticality' project and its theoretical base. BERA symposium, Manchester. Online at www.critical.soton.ac.uk. Accessed 29.2.08

Bruner, J. (1960) *The Process of Education*. Cambridge, MA: Harvard.

Burgess, R.G. (ed.) (1984) *The Research Process in Educational Setting: Ten Case Studies*. Lewes: Falmer Press.

Buruma, I. (2006) *Murder in Amsterdam: The Death of Theo van Gogh and the Limits of Tolerance*. New York: Penguin Books.

Byram, M. (1986) *Minority Education and Ethnic Survival: Case Study of a German School in Denmark*. Clevedon: Multilingual Matters.

Byram, M. (1989a) *Cultural Studies in Foreign Language Education*. Clevedon: Multilingual Matters

Byram, M. (1989b) Intercultural education and foreign language teaching. *World Studies Journal* 7 (2), 4–7.

Byram, M. (1990) Return to the home country: The 'necessary dream' in ethnic identity. In M. Byram and J. Leman (eds) *Bicultural and Trilingual Education: The Brussels Foyer Model*. Clevedon: Multilingual Matters.

Byram, M. (ed.) (1993) *Germany: Its Representation in Textbooks for Teaching German in Great Britain*. Frankfurt aM: Diesterweg.

Byram, M. (1995) Acquiring intercultural competence. In L. Sercu (ed.) *Intercultural Competence: A New Challenge for Language Teachers and Trainers in Europe*. Aalborg: Aalborg University Press.

Byram, M. (1996) Framing the experience of residence abroad: The pedagogical function of the informal interview. *Language, Culture and Curriculum* 9 (1), 84–98.

Byram, M. (1997) *Teaching and Assessing Intercultural Communicative Competence*. Clevedon: Multilingual Matters.

Byram, M. (1999) Source disciplines for language teacher education. In H. Trappes-Lomax and I. McGrath (eds) *Theory in Language Teacher Education* (pp. 70–81). London: Longman.

Byram, M. (2003) On being 'bicultural' and 'intercultural'. In G. Alred, M. Byram and M. Fleming (eds) *Intercultural Experience and Education*. Clevedon: Multilingual Matters.

Byram, M. and Doyé, P. (1999) Intercultural competence and foreign language learning in the primary school. In P. Driscoll and D. Frost (eds) *The Teaching of Modern Foreign Languages in the Primary School* (pp. 138–51). London: Routledge.

Byram, M. and Esarte-Sarries, V. (1991) *Investigating Cultural Studies in Foreign Language Teaching: A Book for Teachers*. Clevedon: Multilingual Matters.

Byram, M. and Feng, A. (eds) (2006) *Living and Studying Abroad: Research and Practice*. Clevedon: Multilingual Matters.

Byram, M. and Risager, K. (1999) *Language Teachers, Politics and Cultures*. Clevedon: Multilingual Matters.

Byram, M. and Zarate, G. (1997) Definitions, objectives and assessment of sociocultural competence. In Council of Europe *Sociocultural Competence in Language Learning and Teaching* (pp. 7–43). Strasbourg: Council of Europe.

Byram, M, Morgan, C. and colleagues (1994) *Teaching-and-Learning Language-and-Culture*. Clevedon: Multilingual Matters

Byram, M., Esarte-Sarries, V. and Taylor, S. (1991) *Cultural Studies and Language Learning: A Research Report*. Clevedon: Multilingual Matters .

Byram, M. and Feng, A. (2004) Culture and language learning: Teaching, research and scholarship. *Language Teaching* 37 (3), 149–168.

Byram, M., Nichols, A. and Stephens, D. (2001) *Developing Intercultural Competence in Practice*. Clevedon: Multilingual Matters.

Canagarajah, A.S. (1999) *Resisting Linguistic Imperialism in English Teaching*. Oxford: Oxford University Press.

Candelier, M. (ed.) (2004) *Janua Linguarum, the Gateway to Languages: The Introduction of Language Awareness into the Curriculum – Awakening To Languages*. Strasbourg: Council of Europe.

Cannadine, D. (2003) *In Churchill's Shadow: Confronting the Past in Modern Britain*. Oxford: Oxford University Press.

Castles, S. (2004) Migration, citizenship and education. In J.A. Banks (ed.) *Diversity and Citizenship Education. Global Perspectives*. San Francisco, CA: Jossey-Bass.

Catteuw, P. (2007) On teaching and assessing ICC by means of a framework of reference for intercultural competence and a development portfolio. Paper presented at the Durham Symposium on Assessment, March.

CERI (Centre for Educational Research and Innovation) (1998) *Human Capital Investment: An International Comparison.* Paris: OECD.

Chan, R. (2007) Context and impact of medium of instruction on attitudes, motivation and academic performance: A secondary school in Hong Kong. Unpublished EdD thesis, University of Durham.

Chryssochoou, X. (2000) Membership in a superordinate level: Re-thinking European Union as a multi-national society. *Journal of Community and Applied Social Psychology* 10, 403–420.

Cinnirella, M. (1996) A social identity perspective on European integration. In G. Breakwell and E. Lyons (eds) *Changing European Identities: Social Psychological Analyses of Social Change.* Oxford: Butterworth Heinemann.

Cinnirella, M. (1997) Towards a European identity? Interactions between the national and European social identities manifested by university students in Britain and Italy. *British Journal of Social Psychology* 36, 19–31.

Collins (1980) *Collins German/English English/German Dictionary* (P. Terrell, V. Calderwood-Schnorr, W.V.A. Morris Breitsprecher, eds). London: Collins.

Commission of Japan's Goals in the Twenty-First Century (2000) *The Frontier Within: Individual Empowerment and Better Governance in the New Millennium.* Online at http://www.kantei.go.jp/jp/21century. Accessed 5.07.

Corbett, J. (2003) *An Intercultural Approach to English Language Teaching.* Clevedon: Multilingual Matters.

Cortazzi, M. and Shen, W.W. (2001) Cross-linguistic awareness of cultural keywords: A study of Chinese and English speakers. *Language Awareness* 10 (2/3), 125–42.

Costanzo, E. (2003) *Language Education (Educazione Linguistica) in Italy: An Experience that could Benefit Europe?* Strasbourg: Council of Europe.

Coulby D. and Jones, C. (2001) *Education and Warfare in Europe.* Aldershot: Ashgate.

Council of Europe (2001) *Common European Framework of Reference for Languages: Learning, Teaching, Assessment.* Cambridge: Cambridge University Press.

Council of Europe (2003) *Guide for the Development of Language Education Policies in Europe: From Linguistic Diversity to Plurilingual Education.* Executive version. Strasbourg: Council of Europe.

Council of Europe (2004) *All European Study on EDC Policies.* DGIV/EDU/CIT (2004) 12. Strasbourg: Council of Europe.

Council of Europe (2005) *Plurilingual Education in Europe. 50 Years of International Cooperation.* Strasbourg: Council of Europe.

Council of Europe (2006) *Plurilingual Education in Europe.* Strasbourg: Council of Europe.

Council of Europe (2007) *Guide for the Development of Language Education Policies in Europe.* Executive version. Strasbourg: Council of Europe.

Council of Europe (in press) *Autobiography of Key Intercultural Encounters.* Strasbourg: Council of Europe.

Council Resolution (2002) Council Resolution of 14 February. *Official Journal C* 050, 23. 02.2002. On WWW at http://eur-lex.europa.eu/LexUriServ/LexUriServ.do?uri=OJ:C:2002:050:0001:0002:EN:PDF. Accessed 29.2.08.

Crawshaw, R. Callen, B. and Tusting, K. (2001) Attesting the self: Narration and identity change during periods of residence abroad. *Language and Intercultural Communication* 1 (2), 101–19.

Cumming, A. (1996) IEA's studies of language education: Their scope and contributions. *Assessment in Education* 3 (2), 179–92.

Curtain, H. and Pesola, C.A. 1994) *Languages and Children: Making the Match*. New York: Longman.

Davies, A (2003) *The Native Speaker: Myth and Reality*. Clevedon: Multilingual Matters.

Davies, I. (1997) Education for European citizenship: A review of some relevant documentation. In I. Davies and A. Sobisch (eds) *Developing European Citizens*. Sheffield: Sheffield Hallam University Press.

Davies, L. (1999) Comparing definitions of democracy in education. *Compare* 29 (2), 127–40.

DeKorne, H., Byram, M. and Fleming, M. (2007) Familiarising the stranger: Immigrant perceptions of cross-cultural interaction and bicultural identity. *Journal of Multilingual and Multicultural Development* 28 (4), 290–307.

Dewey, J. (1916/1985) *Democracy and Education*. Carbondale, IL: Southern Illinois University Press.

DfEE (Department for Education and Employment) (1998) *The Learning Age: A Renaissance for a New Britain*. London: Stationery Office.

DfES (Department for Education and Skills) (2002) *Languages for All: Languages for Life*. London: DfES.

DfES (Department for Education and Skills) (2007) *Languages Review*. London: DfES.

Di Napoli, R., Polezzi, L. and King, A. (eds) (2001) *Fuzzy Boundaries? Reflections on Modern Languages and the Humanities*. London: CILT.

Donmall, B.G. (ed.) (1985) *Language Awareness*. London: Centre for Information on Language Teaching and Research (CILT).

Dörnyei, Z. (1998) Motivation in second and foreign language learning. *Language Teaching* 31 (3), 117–35.

Dörnyei, Z. (2001) *Motivational Strategies in the Language Classroom*. Cambridge: Cambridge University Press.

Dörnyei, Z. and Csizér, K. (1998) Ten commandments for motivating language learners: Results of an empirical study. *Language Teaching Research* 2, 203–229.

Downes, S. (2001) Sense of Japanese cultural identity within an English partial immersion programme: Should parents worry? *International Journal of Bilingual Education and Bilingualism* 4 (3), 165–80.

Doyé, P. (1992) Fremdsprachenunterricht als Beitrag zu tertiärer Sozialisation. In D. Buttjes, W. Butzkamm and F. Klippel (eds) *Neue Brennpunkte des Englischunterrichts* (pp. 280–95). Frankfurt aM: Peter Lang.

Doyé, P. (1993a) Fremdsprachenerziehung in der Grundschule. *Zeitschrift für Fremdsprachenforschung* 4 (1), 48–90.

Doyé, P. (1993b) Neuere Konzepte der Fremdsprachenerziehung und ihre Bedeutung für die Schulbuchkritik. In M. Byram (ed.) *Germany: Its Representation in Textbooks for Teaching German in Great Britain*. Frankfurt aM: Diesterweg.

Doyé, P. (1999) *The Intercultural Dimension: Foreign Language Education in the Primary School*. Berlin: Cornelsen.

Doyé, P. (2008) *Interkulturelles und mehrsprachiges Lehren und Lernen*. Tübingen: Gunter Narr.

Duer, K., Spajic-Vrkaš, V. and Martins, I.F. (2000) Strategies for learning democratic citizenship. DECS/ EDU/ CIT, (2000, 16. Strasbourg: Council of Europe.

Eberhardt, J.L. and Fiske, S.T. (1996) Motivating individuals to change: What is a target to do? In C.N. Macrae, C. Stangor and M. Hewstone (eds) *Stereotypes and Stereotyping*. London: The Guildford Press.

Edwards, J. (1985) *Language, Society and Identity*. Oxford: Blackwell.

Egger, K. (1985) *Zweisprachige Familien in Südtirol: Sprachgebrauch und Spracherziehung*. Innsbruck: Innsbrucker Beiträge zur Kulturwissenschaft.

Ellis, R. (2003) *Task-based Language Learning and Teaching*. Oxford: Oxford University Press.

Eurobarometer (2001–5) *Europeans and Languages: A Survey*. Brussels: European Commission. Online at http://europa.eu.int/comm/education/languages. Accessed 29.2.08.

European Commission (1995) *Teaching and Learning: Towards the Learning Society*. Bruxelles: European Commission.

Evans, C. (1988) *Language People: The Experience of Teaching and Learning Modern Languages in British Universities*. Milton Keynes: Open University Press.

Farr, R.M. and Moscovici, S. (eds) (1984) *Social Representations*. Cambridge: Cambridge University Press.

Felberbauer, M. and Heindler, D. (1995) *Foreign Language Education in Primary School: Report on Workshop 8B*. Strasbourg: Council of Europe.

Feng, A. (2006) Contested notions of citizenship and citizenship education: The Chinese case. In G. Alred, M. Byram, M. Fleming (eds) *Education for Intercultural Citizenship: Concepts and Comparisons*. Clevedon: Multilingual Matters.

Feng, A.W. and Byram, M. (2002) Authenticity in college English textbooks: An intercultural perspective. *RELC Journal* 33/2, 58–84.

Gagel, W. (2000) *Einführung in die Didaktik des politischen Unterrichts* (2nd edn). Opladen: Verlag Leske und Budrich.

Galisson, R. (2000) La pragmatique lexiculturelle pour accéder autrement, à une autre culture, par un autre lexique. *Mélanges CRAPEL* 25, 47–73.

Gardner, R.C. and Lambert, W.E. (1972) *Attitudes and Motivation in Second Language Learning*. Rowley, MA: Newbury House.

Garrett, M.T. (1996) 'Two people': An American Indian narrative of bicultural identity. *Journal of American Indian Education* 36 (1), 1–21.

Gellner, E. (1983) *Nations and Nationalism*. Ithaca, NY: Cornell University Press.

Gellner, E. (1998) *Language and Solitude: Wittgenstein, Malinowski and the Habsburg Dilemma*. Cambridge: Cambridge University Press.

Gilligan, C. (1982) *In a Different Voice*. Cambridge, MA: Harvard University Press.

Giroux, H.A. (1992) *Border Crossings: Cultural Workers and the Politics of Education*. New York: Routledge.

Goffman, E. (1969) *The Presentation of Self in Everyday Life*. London: Allen Lane The Penguin Press.

Goffman, E. (1963) *Behavior in Public Places*. New York: The Free Press.

Gohard-Radenkovic, A. (2001) Comment évaluer les compétences socioculturelles de l'étudiant en situation de mobilité? *Dialogues et cultures* 44, 52–61.

Gouin, F. (1892) *The Art of Teaching and Studying Languages*. London: George Philip and Son.

Goullier, F. (2007) L'impact du *Cadre européen de référence pour les langues* et des travaux du Conseil de l'Europe sur le nouvel espace éducatif européen. Paper at the Council of Europe Policy Forum, Strasbourg, 6–8 February. Online at www.coe.int/lang. Accessed 29.2.08.

Graddol, D. (1997) *The Future of English?* London: The British Council.

Graddol, D. (2006) *English Next: Why Global English may Mean the End of 'English as a Foreign Language'.* London: British Council.

Gruber-Miller, J. and Benton, C. (2001) How do you say MOO in Latin? Assessing student learning and motivation in beginning Latin. *CALICO Journal* 18 (2), 305–38.

Guilherme, M. (2002) *Critical Citizens for an Intercultural World: Foreign Language Education as Cultural Politics.* Clevedon: Multilingual Matters.

Guilherme, M., Pureza, J.M., Paulos da Silva, R. and Santos, H. (2006) The intercultural dimension of citizenship education in Portugal. In G. Alred, M. Byram and M. Fleming (eds) *Education for Intercultural Citizenship: Concepts and Comparisons.* Clevedon: Multilingual Matters.

Habermas, J. (1994) Citizenship and national identity. In B. van Steebergen (ed.) *The Condition of Citizenship.* London: Sage.

Hallet, W. (2001) Fremdsprachenunterricht als 'hybrider Raum': Überlegungen zu einer kulturwissenschaftlich orientierten Textdidaktik. *Zeitschrift für Fremdsprachenforschung* 12 (1), 103–30.

Halsey, A.H., Heath, A.F. and Ridge, J.M. 1980) *Origins and Destinations: Family, Class and Education in Modern Britain.* Oxford: Clarendon Press.

Hargreaves, D. (1982) *The Challenge for the Comprehensive School: Culture, Curriculum and Community.* London: Routledge and Kegan Paul.

Hawkins, E.W. (1981) *Modern Languages in the Curriculum.* Cambridge: Cambridge University Press.

Hawkins, E.W. (1987) *Awareness of Language* (2nd edn) Cambridge: Cambridge University Press.

He, M.F. (2002a) A narrative enquiry of cross-cultural lives: Lives in China. *Journal of Curriculum Studies* 34 (3), 301–321.

He, M.F. (2002b) A narrative enquiry of cross-cultural lives: Lives in Canada. *Journal of Curriculum Studies* 34 (3), 323–342.

He, M.F. (2002c) A narrative enquiry of cross-cultural lives: Lives in the North America academy. *Journal of Curriculum Studies* 34 (5), 513–533.

Herring, R.D. (1995) Developing biracial ethnic identity: A review of the increasing dilemma. *Journal of Multicultural Counselling and Development* 23, 29–38.

Herron, C, Corrie, C., Dubreuil, S. and Cole, S. (2002) A classroom investigation: Can video improve intermediate-level French language students' ability to learn about a foreign culture. *The Modern Language Journal* 86 (1), 36–53.

Himeta, M. (2006) Le paradoxe de la francophilie japonaise. Représentations des enseignants et des étudiants de français au Japon. Thèse de Docteur de l'Université Paris III, France.

Himmelmann, G. (2001) *Demokratie Lernen als Lebens-, Gesellschafts- und Herrschaftsform: Ein Lehr- und Studienbuch.* Schwalbach/Ts: Wochenschau Verlag.

Himmelmann, G. (2003) Zukunft, Fachidentität und Standards der politischen Bildung. Unpublished manuscript. Braunschweig: TU Braunschweig, Institut für Sozialwissenschaften.

Himmelmann, G. (2006) Concepts and issues in citizenship education. A comparative study of Germany, Britain and the USA. In G. Alred, M. Byram and M. Fleming (eds) *Education for Intercultural Citizenship: Concepts and Comparisons.* Clevedon: Multilingual Matters.

Hinkel, R. (2001) Sind 'native-speakers' wirklich die besseren Fremdsprachenlehrer? *Info-DAF* 28 (6), 585–99.

Ho, M-C. (1997) English language teaching in Taiwan: A study of the effects of teaching culture on motivation and identity. Unpublished PhD thesis, University of Durham.

Hobsbawm, E.J. (1992) *Nations and Nationalism since 1780.* Cambridge: Cambridge University Press.

Hobsbawm, E.J. (1994) *The Age of Extremes.* London: Michael Joseph.

Hobsbawm, E.J. (1998) *On History.* London: Abacus.

Hobsbawm, E.J. and Granger, T. (eds) (1983) *The Invention of Tradition.* Cambridge: Cambridge University Press.

Hoffmann, E. (1989) *Lost in Translation: A Life in a New Language.* Harmondsworth: Penguin.

Holcomb, T.K. (1997) Development of deaf bicultural identity. *American Annals of the Deaf* 142 (2), 89–93.

Hsieh, J. (forthcoming) Teaching English as an international and an intercultural English in Taiwan. EdD thesis, University of Durham.

Hu, A. (in press) Interkulturelle Kompetenz: Zum Problem der Dimensionierung und Evaluation einer Schlüsselkompetenz fremdsprachlichen Lernens. In V.Frederking (ed.) *Schwer operationalisierbare Kompetenzen: Herausforderungen empirischer Fachdidaktik.* Hohengehren: Schneider.

Hymes, D. (1971) On communicative competence. In J.B. Pride and J. Holmes (eds) *Sociolinguistics.* Harmondsworth: Penguin.

Ilieva, R. (2001) Living with ambiguity: Toward culture exploration in adult second-language classrooms. *TESL Canada Journal* 19 (1), 1–16.

INCA project (2004) *Intercultural Competence Assessment.* Online at www.inca project.org. Accessed 29.2.08.

Ingram, D. and O'Neill, S. (2002) The enigma of cross-cultural attitudes in language teaching: Part 2. *Babel (AFMLTA)* 36 (3), 17–22, 37–38.

Ingram, M. (2001) Interdisciplinary perspectives in the French civilisation class. *The French Review* 74 (6), 1152–64.

Jackson, J. (2007) Ethnographic pedagogy and evaluation in short-term study abroad. In M. Byram and A. Feng (eds) *Living and Studying Abroad: Research and Practice.* Clevedon: Multilingual Matters.

Jackson, R. (2004) *Rethinking Religious Education and Plurality.* London: RoutledgeFalmer.

James, C. and Garrett, P. (eds) *Language Awareness in the Classroom.* London: Longman.

Jenkins, J. (2000) *The Phonology of English as an International Language.* Oxford: Oxford University Press.

Jiang, W. (2001) Handling 'culture-bumps'. *ELT Journal* 55 (4), 382–90.

Jo, H-Y. (2001) 'Heritage' language learning and ethnic identity: Korean Americans' struggle with language authorities. *Language, Culture and Curriculum* 14 (1), 26–41.

Jogan, M.K., Heredia, A.H. and Aguilera, G.M. (2001) Cross-cultural e-mail: Providing cultural input for the advanced foreign language student. *Foreign Language Annals* 34 (4), 341–46.

Johnstone, R. (2002) *Addressing 'the Age Factor': Some Implications for Languages Policy*. Strasbourg: Council of Europe.

Jordan, S.A. (2001) Writing the other: Transforming consciousness through ethnographic writing. *Language and Intercultural Communication* 1 (1), 40–56.

Kalnberzina, V. (2000) Latvian module: Understanding 'social identity'. In M. Byram and M. Tost Planet (eds) *Social Identity and the European Dimension: Intercultural Competence through Foreign Language Learning*. Graz and Strasbourg: Council of Europe.

Kanno, Y. (2000) Kikokushijo as bicultural. *International Journal of Intercultural Relations* 24, 361–382.

Kawai, Y. (2007) Japanese nationalism and the global spread of English: An analysis of Japanese governmental and public discourses on English. *Language and Intercultural Communication* 7 (1), 37–55.

Kedourie, E. (1966) *Nationalism*. London: Hutchinson.

Kelly, M., Grenfell, M., Gallagher-Brett, A., Jones, D., Richard, L. and Hilmarsson-Dunn, A. (2002) *The Training of Teachers of a Foreign Language: Developments in Europe*. Report to the European Commission. Southampton: University of Southampton.

Kennedy, F. (2007) The intercultural dimension in LOLIPOP. Paper presented at the Durham Symposium on Assessment, March.

Kennedy K. and Fairbrother, P. (2004) Asian perspectives on citizenship education: postcolonial constructions or precolonial values? In W.O. Lee *et al.* (eds) *Citizenship Education in Asia and the Pacific: Concepts and Issues*. Hong Kong: Comparative Education Research Centre and Kluwer Academic.

Kennedy, K.J. (2004) Searching for citizenship values in an uncertain global environment. In W.O. Lee *et al.* (eds) *Citizenship Education in Asia and the Pacific: Concepts and Issues*. Hong Kong: Comparative Education Research Centre and Kluwer Academic.

Koehn, P.H. and Rosenau, J.N. (2002) Transnational competence in an emergent epoch. *International Studies Perspectives* 3 (2), 105–127.

Kohlberg, L., Levine, C. and Hewer, A. (1983) *Moral Stages: A Current Formulation and Response to Critics*. Basel: Karger.

Koike, I, (2004) Japan needs to improve its English strategy. *International Herald Tribune*, 1 December.

Koike, I. and Tanaka, H. (1995) English in foreign language education policy in Japan: Towards the twenty-first century. *World Englishes* 14 (1), 13–25.

Köller, O. and Baumert, J. (2003) *Das Abitur: Immer noch ein gültiger Indikator für die Studierfähigkeit?* Bundescentrale für politische Bildung. Online at www.bpb.de/publikationen/0P7PYG. Accessed 29.2.08.

Kordes, H. (1991) Intercultural learning at school: Limits and possibilities. In D. Buttjes and M. Byram (eds) *Mediating Languages and Cultures*. Clevedon: Multilingual Matters.

Kramer, J. (1997) *British Cultural Studies*. München: Wilhelm Fink.

Kramsch, C. (1993) *Context and Culture in Language Teaching*. Oxford: Oxford University Press.

Kramsch, C. (1995) *Redefining the Boundaries of Language Study*. Boston, MA: Heinle and Heinle.

Kramsch, C. (1998) The privilege of the intercultural speaker. In M. Byram and M. Fleming (eds) *Language Learning in Intercultural Perspective: Approaches Through Drama and Ethnography*. Cambridge: Cambridge University Press.

Kramsch, C. (2003) From practice to theory and back again. In M. Byram and P. Grundy (eds) *Context and Culture in Language Teaching and Learning*. Clevedon: Multilingual Matters.

Küster, L. (2000) Zur Verbindung von Intertextualität und Interkulturalität: Literarische Anregungen auf der Basis von Michel Tourniers Robinsonade. *Zeitschrift für Fremdsprachenforschung* 11 (2), 25–53.

Nuffield (2000) *Languages: The Next Generation*. London: The Nuffield Foundation.

Lantolf, J.P. (1999) Second culture acquisition: Cognitive considerations. In E. Hinkel (ed.) *Culture in Second Language Teaching*. Cambridge: Cambridge University Press.

Lantolf, J.P. (2000) Introducing sociocultural theory. In J.P. Lantolf (ed.) *Sociocultural Theory and Second Language Learning*. Oxford: Oxford University Press.

Lareau, A. (1997) Social-class difference in family–school relationships: The importance of cultural capital. In A.H. Halsey, H. Lauder, P. Brown and A.S.Wells (eds) *Education, Culture, Economy, Society*. Oxford: Oxford University Press.

Leathes Report (1918) *Modern Studies*. A report of the committee on the position of modern languages in the educational system of Great Britain. London: HMSO.

Leung, S.W. and Lee, W.O. (2006) National identity at a cross roads: The struggle between culture, language and politics in Hong Kong. In G. Alred, M. Byram, M. Fleming (eds) *Education for Intercultural Citizenship: Concepts and Comparisons*. Clevedon: Multilingual Matters.

Levin, H.M. and Kelley, C. (1997) Can education do it alone? In A.H. Halsey, H. Lauder, P. Brown and A.S. Wells (eds) *Education, Culture, Economy, Society*. Oxford: Oxford University Press.

Levinson, S.C. (1997) From outer to inner space: Linguistic categories and non-linguistic thinking. In S. Nuyts and E. Pedersen (eds) *Language and Conceptualization*. Cambridge: Cambridge University Press.

Lippmann, W. (1922) *Public Opinion*. New York: MacMillan.

Liaw, M-L. and Johnson, R.J. (2001) E-mail writing as a cross-cultural learning experience. *System* 29 (2), 235–51.

Lloyd, G.E.R. (2002) *The Ambitions of Curiosity: Understanding the World in Ancient Greece and China*. Cambridge: Cambridge University Press.

LoBianco, J. (2003) *A Site for Debate, Negotiation and Contest of National Identity: Language Policy in Australia*. Strasbourg: Council of Europe.

Long, M.H. and Norris, J.M. (2000) Task-based teaching and assessment. In M. Byram (ed.) *Routledge Encyclopedia of Language Teaching and Learning*. London: Routledge.

McNiff, J. (1988) *Action Research: Principles and Practice*. London: MacMillan.

Medgyes, P. (1994) *The Non-native Teacher*. London: Macmillan.

Meierkord, C. (2002) 'Language stripped bare' or 'linguistic masala'? Culture in lingua franca communication. In K. Knapp and C. Meierkord (eds) *Lingua Franca Communication*. Frankfurt aM: Peter Lang.

Méndez García, M. del C. (2006) Citizenship education in Spain: Aspects of secondary education. In G. Alred, M. Byram and M. Fleming (eds) *Education for Intercultural Citizenship: Concepts and Comparisons*. Clevedon: Multilingual Matters.

Meyer, M. (1991) Developing transcultural competence: Case studies of advanced foreign language learners. In D. Buttjes and M. Byram (eds) *Mediating Languages and Cultures*. Clevedon: Multilingual Matters.

Midgley, M. (2003) *The Myths We Live By*. London: Routledge.

Miller, J. (1999) Becoming audible: Social identity and second language use. *Journal of Intercultural Studies* 20 (2), 149–165.

Miller, J. (2003) *Audible Difference*. Clevedon: Multilingual Matters.

Mills, J. (2001) Being bilingual: Perspectives of third generation Asian children on language, culture and identity. *International Journal of Bilingual Education and Bilingualism* 4 (6), 383–402.

Morgan, C. (1993) Attitude change and foreign language culture learning. *Language Teaching* 26 (2), 63–75.

Mundy, K. and Murphy, L. (2001) Transnational advocacy, global civil society? Emerging evidence from the field of education. *Comparative Education Review* 45 (1), 85–126).

Nanz, P. and Steffek, J. (2004) Global governance, participation and the public sphere. *Government and Opposition* 39 (2), 314–35.

NSFLEP (National Standards in Foreign Language Education Project) (1996) *Standards for Foreign Language Learning: Preparing for the 21st Century (SFLL)*, Lawrence, KS: Allen Press.

Niedersächsisches Kultusministerium (1995) *Didaktisch-methodische Empfehlungen für das Fremdsprachenlernen in der Grundschule*. Hannover: Schroedel Schulbuchverlag.

Nold, G. (2006) Central results of the DESI study: Competences in German as L1 and L2 in the context of the German school system. Paper for the Council of Europe.

Norton, B. (2000) *Identity and Language Learning: Gender, Ethnicity and Educational Change*. Harlow: Longman.

Norton, B.P. (1995) Social identity, investment and language learning. *TESOL Quarterly* 29, 9–31.

O'Dowd, R. (ed.) (2007) *On-line Intercultural Exchange: A Practical Introduction for Foreign Language Teachers*. Clevedon: Multilingual Matters.

Oka, H. (2003) English language education in Japan: Ideals and realities. *Bulletin of Foreign Language Teaching Association* 7 (April), 1–20.

Olk, H.M. (2002) Translating culture: A think-aloud protocol study. *Language Teaching Research* 6 (2), 121–44.

Oommen, T.K. (1999) Conceptualising nation and nationality in South Asia. In S.L. Sharma and T.K. Oommen (eds) *Nation and National Identity in South Asia*. New Delhi: Orient Longman.

Osler, A. and Starkey, H. (2005a) *Changing Citizenship: Democracy and Inclusion in Education*. Maidenhead: Open University Press.

Osler, A. and Starkey, H. (eds) (2005b) *Citizenship and Language Learning: International Perspectives*. Stoke on Trent: Trentham Books.

Outhwaite, W. (2006) *The Future of Society*. Oxford: Blackwell.

Parmenter, L. (2003) Describing and defining intercultural communicative competence: International perspectives. In M. Byram (ed.) *Intercultural Competence*. Strasbourg: Council of Europe.

Parmenter, L. (2006) Beyond the nation? Potential for intercultural citizenship in Japan. In G. Alred, M. Byram and M. Fleming (eds) *Education for Intercultural Citizenship: Concepts and Comparisons*. Clevedon: Multilingual Matters.

Paulston, C.B. (1992) *Sociolinguistic Perspectives on Bilingual Education*. Clevedon: Multilingual Matters.

Pavlenko, A. (2003) 'Language of the enemy': Foreign language education and national identity. *International Journal of Bilingual Education and Bilingualism* 6 (5), 313–331.

Pavlenko, A. and Lantolf, J.P. (2000) Second language learning as participation and the (re)construction of selves. In J.P. Lantolf (ed.) *Sociocultural Theory and Second Language Learning*. Oxford: Oxford University Press.

Pennycook, A. (1994) *The Cultural Politics of English as an International Language*, London: Longman.

Phillipson, R. (1992) *Linguistic Imperialism*, Oxford: Oxford University Press.

Phillipson, R. and Davies, A. (1997) Realities and myths of linguistic imperialism. *Journal of Multilingual and Multicultural Development* 18 (3), 238–48.

Phipps, A. and Gonzales, M. (2004) *Modern Languages: Learning and Teaching in an Intercultural Field*. London: Sage.

Poston, W.S.C. (1990) The biracial identity development model: A needed addition. *Journal of Counselling and Development* 69, 152–155.

President's Commission (1979) *Strength through Wisdom: A Critique of US Capability*. A report to the President from the President's Commission on Foreign Language and International Studies. Washington, DC: President's Commission.

Puren, C. (2000) France. In M. Byram (ed.) *Routledge Encyclopedia of Language Teaching and Learning*. London: Routledge.

Qi, D.S. (2001) Identifying and bridging cultural prototypes: Exploring the role of collaborative dialogue in second language lexical meaning acquisition. *The Canadian Modern Language Review* 58 (2), 246–72.

Qualifications and Curriculum Authority (1998) *Education for Citizenship and the Teaching of Democracy in Schools*. London: DfEE.

Rao, Z. (2002) Chinese students' perceptions of communicative and non-communicative activities in the EFL classroom. *System* 30 (1), 85–105.

Reason, P. and Bradbury, H. (2000) *The Handbook of Action Research: Participative Inquiry in Practice*. London: Sage.

Reid, W.A. (2000) Curriculum as an expression of national identity. *Journal of Curriculum and Supervision* 15 (2), 113–122.

Risager, K. (1994) International cultural studies at Roskilde University. In M. Byram (ed.) *Culture and Language Learning in Higher Education*. Clevedon: Multilingual Matters.

Risager, K. (2003) *Det nationale dilemma i sprog- og kulturpædagogikken Et studie i forholdet mellem sprog og kultur*. Copenhagen: Akademisk Forlag.

Risager, K. (2006) *Language and Culture Global Flows and Local Complexity*. Clevedon: Multilingual Matters.

Risager, K. (2007) *Language and Culture Pedagogy: From a National to a Transnational Paradigm*. Clevedon: Multilingual Matters.

RobertCollins (1987) *RobertCollins French/English English/French Dictionary* (2nd edn) (B.T. Atkins, A. Duval and R.C. Milne, eds). London: Collins/Paris: Le Robert.

Roberts, C., Barro, A., Byram, M., Jordan, S. and Street, B. (2001) *Language Learners as Ethnographers: Introducing Cultural Processes into Advanced Language Learning.* Clevedon: Multilingual Matters.

Rohrbach, R. and Winiger, E. (2001) Tandem statt Unterricht. *Babylonia* 3, 64–68.

Rohrschneider R. and Dalton, R.J. (2002) A global network? Transnational co-operation among environmental groups. *Journal of Politics* 64 (2), 510–33.

Ryle, G. (1949) *The Concept of Mind.* London: Hutchinson.

Saville, N. (2005) An interview with John Trim at 80. *Language Assessment Quarterly* 2 (4), 263–88.

Schnapper, D. (2002) Citizenship and national identity in Europe. *Nations and nationalism* 8 (1), 1–14.

Schreiner, M. (2007) Inhalte und Ziele des kulturkundlichen Englischunterrichts der Jahre zwischen den Weltkriegen. Paper presented at the conference Looking Ahead with Curiosity: Visions of Languages in Education. Johann Wolfgang Goethe-Universität, Frankfurt aM, 28 April–1 May.

Schulz, R. (2001) Cultural differences in student and teacher perceptions concerning the role of grammar instruction and corrective feedback: USA-Colombia. *The Modern Language Journal* 85 (2), 244–58.

Schulz, R.A. (2007) The challenge of assessing cultural understanding in the context of foreign language instruction. *Foreign Language Annals* 40 (1), 9–26.

Schulz, R., Lalande, J.L., Dykstra-Pruim, P., Zimmer-Loew, H. and James, C.J. (2005) In pursuit of cultural competence in the German language classroom: Recommendations of the AATG task force on the teaching of culture. *Die Unterrichtspraxis: Teaching German* 38 (2), 172–181.

Scollon, R. and Scollon, S.W. (1995) *Intercultural Communication.* Oxford: Blackwell.

Searle, J. (1995) *The Construction of Social Reality.* Harmondsworth: Penguin.

Seidlhofer, B. (2003) *A Concept of International English and Related Issues: From 'Real English' to 'Realistic English'?* Strasbourg: Council of Europe.

Sellar, W.C. and Yeatman, R.J. (1993) *1066 and All That.* London: Mandarin.

Sercu, L. (2000) *Acquiring Intercultural Communicative Competence from Textbooks.* Leuven: Leuven University Press.

Sercu, L. Bandura, E., Castro, P., Davcheva, L., Laskaridou, C., Lundgren, U., Mendez Garcia, M. and Ryan, P. (2005) *Foreign Language Teachers and Intercultural Competence An International Investigation.* Clevedon: Multilingual Matters.

Seward, G. (1958) *Clinical Studies in Culture Conflict.* New York: The Ronald Press Co.

Sherif, M. and Sherif, C. (1969) *Social Psychology.* New York: Harper and Row.

Shorter Oxford (1944) *The Shorter Oxford English Dictionary* (3rd edn) (W. Little, H.W. Fowler and J. Coulson, eds). Oxford: Clarendon Press.

Singleton, D. and Lengyel, Z. (eds) (1995) *The Age Factor in Second Language Acquisition.* Clevedon: Multilingual Matters.

Skeie, G. (2003) Nationalism, religiosity and citizenship in Norwegian majority and minority discourses. In R. Jackson (ed.) *International Perspectives on Citizenship, Education and Religious Diversity.* London: RoutledgeFalmer.

Skender, I. (1995) Eléments culturels dans l'apprentissage/l'enseignement des langues étrangères. In M. Vilke (ed.) *Children and Foreign Languages.* Zagreb: University of Zagreb, Faculty of Philosophy.

Smith, R. (2001) Group work for autonomy in Asia: Insights from teacher-research. *AILA Review* 15, 70–81.

Snow, D. and Byram, M. (1997) *Crossing Frontiers: The School Study Visit Abroad.* London: Centre for Information on Language Teaching and Research.

Sommer, T. (ed.) (2004) *Leben in Deutschland: Eine Entdeckungsreise in das eigene Land.* Hamburg: Rowohlt.

Spencer, J.A. and Jordan, R.K. (1999) Learner-centred approaches in medical education. *British Medical Journal* 318, 1280–83.

Spradley, J. (1979) *The Ethnographic Interview.* New York: Holt, Rinehart and Winston.

Standish, P. (2002) Preface. *Journal of Philosophy of Education* 36 (3), i–iv.

Stangor, C. and Schaller, M. (1996) Stereotypes as individual and collective representations. In C.N. Macrae, C. Stangor and M. Hewstone (eds) *Stereotypes and Stereotyping.* London: The Guildford Press.

Starkey, H. (2002) *Democratic Citizenship, Languages, Diversity and Human Rights.* Strasbourg: Council of Europe. .

Tajfel, H. (ed.) 1978) *Differentiation Between Social Groups.* London: Academic Press.

Tajfel, H. (1981) *Human Groups and Social Categories: Studies in Social Psychology.* Cambridge: Cambridge University Press.

Takagaki, Y. (2001) Des phrases mais pas de communication: Problème d'organisation textuelle chez les non-Occidentaux: Le cas des japonais. *Dialogues et Cultures* 44, 84–91.

Tarp, G. (2006) Student perspectives in short-term study programmes abroad: A grounded theory study. In M. Byram and A. Feng (eds) *Living and Studying Abroad: Research and Practice.* Clevedon: Multilingual Matters.

Taylor, A.J.P. 1965) *English History 1914–1945.* Oxford: Clarendon Press.

Taylor, C. (1971) Interpretation and the sciences of man. *The Review of Metaphysics* 25 (1), 3–51.

Taylor, R. (2006) Investigating the role of connotation in communication and miscommunication within English as a lingua franca and consequent implications for teaching. Unpublished PhD thesis, University of Durham.

Tonnies, F. (1887/1963) *Community and Society: Gemeinschaft und Gesellschaft.* New York: Harper and Row.

Tost Planet, M. (1997) Objectives and contents. In P. Doyé and A. Hurrell (eds) *Foreign Language Education in Primary Schools.* Strasbourg: Council of Europe.

Trim, J.L.M. (2006) *Modern Languages in the Council of Europe 1954–1997.* Strasbourg: Council of Europe.

Truscott, S. and Morley, J. (2001) Cross-cultural learning through computer-mediated communication. *Language Learning* 24, 17–23.

UNESCO (The Delors Report) (1996) *Learning: The Treasure Within.* Paris: UNESCO.

Valdez, J.N. (2000) Psychotherapy with bicultural hispanic clients. *Psychotherapy* 37 (3), 240–246.

van Ek, J. 1986) *Objectives for Foreign Language Learning* (Vol. 1): *Scope.* Strasbourg: Council of Europe.

van Gunsteren, H. (1996) Neo-republican citizenship in the practice of education. *Government and Opposition* 31 (1), 77–99.

van Lier, L. (1995) *Introducing Language Awareness.* Harmondsworth: Penguin.

von Humboldt, W. (1836/1988) *On Language.* Cambridge: Cambridge University Press.

von Wright, G.H. (1971) *Explanation and Understanding*. London: Routledge and Kegan Paul.

Wagner, A. (2004) Redefining citizenship for the 21st century: From the national welfare state to the UN global compact. *International Journal of Social Welfare* 13, 278–286.

Walat, M. (2006) Towards an intercultural frame of mind: Citizenship in Poland. In G. Alred, M. Byram, M. Fleming (eds) *Education for Intercultural Citizenship: Concepts and Comparisons*. Clevedon: Multilingual Matters.

Ward, C., Bochner, S. and Furnham, A. (2001) *The Psychology of Culture Shock* (2nd edn). London: Routledge.

Wetherell, M. (1996) Group conflict and the social psychology of racism. In M. Wetherell (ed.) *Identities, Groups and Social Issues* (pp. 217–18). London: Sage.

Wiegand, P. (1992) *Places in the Primary School*. London: Falmer Press.

Wierzbicka, A. (1997) *Understanding Cultures through Key Words: English, Russian, Polish, German and Japanese* Oxford: Oxford University Press.

Williams, R. (1961) *The Long Revolution*. London: Chatto & Windus.

Winch, P. (1964) Understanding a primitive society. *American Philosophical Quarterly* 1 (4), 307–24.

Woodhall, M. (1997) Human capital concepts. In A.H. Halsey, H. Lauder, P. Brown and A.S. Wells (eds) *Education, Culture, Economy, Society*. Oxford: Oxford University Press.

Wringe, C. (2007) *Moral Education: Beyond the Teaching of Right and Wrong*. Dordrecht: Springer.

Yakhontova, T. (2001) Textbooks, contexts and learners. *English for Specific Purposes* 20 (5), 397–415.

Yamada, E. (2008) Fostering criticality in a beginners' Japanese language course. A case-study in a UK Higher Education Modern Languages Degree programme. Unpublished PhD, University of Durham.

Zarate, G. (1993) *Représentations de l'étranger et didactique des langues*. Paris: Hachette.

Zarate, G. (2003a) Identities and plurilingualism: Preconditions for recognition of intercultural competences. In M. Byram (ed.) *Intercultural Competence* (pp. 85–118). Strasbourg: Council of Europe.

Zarate, G. (2003b) The recognition of intercultural competences: From individual experience to certification. In G. Alred, M. Byram, M. Fleming (eds) *Intercultural Experience and Education*. Clevedon: Multilingual Matters.

Zarate, G. and Gohard-Radenkovic, A. (eds) (2004) *La Reconnaissance des compétences interculturelles: De la grille à la carte*. Paris: Didier.